The Future of Think Tanks and Policy Advice Around the World

James McGann

The Future of Think Tanks and Policy Advice Around the World

palgrave
macmillan

James McGann
University of Pennsylvania
Philadelphia, PA, USA

ISBN 978-3-030-60378-6   ISBN 978-3-030-60379-3   (eBook)
https://doi.org/10.1007/978-3-030-60379-3

This Palgrave Macmillan imprint is published by the registered company Springer Nature
Switzerland AG
The registered company address is: Gewerbestrasse 11, 6330 Cham, Switzerland

ACKNOWLEDGEMENTS

I would like to thank my very dedicated and able research interns from the University of Pennsylvania and the 70 interns from colleges and universities from across the US and around the world for their assistance collecting data and conducting background research for this book. I would like to especially thank Varsha Shankar who provided invaluable help with the editing of the early drafts of the manuscript and shepherding the book and the flock of 64 authors from start to finish. I also want to thank the 64 CEOs of think tanks that provided thought provoking and forward looking essays for this book. Additionally I want to thank the Lauder family and especially Ambassador Ronald S. Lauder and Martin Haas, director of the Lauder Institute, for their support and encouragement of my research. Finally, I want to thank Maya, my daughter, and Emily, my wife, for their patience and understanding for the nights and weekends I spent away from them working on this book.

CONTENTS

Conclusions

Introduction and Background

James McGann

Abstract James McGann, Director of the Think Tanks and Civil Societies Program, Lauder Institute for Management and International Studies, University of Pennsylvania in Philadelphia, PA, explores the Future of Think Tanks and Policy Advice around the World.

Keywords Advocacy tanks · Canada · Civil society · Mexico · NGOs · Policy advice · Policy advocates · Policy research organization · Public engagement · Research institutions · Thailand · Think tanks

The changes we continue to witness in the twenty-first century are proving to be far more revolutionary, dynamic, and impactful than any before. Far from what many believed to be the post-Cold War "End of History," we are undergoing seismic shifts in technology, culture, and geopolitics. These developments reach across national borders into every aspect of society. Think tanks, a core sector of public and international affairs, are no exception.

J. McGann (✉)
Think Tanks and Civil Societies Program, Lauder Institute for Management and International Studies, University of Pennsylvania, Philadelphia, PA, USA

© The Author(s) 2021   1
J. McGann, *The Future of Think Tanks and Policy Advice Around the World*, https://doi.org/10.1007/978-3-030-60379-3_1

What exactly are think tanks, and how are they different from other organizations? During the fifty years that the body of literature grappling with the etymology of the "think tank" has existed, a wide consensus has gradually developed toward a broad definition that identifies a number of core institutional characteristics. However, even at a broad level, attempts to define and/or categorize think tanks has sparked much debate over the meaning of basic terms such as "public policy research," "think tank" and "advocacy." There is no wonder, then, that a struggle exists among think tanks concerning their role in the policymaking process; are they academics, advisors or advocates? This debate reflects the inherent tension between the world of ideas and the world of politics or the clash of academic and policy cultures. While there is a general consensus at the broadest level of scholarly attempts to define the term "think tank" (irrespective of the aforementioned debate), when scholars seek to refine the definition to a more specific level, a number of points of contention emerge. At the broadest level, think tanks are institutions that provide public policy research, analysis, and advice. For the purposes of this book, we will define think tanks as public policy research, analysis, and engagement institutions that generate policy-oriented research, analysis, and advice on domestic and international issues which enable policymakers and the general public to make informed decisions about public policy issues. Think tanks may be affiliated or independent institutions and are structured as permanent bodies, not ad hoc commissions. These institutions often act as a bridge between the academic and policymaking communities, providing a voice that translates applied and basic research into a language and form that is understandable, reliable, and accessible for policymakers and the public.

Whether it is changing their goals, sources of funding, or use of technology, think tanks are a part of this global evolution. The purpose of this text is to explore the changing landscape that think tanks find themselves in. Navigating the rapidly approaching future poses many challenges to the sector, but with these obstacles come opportunities for the most savvy competitors to distinguish themselves and leave profound impacts on civil society. To further an understanding of these challenges, it is vital to hear the perspectives and ideas of those currently in the midst of this changing landscape. For this purpose, presidents from top think tanks across the world have contributed essays detailing their own experiences and expectations for their institutions and the think tank community in a broader sense. These writings give a glimpse into a myriad of different perspectives

surrounding the evolution of think tanks, and have the unique characteristic of being written by those who not only study the subject, but are
actively engaged in shaping its future. This allows the reader to better
understand not only the directions that think tanks may take as they
move into the future, but also the rationals or beliefs guiding these new
directions.

The History of Think Tanks

The beginnings of think tanks can be traced back to the late nineteenth and early twentieth centuries when a number of institutions
had already taken root in Great Britain and the United States with
the aim of "helping policy-makers navigate their way through complex
policy problems" in the years leading up to The Great War (Hernando
et al. 2018: 125). Think tanks first emerged during the Progressive era
in an attempt to professionalize government—they were initially non-
partisan and provided government officials with unbiased policy advice
(McGann and Sabatini 2010: 42). Their main purpose was to provide
well-researched policy proposals that were aimed at solving social issues
(Troy 2012). Despite the proliferation in both the United States and
Europe, the underlying objective remained largely universal: provide
governments with expert, nonpartisan, disinterested advice (McGann and
Sabatini 2010: 43). Think tanks attempted to stay "detached from the
political process because of their commitment to preserve their intellectual and institutional independence and not influence policy decisions
directly" (Ahmad 2008: 532).

The term "think tank" itself was introduced in the United States
during World War II to characterize the secure environment in which
military and civilian experts were situated so that they could develop
invasion plans and other military strategies. The use of the term was
expanded in the 1960s to describe other groups of experts who formulated various policy recommendations, including some research institutes
concerned with the study of international relations and strategic questions
(Dickinson 1972). By the 1970s, the term think tank was applied to those
institutions focusing not only on foreign policy and defense strategy, but
also on current political, economic, and social issues. These new think
tanks were far more focused on particular issues than their predecessors,
hence, the 1970s revealed Western countries that had become increasingly more receptive to think tank advice. As voters began to assume

stances on specific issues, demand for research regarding the various view-points expanded. These issue-specific think tanks often established sites outside the individual country of origin and fostered formal relationships with international institutions. Their staff included specialists, advocacy experts, and academics. Not surprisingly, these think tanks blurred the lines between the original concept of a think tank (which was academic) with that of an advocacy group (McGann and Sabatini 2010: 43).

Think tanks now operate in a variety of political systems, engage in a range of policy-related activities, and comprise a diverse set of institutions that have varied organizational forms. As of December 8, 2018, 8248 academically oriented research institutions, contract research organizations, policy advocates, and political party affiliated think tanks can now be found in 188 countries (McGann and Whelan 2020). While their organizational structure, modes of operation, targeted audience or market, and means of support may vary from institution to institutions and from country to country, most think tanks share a common goal of producing high-quality research and analysis that is married to some form of public engagement.

Types of Think Tanks

Of the 8248 think tanks across the globe, there are countless distinctions which separate individual institutions from their peers (McGann 2020). Recognizing the factor that distinguishes one think tank from another is crucial for understanding where to find the niche repositories of information required for modern policymaking. While each institution is unique, it is useful to categorize them based on certain criteria. Some of the most relevant categories for defining different types of think tanks are their geographic scope, thematic focus, and institutional structure.

Regarding the geographic scope of think tanks, it is reasonable to separate these institutions by scope into those which primarily operate on a domestic, regional, or international level. Domestic think tanks tend to restrict their research to subjects pertaining to a specific nation. An example of one such institution would be the Egyptian Center for Economic Studies, which consistently outputs information pertaining to Egyptian economics. For all institutions that fit this categorization, it is important that they not become too siloed by exclusively focusing on their nation of interest. In an increasingly globalized world, domestic economic developments can have dramatic impacts on seemingly unrelated countries. Whether it be oil price wars, pandemics, or financial crashes, modern geopolitical analysis is a necessary component for any think tank's research.

Fortunately for those domestic institutions, their work is an invaluable segment of this process. Regional and international developments are the sum of internal state policies and politics. By continuing to offer analysis on individual states, domestic think tanks represent a vital portion of the global knowledge community.

Regional think tanks, like their domestic counterparts, also offer valuable insights that would likely be overlooked were it not for their specific geographic scope. For example, the Al Jazeera Center for Studies provides some of the highest quality research pertaining to the Middle East. The benefit of regional institutions is that they may offer perspective on issues which are too broad to be understood from solely a national perspective but also too geographically specific to be relevant to global research. Examples of such issues include analysis on the Arab Spring in the Middle East, economic migration in Central and South America, and demographic challenges for East Asia.

Global think tanks, laying claim to the broadest geographic scope, often must limit their research by other factors. Typically, they do so by restricting their thematic focus to a particular family of issues. International think tanks focus heavily on issues that transcend borders, for example education, environment, and economic stability. With research results and advocacy, these problems can either be brought back into the international spotlight to be further improved upon—as Brookings has done with education—or can call attention to newly identified international issues, such as governmental inefficiency (Wihardja 2014; Winthrop 2014).

The key challenge facing think tanks that are primarily focused on global issues is the risk of overextension. To maintain integrity and academic-quality work products, many global-scale think tanks implement measures—like CSIS's performance index or Brooking's stakeholder model for the Global Compact on Learning project—to check researchers' freedom and give an incentive for high-quality work (Wihardja 2014; Winthrop 2014).

Global think tanks can take hands-on or hands-off approaches to resolving international issues. A hands-on approach includes whistle-blowing through treaties and taking the initiative to apply knowledge to policy. The existence of international treaties, agreements, and associations between countries allows policy networks to form, and global think tanks to work with colleagues and governments in other nations; for instance, CEIP took a hands-on approach in working directly with the Vatican Library to improve education (Hary 1996). Meanwhile, Brookings exemplifies a less direct approach with its Global Compact on Learning project. After conducting research, the institute aimed to serve as a "neutral convener" to facilitate dialogue without having complete control of the issue (Winthrop 2014).

Navigating a variety of global issues and regions poses a unique challenge for global think tanks, which domestic policy research institutes do not face. Various global think tanks have distinct approaches to conducting research in the international sphere, which emphasizes that multiple paths can be taken to "go global." Flexibility in structure and diversity in funding is critical to tackle the politics of different regions and international issues.

Think tank networks have become especially important to the success of global think tanks. There are three general types of think tank networks: "Open Assembly, Association of Think Tanks Under Donor Leadership or Official Patronage, and Association of Think Tanks Under Single Organization Leadership" (Struyk 2002: 631). Open Assembly is the most loosely structured and intended mainly for information sharing, while the other two have more structure and exclusive membership. Environmental NGOs in North America have used the Open Assembly structure to effectively share information between the USA, Canada, and Mexico, in order to put pressure on governments to effectively police environmental breaches and implement policy on environmental preservation (Pacheco-Vega 2015). Even a loosely structured think tank network can have a large impact on a shared issue between borders; the ENGOs in North America have shown that correct management and dedication to a global issue within a network can lead to significant shifts in policy.

Due to the nature of global issues, it is extremely improbable that one nation could single-handedly solve a problem in all regions of the world. Because of this handicap, think tank networks become important in facilitating knowledge sharing between policy research centers in multiple regions of the world. This collaboration between researchers and regions allows for a much more successful outlook on the ability to solve a shared problem.

As previously referenced, another way think tanks may distinguish themselves is by utilizing a particular thematic focus. The most common areas of interest are security, economic development, and human rights or cultural issues. Unlike geographic scope, it is common for global think tanks to straddle these lines and offer research output pertaining to multiple issues. That being said, institutions are often renowned for their niche expertise, and while one think tank may offer valuable analysis on multiple themes, they are likely to be identified for one field in particular.

Institutions that focus primarily or entirely on security typically offer analysis on military capabilities, potential flashpoints, strategic posturing, and conflict mitigation or resolution. An example of one such institution would be the Institute for National Security Studies, an Israeli think tank focused on Israeli national security. For any think tank operating in this sphere, a difficult yet crucial challenge is understanding both sides of potential or ongoing conflicts. This challenge is only compounded if the institution in question is primarily focused on a singular nation or funded in whole or in part by a government.

These conditions can often make it difficult to source information from the other side of a conflict, and having perspective into only half of a security dilemma makes offering valuable analysis difficult. Thus making the formation of inter-institutional relationships extremely important for security-focused think tanks. These relationships can be between think tanks, but any communication channel that reaches over to the other side of a security issue is worthwhile. In addition to bolstering the quality of research, inter-institutional connections also offer the opportunity for track II diplomacy, by which security think tanks may play a more active role in the policymaking process.

Another popular theme for think tanks is economic development. Institutions that choose this focus primarily publish research pertaining to economic issues of trade, education, resource management, industry regulation, and any other topics deemed pertinent for sustaining or expanding the economic growth of their chosen region. One example of these institutions is the Thailand Development Research Institute, which is dedicated to furthering economic development in Thailand. A central challenge facing these institutions is being able to identify and provide analysis for issues which at first do not appear economic in nature. This is important because often issues that are not inherently economic such as pandemics, natural disasters, and demographic shifts have the most profound economic impacts. To stay ahead of these extremely important issues, it is necessary that economics-focused institutions continuously scan the broader policy community for topics which are likely to eventually impact their work.

The final thematic concentration to be considered is human rights and cultural issues. These institutions often offer research on ethnic, religious, or gender-based discrimination and violence, democratization and authoritarianism, or general human rights issues. The Center for Democracy and Development is an example of one such institution, which offers research on the aforementioned topics pertaining to West Africa. A unique challenge facing think tanks that pursue this line of research is political and institutional animosity or lack of support. Unlike topics such as security and economic development, there are little to no vested interests in advancing or protecting human rights. In many cases, these institutions can face blatant or discreet opposition from governments or other political entities. As a result, accessing funding, establishing communication channels, and conducting operations become far more difficult. To mitigate these opposing forces, it is particularly important for think tanks conducting human rights research to generate support from the general public so as to pressure governments to support them (at best) and permit their presence (at worst).

Like think tanks with specific geographic foci, global institutions that dedicate their research to a common theme must be willing to communicate outside their silo. There is immense value to dedicating an institution to one of these fields, but it is also crucial to recognize that security, economics, and human rights are all deeply interconnected. How can an economy and population prosper if their physical security is at risk? How can a nation be secure with a discontent citizenry and volatile economy? Understanding not only the complex nuances of an institution's area of expertise, but also having a general understanding of how other factors come into play, is critical for consistently delivering the most pertinent policy analysis and recommendations.

Another axis on which think tanks can be defined is described in R. Kent Weaver's *The Changing World of Think Tanks*. Weaver's reflections on the changing world of think tanks, or even just his acknowledgment of the fluidity of the domain, introduce into the literature a number of useful concepts and areas of focus that allow us to capture the diversity of the think tank domain in the most distilled manner possible. Weaver's work focuses on think tanks with organizational independence, and he asserts that institutions in this group follow one of three organizational models: Universities Without Students, the Contract Researcher, and Advocacy Tanks (1989: 563). Building on Orlans' notion of think tanks as "non-degree granting" institutions, "university without students"-model think tanks rely heavily on academics as researchers, have private sector funding, and primarily produce book-length studies, academic monographs, and journal articles (1972: 3). This type of think tank is typically funded by foundations, corporations, and individuals, with their agendas set internally as part of a bottom-up process in which the researchers themselves play an important role. According to Weaver, this type of think tank generally maintains a long-term focus and seeks to change elite opinion (Weaver 1989: 564). Traditional examples of this type of think tank are The Brookings Institution and The American Enterprise Institute (AEI), with a "new breed" represented in the Carnegie Endowment for World Peace and the Center for Strategic and International Studies (CSIS).

Contract researcher think tanks, like Universities Without Students, practice objective analysis with a "heavy reliance on academics as researchers," emphasizing rigorous social science methods (Weaver 1989: 568). With a reputation for objective research, these institutions provide a useful external voice to supplement their clients' own work. Where Contract Researchers and Universities Without Students differ, however, is in their sources of funding, research agendas, and output. Contract researchers mainly receive their funding from, and produce reports for, specific government agencies; and their research agenda is thus steered by those agencies. In the late 1980s, this assertion was novel, and one that broke with the previous consensus, established by Levien and Dror, that one of the defining characteristics of think tanks was their research freedom (Levien 1969; Dror 1980). Indeed, many of the studies produced by these think tanks are not made available to the general public unless the agencies involved consent to their release. Institutions that best exemplify this type of think tank are the Rand Corporation and the Urban Institute.

Weaver's final category, Advocacy Tanks, differ in a number of ways from the preceding categories and, at the time of the publication of his article, were a relatively new phenomenon. Weaver contends that, while Universities Without Students and Contract Researchers were the predominant models operative in the think tank domain in the 1970s–1980s, they were supplanted by the proliferation of advocacy tanks in the 1980s (Weaver 1989). This new breed of think tank was unabashedly partisan and ideological, and prioritized putting a "spin on existing research" over the production of original research (Weaver 1989). In the words of Weaver, they "combine a strong policy, partisan or ideological bent with aggressive salesmanship and an effort to influence policy debates," decreasing their academicism in favor of increasing their accessibility to policymakers (Weaver 1989: 567). Advocacy tanks frequently draw their resources disproportionately from sources linked to specific interests (e.g., corporations for conservative think tanks, labor unions for liberal think tanks). Their staff, in comparison, are typically drawn more heavily from government, political parties, and interest groups than from university faculties, and may be less credentialed in terms of social science expertise. Their products, normally in the form of policy briefs or white papers, tend to advocate a particular policy, in contrast to the academic tomes that are associated with the more academic think tanks. This medium of communication tends to be more condensed, concise, and clearly illustrates policy implications and options. Examples of this type of think tank can be found on the right in the Heritage Foundation (HI) and on the left in the Center for American Progress (CAP).

Expectedly, Weaver's broader treatment of "think tank" aligns fairly concordantly with his predecessors. To Weaver, "think tanks" play a number of defining roles: they are sources of policy-primed ideas, evaluation of policy proposals and government programs, personnel (they are "hospitals for governmental casualties") and punditry. That said, Weaver also acknowledges a number of inherent tensions within the concept that he perceives will be the subject of future debate. He acknowledges the politicization of the think tank domain as a future point of contention, identifying the contradiction between the image of academic objectivity that public policy research institutions seek to garner and (a) the organizational form that advocacy think tanks represent and (b) the survival impulse to satisfy budgetary necessity. Weaver also identifies the distinctly Anglo-American character and lack of portability of current definitions as a foreboding etymological difficulty (Weaver 1989). Finally, while he admits the irreconcilability of each of his aforementioned models with each other, he asserts that newly established "think tanks" are beginning to hybridize to some degree (Weaver 1989). It remains, however, that Weaver is to be credited primarily for his redefinition of the conventional approach to defining "think tank." Indeed, he acknowledges the diversity of think tanks and the subsequent need for a typology that accounts for both their inter-categorical uniqueness and intra-categorical diversity.

THE GLOBAL ISSUES THINK TANKS FACE

Incorporating Disruptive Technology

Technological development continues to dynamically alter global civil society, disrupting previously sedentary industries and organizations, and the think tank sector is no exception to this trend. Innovations in information technology have redefined how think tanks can and should operate, inviting in a host of challenges for the unprepared and a plethora of opportunities for those organizations ready to seize new advantages.

The principal factor that must be considered is the ease of access by which parties may locate, create, and disseminate information. The roots of this development extend back to the origins of the internet, but have been vastly accelerated by the emergence of search engines, new media platforms, and smart devices, which have exponentially increased the amount of information instantaneously available to citizens and experts alike. The most impactful effect that these changes have had on the think tank sector so far is the increasing difficulty in reaching policymakers.

A byproduct of the surge of information available to policymakers has been a necessary shortening of their related attention spans. Gone are the days of policymakers dissecting academic journals or robust policy reports, which were typically the output of the think tank sector. In this new, fast-paced reality, one must be concise and easily digestible to be heard. This must be how think tanks adapt their knowledge products.

The common output of think tanks is rapidly changing. Once articulated in the form of books, journal articles, congressional testimony, op-eds, and conference papers, Montoya and Swanger contend that the policy-oriented product of public policy research organizations is increasingly being distributed by way of electronic media, such as blogs, websites, and databases (Montoya and Swanger 2007).

There is still a place for long-form, detail-focused work, which is critical for crafting effective policy. This place, however, is not on the desks of politicians. In its place, think tanks must provide shorter and more direct content, such as videos or infographics, which articulate their most important research findings. If think tanks fail to adapt in this way, their competition will supersede them.

These competitors, be they private lobbyists, political advocacy groups, law firms, or anyone else, have only been bolstered by these new technological developments. The previously held policy advice oligopoly think tanks enjoyed in much of the world is being challenged. To remain influential, think tanks must broaden their consumer base to include not only government and intelligence, but also the public at large.

Social media, both a technological and cultural development, has accelerated the politicization of society. This redistribution of political capital must also be addressed in think tank strategy. Fortunately, the reforms necessary to retain policymaker attention are the same as those needed to break into social media and the public consciousness. Principally, what is required is the diversification of knowledge products to include shorter form multimedia content. Generating public support for policy recommendations adds pressure on governments to take think tanks and their work seriously, which could be an invaluable asset in nations where governments are unsupportive or even hostile toward the think tank sector.

A major challenge facing think tanks relates to their financial capacity to incorporate the human capital necessary to adapt to these new demands. Besides ongoing sociocultural changes, think tank research must also adapt to the surges of big data which will continue to increase exponentially in the coming 5G revolution. To account for all of these requirements will necessitate that think tanks incorporate into their operations: multimedia experts, public relations specialists, and data scientists along with their traditional teams of social scientists. At a time when institutional funding is notoriously difficult to acquire, only the largest think tanks will be able to host all of these specialists in-house.

Fortunately, emerging technologies and organizational models offer think tanks a means to incorporate specialists into their production cycles without incurring heavy payroll costs. Work-sharing technologies, such as real-time cloud editing provided through Google Suite, have made cross-institutional collaboration more viable than ever before. By utilizing such technology, think tanks gain a number of options relating to whom they collaborate with. For specific needs, they could contract the work of multimedia or public relations firms. More generally, and likely more valuable, they may pool resources together with other think tanks that compliment their own deficiencies.

A beneficial byproduct of utilizing work-sharing systems is that they make internal operations more flexible and resilient. This is particularly valuable in times of crisis, such as the COVID-19 pandemic, during which researchers are unable to work on-site. By utilizing these systems, researchers are able to work remotely, maintaining project release expectations during times when they are most needed. However, these advantages are not only limited to crises. The digitization of workflow also enables employees to work without regard for geographic limitations, meaning that employees can continue producing content while attending international conferences, conducting on-site research, or performing other tasks that take them away from their office.

For any modern institution, maintaining technological relevance is a necessity. For think tanks, this takes the form of developing their capacities to reach larger audiences through multimedia communication, bolstering their research by incorporating big data, and remaining solvent by utilizing work-sharing services. Think tanks that fail to adapt to the new realities of their sector and the world will fall from relevance, while those who take advantage of these new opportunities will see their influence grow and their policy advice shape the world.

Funding

Although the number of think tanks has grown precipitously in the past decades, there have been immense organizational obstacles that have deterred the growth of the industry. (McGann 2018). By their very nature, global or transnational think tanks face truly global challenges in their quest to influence and affect the various policymaking processes. While their global presence may enable them to deal more efficiently and effectively with certain obstacles with which traditional think tanks may struggle, being global brings with it a host of additional considerations and challenges.

Compiled research on think tank impact provides the foundation for analysis of such challenges facing global think tanks (McGann 2008). Evidence from this research illuminates the following obstacles to think tank impact, distilled from the responses from a primary survey of think tanks globally: lack of institutional support, lack of access to information, lack of public funding, lack of technology, and lack of relationships with government officials. Funding was, by far, the most frequently identified challenge; 120 think tanks, or 75% of the responding total, listed a lack of funding as a serious hindrance (McGann 2006).

Increased competition for funding among think tanks exacerbates their funding challenges. This competition is further exacerbated by the fact that said funding is often available in less than desired amounts. In many cases, these organizations must compete for a decreasing amount of funding. This inverse relationship creates an interesting dilemma for any think tank: in order to fulfill their mission of improving public policy, think tanks must operate in two distinct but overlapping markets. These markets are, of course, funding and policy advice. Money is the most reliable "carrier of interests," and it is important to ensure that adequate funding creates significant incentives for think tanks and networks to carry out the following functions globally: communicate knowledge (informative function), advocate values (normative function), and lobby for interests (affective function) (Schneider 2003).

The exact sources of think tank funding can be quite diverse and the global expansion of think tanks has only increased the overall complexity of the funding issue. Project-based funding is, and will likely remain, critical for global think tanks. However, it remains imperative that these institutions continue to seek out and secure a consistent inflow of funds for the administrative staff, rent, communication, and other aspects that inevitably consume a good deal of financial capital. The costs associated with establishing and operating a global think tank present a major challenge for think tanks that have gone global. In addition, transnational think tanks involve complex legal, management, and staffing issues. Unfortunately, these global operational centers are not subject to uniform regulation because each country has a unique set funding, labor, and legal requirements.

Since foreign funding is an essential element of a global think tank's overall financial resource pool, it is perhaps wholly unsurprising to find that there is often intense competition for it. Funding and financial independence are an incredibly complex set of issues, as they often directly affect a think tank's credibility as well as their ability to operate in difficult and occasionally hostile environments, such as those found under authoritarian regimes. Ascertaining the potential for private and public international donors may also be problematic if there is a significant shortage of overall financial resources for the country in which a think tank is considering expanding its operations. The absence or limited supply of financial support hinders a global think tank's ability to have the resources necessary to substitute for and diversify domestic funding. The funding issue is further complicated by the fact that many host countries often view think tanks that are supported entirely by foreign donors as "outside agitators" (McGann and Sabatini 2010: 108).

These organizations find it extremely difficult to raise funds for independent policy research, and donors often find it difficult to continue to sponsor an operation that does not produce immediate, quantifiable results. Attracting donors who do not have an immediate or direct interest in a project also proves difficult. Even if funding is secured, these think tanks face the additional challenges of finding a niche in the "global marketplace of ideas" and translating the ability to gather information or consult on policy into the ability to affect or implement policy change. Once these institutions have distilled valuable ideas from the plethora of available information available, they must work to get government actors and those in positions of official authority to utilize these ideas and produce results. Creating objectives and defining an agenda can be a potential complication for both think tanks and policy networks; protraction and a subsequent loss of focus are potential issues that inevitably arise due to the considerable start-up costs and the time required to produce and promote viable and visible results.

Additional considerations, such as sudden changes in funder interests, are present as well. These shifts in funder interests are serious risks to sustainable funding for think tank operations. Think tanks are committed to ensuring quality research in order to strengthen the perception that their products can be trusted. This trust is derived from the label of most think tanks as nonprofits; they are not driven to maximize profit, which could compromise their work product (Stone 2013). Where the expanse of funding opportunities is lacking, think tanks face the difficulty of remaining independent from governments (Dabrowski 2014). In many countries, there is a continuing risk of a return to authoritarian governments that will not tolerate independent voices that might criticize the regime. Even for think tanks, challenging politically insecure governments in countries with weak democratic traditions and institutions remains a risky business.

References

Introduction

Ahmad, Mahmood. 2008. US Think Tanks and the Politics of Expertise: Role, Value and Impact. *The Political Quarterly* 79 (4): 529–555.

Dabrowski, Marek. 2014. Center for Social and Economic Research (CASE): Think Tanks in the Era of Globalization. In *How Think Tanks Shape Social Development Policies*, ed. J.G. McGann, A. Viden, and J. Rafferty, 213–230. Philadelphia, PA: University of Pennsylvania Press.

Dickinson, Paul. 1972. *Think Tanks*. New York: Atheneum.

Dror, Yehezkel. 1980. Think Tanks: A New Invention in Government. In *Making Bureaucracies Work*, ed. Carol H. Weiss and Allen H. Barton, 139–152. Beverly Hills, London: Sage.

Hary, Nicoletta M. 1996. American Philanthropy in Europe: The Collaboration of the Carnegie Endowment for International Peace with the Vatican Library. *Libraries & Culture* 31 (2): 364–379.

Hernando, M.G., P. Hartwig, and D. Stone. 2018. Think Tanks in 'Hard Times'—The Global Financial Crisis and Economic Advice. *Policy and Society* 37 (2): 125–139.

Levien, Roger E. 1969. Independent Public Policy Analysis Organization—A Major Social Invention. In *Rand Papers Series*, ed. Rand Corporation. Santa Monica: Rand Corporation.

McGann, James G. 2006. Think Tanks and Civil Societies 2006 Survey. University of Pennsylvania.

McGann, James G. 2008. *Think Tank Assessment Study; Initial Global Trend Report*. Philadelphia: Think Tanks and Civil Societies Program, Foreign Policy Research Institute.

McGann, James G. 2020a. *2019 Global Go to Think Tank Index Report*. Philadelphia: Think Tanks and Civil Societies Program, University of Pennsylvania.

McGann, James G., and L.C. Whelan. 2020. *Global Think Tanks: Policy Networks and Governance*. New York: Taylor & Francis.

McGann, J.G., and R. Sabatini. 2010. *Global Think Tanks: Policy Networks and Governance*. New York: Routledge.

Montoya, S., and R. Swanger. 2007. Ideas for Policymakers: Enhancing the Impact of Think Tanks. *Pardee RAND Graduate School: Policy Insight* 1 (2): 1–2.

Orlans, Harold. 1972. *The Nonprofit Research Institute: Its Operation, Origins, Problems, and Prospects*. New York: McGraw-Hill.

Pacheco-Vega, Raul. (2015). Transnational Environmental Activism in North America: Wielding Soft Power Through Knowledge Sharing? *Review of Policy Research* 32 (1): 146–162.

Schneider, Jiri. 2003. Globalizations and Think Tanks; Security Policy Networks. In *Proceedings from the SAREM International Seminar*, May 30, Istanbul, Turkey.

Stone, Diane. 2013. *Capturing the Political Imagination: Think Tanks and the Policy Process*. London: Routledge.

Struyk, R.J. 2002. Management of Transnational Think Tank Networks. *International Journal of Politics, Culture, and Society* 15 (4): 625–638.

Troy, T. 2012. Devaluing the Think Tank. *National Affairs*, Winter 2012. https://www.nationalaffairs.com. Accessed 23 March 2020.

Weaver, Kent R. 1989. The Changing World of Think Tanks. *Political Science and Politics* 22 (3): 563–578.

Wihardja, M.M. 2014. Center for Strategic and International Studies (CSIS): Shaping Development Policy in a Globalized World. In *How Think Tanks Shape Social Development Policies*, ed. J.G. McGann, A. Viden, and J. Rafferty, 185–199. Philadelphia, PA: University of Pennsylvania Press.

Submission

McGann, James G. 2018. 2018 Latin America Think Tank Summit Report: Think Tanks: A Bridge Over Troubled Waters and Turbulent Times. TTCSP Global and Regional Think Tanks Summit Reports. https://repository.upenn.edu/cgi/viewcontent.cgi?article=1022&context=ttcsp_summitreports.

McGann, James G. 2020. 2019 Global Go to Think Tank Index Report. TTCSP Global Go to Think Tank Index Reports.

Africa Region

The 612 think tanks operating in Africa have an enormous range of policy issues to analyze in the coming years. African populations are the fastest-growing and least wealthy in the world, presenting a monumental challenge for resource distribution. This dilemma is only compounded by the fact that Africa is also expected to be one of the regions worst affected by climate change, making the few available resources even scarcer. With ongoing security threats from civil wars, religious terrorism, and ethnic conflicts, Africa is perhaps more in need of objective, fact-based policy solutions than any other region of the world.

The Future of Think Tanks in Africa

Vasu Gounden and Cedric de Coning

Abstract Vasu Gounden, Executive Director and Cedric de Coning, Senior Advisor at The African Centre for the Constructive Resolution of Disputes in Durban, South Africa, explore the Future of Think Tanks and Policy Advice around the World.

Keywords African think tanks · Brazil · China · Civil society · India · NGOs · Policy advice · Research centers · Research institutions · Russia · South Africa · Think tanks

A decade from now, when we reflect on the role think tanks played and the environment they operated in, it may not be inappropriate to paraphrase Charles Dickens and say that for think tanks, "it was the best of times, it was the worst of times... it was the epoch of belief, it was the epoch of incredulity... it was the spring of hope, it was the winter of despair."

In many ways, this is the best of times and it is the worst of times for think tanks. The sheer breadth and depth of knowledge that exists today

V. Gounden (✉) · C. de Coning
The African Centre for the Constructive Resolution of Disputes,
Durban, South Africa

© The Author(s) 2021
J. McGann, *The Future of Think Tanks and Policy Advice Around the World*, https://doi.org/10.1007/978-3-030-60379-3_2

21

and the technological tools available to mine that knowledge certainly make this one of the best times for think tanks to execute their mandate of providing critical thought and evidence-based policy advice. However, on the other hand, precisely because there is this breadth and depth of knowledge and tools to mine information, and the fact that these are easily accessible to everybody, including policymakers and competitive entities like law firms, PR companies, etc., the value of think tanks can be and often is diminished. While this has a negative impact on think tanks, the more critical impact is the effect that this has on the quality of policy advice.

THE ROLE OF THINK TANKS IN AFRICA

When we reflect on the role of civil society in Africa, we rarely think about the role of think tanks. We tend to consider the role of NGOs that advocate for specific norms or that represent certain interest groups. However, think tanks play an important role in the development, adaptation, and enhancement of Africa's peace and security, governance, and development. ACCORD, ISS, IPSS, CCCPA, KAIPTC, and others have been particularly active in the peace and security and conflict resolution realms, so we will use that experience when we reflect on the future of think tanks, but all domains are, of course, closely interrelated.

Not all think tanks have the same DNA. Some like ISS are perhaps more research- and policy-orientated, while others like CCCPA and KAIPTC are perhaps more practice-orientated. ACCORD, IPSS, and others straddle both worlds. We have been, and remain, engaged in supporting international mediation, peacemaking and peacekeeping efforts, national dialogue processes, national and local capacities for peace and local mediation, and conflict resolution mechanisms. Most recently, our focus is on tracking COVID-19 related conflict trends and developing analysis and interventions to prevent social unrest and violent conflict that may be the result of the spread of the virus or the efforts to contain it. Our practice is informed by our research and policy work, which in turn informs our research, policy, and training initiatives.

OPERATING SPACE

When one considers the future of think tanks in Africa, a typical concern may be that the space think tanks have to contribute practical or policy solutions is assumed to be dominated by government. In our now 27 years of experience, this has rarely been a real problem. Governments and governmental multilateral institutions are important stakeholders that any think tank operating in Africa has to engage with. In our experience, most governments in Africa, along with institutions like the African Union and the regional economic communities we have worked with, are keen to engage with ideas and solutions, and are looking for partners that can deliver and are willing to experiment with new and innovative approaches to challenges that they themselves have been struggling with. ACCORD has, for example, worked with the African Union on scoping climate-related security risks, establishing women peace and security networks, building mediation capacity, and supporting the development of peace operations doctrine.

This is perhaps not so surprising if you consider that many of the staff, officers, and diplomats that work in these governments and institutions have been educated and trained by Africa's regional centers of excellence, think tanks, and universities. This education and training is based on theoretical, normative, critical, and problem-solving research with foundations reaching back hundreds of years. The daily work of the staff, officers, and diplomats is further informed by research undertaken by think tanks.

In the peace and security context, they study specific conflict situations or regional conflict systems to identify and analyse the causes and drivers of conflicts. They research phenomena such as the emergence and dynamics of rebel groups, insurgencies, and violent extremism. They also study the ideas, norms, theories of change, processes, and mechanisms that institutions like the African Union and the regional economic communities employ to prevent, manage, and resolve conflicts. In the process, think tanks also contribute to identifying best practices and learning lessons about which approaches have better results than others. ACCORD and other African think tanks have, for instance, participated in African Union strategic assessments, best practice studies, and lessons learned initiatives. In these ways, think tanks help identify new challenges, monitor trends, and study trajectories that help these institutions to adapt to changes in their environment.

These roles that think tanks play in supporting Africa's peace and security architecture are not unique to Africa. ACCORD has provided similar support to the United Nations, the European Union, and national governments.

WHY DO GOVERNMENTS AND MULTILATERAL INSTITUTIONS NEED THINK TANKS?

Some question why institutions need this kind of support from think tanks. Is it an indication that there is a lack of capacity in these institutions? In fact, precisely the contrary is true. The countries and institutions with the most capacity in the world are also the ones with the largest budgets for research and development, and the ones that have the most engagement with academic institutions, think tanks, and research institutions.

It would be uneconomical and inefficient for multilateral and national institutions to maintain in-house expertise on all the range of topics and issues that make up the peace and security landscapes of today and tomorrow. It is much more economical and effective for these multilateral and national institutions to engage that expertise as needed. A symbiotic relationship between researchers, practitioners, and policymakers has thus developed in most disciplines, and the area of peace and security is no exception.

However, someone must make the investment and bear the cost of maintaining such expertise. In most countries, this is done by government support to institutions of higher learning as well as through the establishment of national research foundations or other mechanisms that fund research. Some multilateral institutions, like the European Union, also provide research funding, while others rely on their member states and play a role in coordinating and facilitating research among them.

It is interesting, in this context, for instance, to note the attention given to research collaboration by the BRICS (Brazil, Russia, India, China, and South Africa) grouping, who have regular meetings of think tanks, academic institutions, research foundations, and university principals. In the case of Africa, in addition to national-level support for research, several international partners also support research, education, and training. However, funding has also become challenging for think tanks. This is driven by increased competition for funding among think tanks, by funding cuts from donor agencies, and competition with other entities like NGOs, CBOs, and for-profit consulting firms. This has forced many think tanks to become quasi-commercial. This orientation comes with its own set of challenges in setting priorities and managing the organizations' rigorous ethical and professional standards. Funding has also led think tanks to rethink their organizational model by insourcing very expensive and high-quality research skills so that they have the benefit of this expertise without the cost of retaining those skills full-time.

THE FUTURE OF THINK TANKS IN AFRICA

Academic institutions, think tanks, and research centers thus play an important role in supporting, innovating, and enhancing Africa's peace and security architecture. This role may be mostly invisible, but it is nevertheless crucial for ensuring that there is an ongoing process of analysis, feedback, and adaptation that helps Africa's peace and security institutions to coevolve with the changing dynamics of their peace and security environment.

As the outbreak of the COVID-19 pandemic in 2020 showed, the role of think tanks in Africa is likely to become even more important in the future, taking into account a number of significant trends, such as a changing international global order and an increasingly integrated African continent, but also a continent facing a number of significant challenges and opportunities, including population growth, urbanization, technological developments, the knowledge economy, and perhaps the most significant: climate change.

These challenges are fast converging in Africa and presenting governments with challenges that are increasingly beyond their ability to respond to alone. Some governments work with think tanks, research institutions, and the private sector to address these challenges together. There are others, however, that see think tanks as a problem because they generate data that may expose policy gaps, mismanagement, and corruption. In a global environment of growing polarization and authoritarianism, a clampdown on think tanks is not far fetched and in some countries, is already occurring.

These challenges will provide new opportunities for think tanks to prove their value by providing quality, evidence-based research, policy advice, and support to governments and multilateral institutions. Many think tanks in Africa have taken on a more active role that goes beyond providing research, to one that works with governments to turn knowledge into policy and practice. These are some of the ways in which think tanks in Africa have, and will continue into the future, to contribute to the peace, security, and development agenda so that we can turn an approaching Dickensian winter of despair into a spring of hope.

The Future of African Think Tanks

Emmanuel Acquah

Abstract Emmanuel Acquah, CEO of The Africa Centre for Entrepreneurship and Youth Empowerment in Accra, Ghana, explores the Future of Think Tanks and Policy Advice around the World.

Keywords Civil society organizations · Digital platforms/Digitization · Ghana · Policy advice · Think tanks

Think tanks have had an overwhelming impact over the years in the spheres of urbanization, industrialization, poverty alleviation, and international terrorism. Despite this development, think tanks, especially those from Africa, face challenges such as fragmented and partisan interpretation of policies by political parties and their followers; ownership, privacy, and free flow of big data; inadequate domestic funding; technological advancement that does not ensure even dissemination of information, especially to poor and deprived communities; and limited availability of experts, which require think tanks to hire more middle managers.

E. Acquah (✉)
The Africa Centre for Entrepreneurship and Youth Empowerment,
Accra, Ghana

© The Author(s) 2021
J. McGann, *The Future of Think Tanks and Policy Advice Around the World*, https://doi.org/10.1007/978-3-030-60379-3_3

Think tanks are widely known for their subject matter expertise and assistance in policymaking. Over the years, think tanks have carved a niche for themselves as being independent and fair. Rich information, based on qualitative and quantitative research and findings, has been a bedrock for think tanks.

As former Canadian Senator Hugh Segal suggested, think tanks are at their worst when they are narrowly ideological and consistently generate predictable findings on any question despite evidence to the contrary. Think tanks that demonstrate such behavior should be discounted.

Owing to increasing digitization, many people now have access to mobile phones and the internet. With this, vast quantities of data are generated by daily economic and social connections. Despite the benefits that think tanks could gain from the big data of daily interactions, matters such as privacy, personal data, and ownership of data are major challenges that think tanks must overcome. New regulations enacted to curb risks associated with big data may hinder the free flow of data and cause data specialists to face unemployment as more effective communication tools automate away their positions.

The rise of law firms, advocacy groups, public relations firms, nontraditional media sources, and companies like Google has shaped the quality of work by think tanks. The existence of these institutions has supported the production and circulation of ideas and has created easy access to secondary data. However, there is a sharp contrast between think tanks and these groups. Differences in ideology, work ethics, interests, and management style create the challenge that ideas generated by these institutions are often based on what promotes their cause. Since these institutions are partially motivated by profit maximization, unlike think tanks who rely on donor funding and provide evidence-based policy work, the content of these groups is questionable. This makes think tanks more relevant and credible than the latter. Despite this, the role of these groups in creating a climate of ideas cannot be ignored. Based on their popularity and accessibility, politicians sometimes ride on the shoulders of these groups and reference claims that may not be true. So long as think tanks remain factual, the likes of Facebook and other digital platforms should be an enabler for quality discourse.

Factors Influencing Hiring
Policies of Think Tanks

Just like in any effective organization, a think tank's Human Resource Management team is directed to ensure that skilled and competent people are employed, human capital is retained, and personnel are engaged efficiently. In the late 1900s and early 2000s, the strong connection between think tanks and traditional universities made it possible for think tanks to have direct engagement with experts on particular subject matters. Usually, these experts are limited to a particular field of study. The cost associated with hiring these experts is of great concern to think tanks in Africa. Currently, most think tanks that I have come across in Africa work with middle managers as staff and appoint distinguished academicians to be part of their Board Directors or as Fellows.

Think tanks focus on middle managers due to their creativity and willingness to try new things and pick up extra responsibilities, such as managing and leading high-performance teams on research projects.

In Africa, due to the scattered nature and difference in ideologies of political parties, it is very easy for individuals to pick sides on a particular matter, tagged in partisan colors. Polarization in Africa exists both in elite and general forms. That is to say, there is a battle of ideas between the political philosophies upon which these political parties were founded. This is seen further in the arguments in which their followers engage. There are increasing verbal attacks on think tanks, especially those whose mission includes popularizing their policies to effect change, due to the fragmented and polarized political climate. A government in power expects little or no critique from think tanks, particularly when their policies have been widely accepted by the majority of the populace and even their political rivals. An example of this is a decision by the Electoral Commission of Ghana to commence a new voter register exercise. A group of Civil Society Organizations, including a think tank, has widely been the object of criticism and derogatory words, as can be seen in the comment section of a news report from Ghanaweb. On the other hand, there are others who agree with this call made by Civil Society Organizations because it is supportive of their political party.

Think tanks that engage the government directly also find it difficult for the government to accept and implement the reforms they promote. Politicians are compelled to act in favor of the masses; thus, due to the mindset of winning the next election, any policy which only proves to be effective, yet not popular, is swept under the carpet.

Evolution of Funding for Think Tanks in Africa

Locally, Civil Society Organizations find it difficult to raise funds. This stems from the fact that corporations and foundations are not interested in being chastised politically. For example, during ACEYE's first year of operation, proposals for funding from two organizations did not meet any consideration. Prior to this, two staff members from these organizations had already explained that if there was going to be a rejection of the proposal, it would be on the basis of its legal implications. The take-away from these conversations is that some corporations see think tanks as a pressure group. There are also issues regarding misalignment between corporate social responsibilities and the role of think tanks. As such, there are few organizations supporting the work of think tanks. There is a need for conscious effort for more local funding schemes. This is an effect of how polarized the continent is. Citizens often interpret issues of objectivity on partisan lines. Funding strategies have also metamorphosed in recent times. Some funders are interested in institutional funding, while others focus on project-based funds. So far as donors remain flexible with their funding options, think tanks have room to operate freely.

The fate of think tanks in Africa is heavily reliant on the niche that they have carved for themselves. For example, the President of the Center for International Governance Innovation (CIGI), Rohinton Medhora, was once asked a question, "What Are Think Tanks Good For?" His answer was to the point, "influence peddling, in the best sense of the term." He went on to stress that while one could question the tactics and motivations behind how and who think tanks influence, the bottom line was that they are in the business of pushing for change through ideas and networks. The litmus test of a good think tank, according to Medhora, was not whether it was "right, left, liberal or not, but whether it was proposing evidence-based discussion." Today, think tanks in Africa have contributed to the socioeconomic advancement of the continent through alternative, effective policies and interventions in the areas of education, health, poverty alleviation, freedom, and regional integration, among other things. This is evident in works done by organizations such as the Africa Center for Entrepreneurship and Youth Empowerment (popularly known as ACEYE): *ACEYE calls on ECOWAS to prioritize youth employment as a sustainable means to fight terrorism.*

In conclusion, the future of think tanks will be shaped by the push and pull of donor demands, the quality of their teams, technological advancement, their partnerships, and their resilience in the face of a polarized and fragmented continent.

The Future of Think Tanks and Policy Advice: An African Perspective

Ufo Okeke-Uzodike

Abstract Ufo Okeke-Uzodike, Executive Director of the African Heritage Institution in Enugu, Nigeria, explores the Future of Think Tanks and Policy Advice around the World.

Keywords African think tanks · Civil society organizations · Ghana · Kenya · Nigeria · Policy advice · Policy experts · Policy formulation · Rwanda · South Africa · Think tanks · Transparency

Globally, humans are at crossroads in the twenty-first century. We are witnessing momentous developments across a spectrum of severe economic challenges, institutional realignments (Brexit), tumultuous climatic changes, sociocultural and political conflicts, insecurity, terrorism, extreme inequality, poverty, social exclusions, and gender-based discriminations. In fact, the very existence of nation-states (as currently constituted) appears to be under severe pressure as challenges mount and it becomes increasingly clear that many policymakers are overwhelmed. These policymakers lack coherent or effective responses to growing expectations and demands from increasingly aware and aggressive

U. Okeke-Uzodike (✉)
African Heritage Institution, Enugu, Nigeria

33

constituencies for jobs, salary increases, service delivery, quality of life improvements, etc. This questioning of the legitimacy of policymakers and other constituted authority often belies the objective reality of competing needs and severe budgetary limitations for problem-solving. Such problems are despite the impact of technology-driven innovations in communication systems, which have created new tools to facilitate dissent while encouraging collective actions.

Threatened by the prospect of losing control, governments have become increasingly defensive, short-sighted, conservative, and opportunistic as they grope for answers. They have also resorted to populist postures and the use of sound bites, catchphrases and, often, contempt and cynicism directed at real and perceived opponents, including the probing of dissenting think tanks. In the process, there has been a growing shift away not only from concrete results, transparency, and accountability but also, particularly, from meaningful understanding of the partnership and contributing roles of think tanks for all societies and nations. Thus, think tanks are being subjected increasingly to various forms of bureaucratic and regulatory restrictions, aimed at controlling them, reducing, or even stifling their critical voices for evidence-based policies and reforms.

The net effect is that government funding sources are increasingly drying up where they once existed, or out of the question where they were merely being contemplated. These realities are despite considerable national growth in government budgets over the past few decades. These challenges are made worse by the exponential global increase in the number of think tanks which, expectedly, has created greater competition for available resources.

THINK TANKS IN A CHANGING OPERATIONAL ENVIRONMENT: PLANNING FOR THE FUTURE IN AFRICA

Although think tanks around the world are increasingly struggling for survival, the situation appears more serious for think tanks in Africa, a region with some of the greatest needs for policy influence and redirection. The resulting environment of uncertainty and public frustrations has served to increase questions about the historic role and usefulness of African think tanks. Indeed, many of them, such as the African Heritage Institution (AfriHeritage) or the African Center for the Constructive Resolution of Disputes (ACCORD), are demonstrably change-drivers and are protectors of the regional or public interest and conscience. The situation is further worsened due to rising demands by donor organizations for short-term and project-specific funding, accountability, and evidence of impact. In Africa, many donor agencies are so keen to maximize outputs and outcomes that they ignore organizational health and growth issues by insisting on low overheads of about 10% and even the recipient's own contributions toward the completion of the project. Such conditions have led some analysts to raise serious questions about think tanks and their survival. In 2010, for instance, Michael Tanji declared that think tanks are dead as we know them: "The Think Tank Is Dead: Long Live the Think Tank" (2010).[1] Writing five years later (October 5, 2015) in the Washington Post, Amanda Bennett asked very seriously: "Are Think-Tanks Obsolete?"[2] However, writing about two weeks later (October 21, 2015) in *The National Interest*, James Jay Carafano disagreed with Bennett and Tanji but acknowledged that think tanks must adjust to a fast-changing operational environment: "Think-Tanks Aren't Going Extinct. But They Have to Evolve."[3]

Indeed, think tanks have never been more needed and relevant than now: a vastly more dynamic and often technologically bewildering world where many of the old rules no longer apply. As James McGann (Bennett 2015) underscored, "the old adage 'research it and write it and policy-makers will beat a path to your door,' is no longer the case." Think tanks must either adjust to objective conditions, by shifting away from traditional precepts, or perish. Globally, many think tanks face varied combinations of serious challenges: funding; independence and autonomy; quality and capacity; and impact/effectiveness. These challenges are especially salient for African think tanks that are saddled with additional issues:

[1] Tanji, Michael. 2010. The Think Tank Is Dead: Long Live the Think Tank. http://www.haftofthespear.com/wp-content/uploads/2010/08/The-Think-Tank-is-Dead-Final-Online.pdf. Accessed 8 February 2020.

[2] Bennett, Amanda. 5 October 2015. Are Think Tanks Obsolete? *Washington Post: In Theory*. https://www.washingtonpost.com/news/in-theory/wp/2015/10/05/are-think-tanks-obsolete/. Accessed 7 February 2020.

[3] Carafano, James Jay. 21 October 2015. Think Tanks Aren't Going Extinct: But They Have to Evolve. *The National Interest*. https://nationalinterest.org/feature/think-tanks-arent-going-extinct-they-have-evolve-14137. Accessed 8 February 2020.

ineffective boards and excessive founder interferences on routine administrative matters or on-the-ground strategies despite a desperate need to tackle searing problems. Largely starved of funding, many African think tanks' operational environments are often dire, heavily contested, or desperate. This situation usually leaves them fragile and vulnerable as relatively weak governments plot their own survival in the face of social turmoil and increasingly outspoken, demanding, and insistent electorates. Sadly, when pressured, governments often see think tanks as detractors or enemies rather than development partners. In fact, many African governments (including Nigeria's) are challenging the autonomy of independent non-state civil society organizations such as think tanks. Although many think tanks such as AfriHeritage persist with their efforts, some others align under pressure in order to avoid proscription or trumped-up charges, or in expectation of government favors. Given this array of problems, many African think tanks are faced with strategic and operational challenges that they must redress or fail.

KEY STRATEGIC CHALLENGES
FACING AFRICAN THINK TANKS

1. **New Innovations in Technology and Communications**: Faced perennially with funding and staffing challenges, many African think tanks cannot keep up with changes in technology, communications, big data, and data visualizations. While some peers elsewhere are updating their business models, skill sets, and other innovations, many African think tanks are typically either in survival mode or deeply entangled in low-reward projects, and thus unable to engage emerging developments, opportunities, and threats. There are also serious issues around how they should adjust to highly intense and desirable technological innovations which require training and deeper pockets. Consequently, they often lack the competitive edge or capacity necessary for quick distilling reactions and impactful responses to emerging issues and developments. For AfriHeritage and many other African think tanks, bridging efforts for such gaps typically depends on savings from consultancies as well as careful planning and difficult choices (where possible).

2. **Emergent Competition**: As with their global peers, African think tanks are faced with vastly changed operational and competitive environments in which other organizations—YouTube, advocacy

groups, financial organizations, social media, public relations firms, bloggers, Google, news platform and networks, etc.,—have transformed and accelerated news analyzes and information delivery cycles so profoundly that they are often faced with packaging and disseminating comparatively stale documents and assessments of critical issues. In a world of smartphones and news-and-analysis-as-it-happens, traditional research and publishing processes are increasingly outdated, slow, bulky, tedious, and unwelcome by information-loaded policymakers and the general public who prefer summaries and soundbites. So, instead of the previous near-dominance of the ideas industry, think tanks are now compelled to subsist within a saturated environment, where different and more innovative competitors often hold sway. One analyst aptly underscored that the ideas merchants are "struggling to be heard" (Bennett 2015). For a growing number of African think tanks, this has meant reducing or eliminating hard-copy based publications and gravitating toward online newsletters, e-books, e-journals, and e-libraries.

3. **Think Tank Strategy and Structure**: Faced with global, rapid, and profound changes in their operational environments, many think tanks have been slow to change their operational structures and strategies with respect to their business models, focal points, and delivery arrangements. Indeed, AfriHeritage and other African think tanks often struggle with appropriate adjustments and traction due to their arrays of challenges, especially their routinized inability to retain qualified staff with cutting-edge training and skills. Often, this is despite years of training and investments in staff development. For instance, laboring over the years to nurture many of its staff toward higher degree qualifications, AfriHeritage's lack of strong career paths for mid-level staff, and its demonstrably weak benefits structure and lower salaries for many staff members combine to render it comparatively noncompetitive vis-à-vis universities, international organizations, and aid agencies.

4. **Impact of Changing Political Environment**: Besides being ignored or neglected in many countries, some African think tanks face stifling, politically motivated, regulatory, and internal administrative policy instruments by governments (including Nigeria's) with the view to limit think tank independence and control their abilities to challenge government policy failures and service delivery

issues, and diffuse or weaken opposition political parties. Arguably, these pushbacks from government are net outcomes of the changed Western political environments of resurgent conservative political parties and governments, which have relaxed previous pressures on human rights-abusing governments. This new environment has weakened the work and capacity of think tanks as proponents for evidence-informed policymaking and transformative change. Hence, with the exception (arguably) of a few countries such as South Africa, Ghana, Rwanda, and Kenya, most independent think tanks in Africa are largely marginal in the calculations, activities, and policy formulation processes of governments and political organizations. This harsher operational environment has forced AfriHeritage and many other African think tanks to look for ways to collaborate more effectively, at least with respect to addressing the existential threats facing them domestically. Alive to the political nature of the threats, many think tanks have not only refused to be intimidated, but also have remained adamant on prioritizing their operational mandates.

5. **Impact of Funding Options and Environment**: Funding is the lifeblood of think tanks. Indeed, no organization can thrive or stay healthy without adequate and sustained financial resources. Funding has direct implications not only for research work and programming, but also for rental and administrative costs, human resources, and staff development. Unfortunately, most African governments do not have dedicated budgets for independent think tanks. As such, many think tanks must rely on external funding and consultancies to keep afloat. The sources, types, and duration of funding are hugely important for think tanks, especially in Africa. For instance, the innovative IDRC-TTI model with its renewable five-year awards was particularly good for grantees such as AfriHeritage and the Institute of Economic Affairs in Ghana. This was because it enabled them to operate more credibly as think tanks. While there were a few hitches and challenges over the 10-year support received by most grantees, it made a marked difference for grantees with respect not only to research quality, advocacy, and impact, but also on planning, staff capacity-building and higher degree qualifications, and the all-important matter of improved organizational performance through institution building. This contrasts sharply with other grants, which are typically rare and short-term, and standard funding arrangements that tend to be one-off, short-term, and

project based. The latter often entails institutional overhead of about 10%, which means that organizations are constantly cash-strapped, short-term and project-focussed, and consistently spending scarce intellectual resources on proposal preparations. Long-term support is important for think tanks generally. For African think tanks, such support is indispensable not only for organizational effectiveness, but also for institutionalization and long-term sustainability. TTI support was especially helpful for AfriHeritage because it enabled the organization to leverage some of its resources more creatively for complimentary activities.

6. **Think Tank Value Addition**: Think Tanks are not just storage banks for ideas; they are change-drivers in all societies. By canvassing for evidence-informed discussions and policymaking, think tanks are catalysts for transformative change and development. Their value additions rest particularly in their ability to reframe or set agendas through policy evidence and innovations by mobilizing subject experts, incubating and sharing ideas, and driving policy issues. Sadly, many African think tanks are often unable to play those critical roles as effectively and consistently as peers elsewhere. The often complex reasons include: inadequate trust of think tanks due to suspicion that they may be stooges used instrumentally by local political rivals for political sabotage; that foreign government interests may be using local think tanks to remove the sitting government for hegemonic reasons or in pursuit of foreign national interests; that there is a need to limit the probing eyes and questioning tendencies of think tanks and other organizations that may ask problematic questions about accountability and transparency on government activities, which are best kept as internal matters; and that government ministries and departments have numerous policy experts with the capacity to handle policy issues effectively. Many African think tanks operate in hostile environments where their mere existence may pose significant problems for dishonest officials and policymakers; hence, their tension-riven relationships, and the associated government efforts to control think tank activities.

Without a doubt, think tanks are genuine instruments for transformative change around the world. This is no different for African think tanks, which continue to perform at relatively high levels despite working in comparatively hostile operational environments. They are often denied support funding, access to information and key officials and, often, independence and autonomy. While some African think tanks are spared some of those challenges, many others have had to deal with these or even worse challenges. For me, those challenges do reflect considerably my own experiences since joining AfriHeritage in August of 2016. Yet, the organization and many of its peers in Africa persevere and persist through hard work and incredible sacrifices. Hence, there is a need to reflect thoughtfully and methodically on how best to manage and steer African think tanks away from harm's way and toward sustainability and a more contributing outlook and effectiveness for Africa's continued economic, political, and social transformation.

References

Submissions

Bennett, Amanda. 5 October 2015. Are Think Tanks Obsolete? *Washington Post: In Theory*. https://www.washingtonpost.com/news/in-theory/wp/2015/10/05/are-think-tanks-obsolete/. Accessed 7 February 2020.

Carafano, James Jay. 21 October 2015. Think-Tanks Aren't Going Extinct. But They Have to Evolve. *The National Interest*. https://nationalinterest.org/feature/think-tanks-arent-going-extinct-they-have-evolve-14137. Accessed 8 February 2020.

Tanji, Michael. 2010. The Think Tank Is Dead: Long Live the Think Tank. file:///G:/New%20NIOU/Research/think%20Tank%20Matters/The-think-Tank-is-Dead-Final-Online.pdf. Accessed 8 February 2020.

Bringing Think Tanks into the Digital Era

Idayat Hassan

Abstract Idayat Hassan, Director of the Centre for Democracy and Development in Lagos, Nigeria, explores the Future of Think Tanks and Policy Advice around the World.

Keywords African think tanks · Civil society · Nigeria · South Africa · Think tanks · Transparency

In the last thirty years, technological development has revolutionized societies and democratized participation. Information and communication technology (ICT) is reshaping the way businesses create products and capture value; how and where we work; and how we innovate, interact, and communicate with each other. Cloud computing, platform technologies, big data and analytics, social and collaborative systems and artificial intelligence are fuelling and accelerating a new era of digital business transformation. They are prompting businesses to invent new business models and reimagine how they deliver value to their customers and the

I. Hassan (✉)
Centre for Democracy and Development (CDD), Lagos, Nigeria

© The Author(s) 2021   41
J. McGann, *The Future of Think Tanks and Policy Advice Around the World*, https://doi.org/10.1007/978-3-030-60379-3_5

market. Industry boundaries are expanding and blurring and relationships with business partners are being redefined.[1]

Technology has elevated civic techs, intelligence companies, and political risk consultants above think tanks in Africa. Their ability to do rapid research, simplify data, and readily provide it to governments and the public has increased their influence and reach. However, think tanks are slowly catching on to the use of new technologies that can help to increase the volume and velocity of information flows (McGann 2019: 18). The ability to illustrate project activities or findings through graphics and data visualization is becoming an essential part of think tank communications. Data visualization enables the transformation of unstructured data into different types of more interactive visual content. Think tanks now use interactive websites, infographics, podcasts, social media aggregator tools, and videos to reach the public, policymakers, and their staff.

The one-page infographic which captures key findings or recommendations has become a particularly effective way of gaining the attention of policymakers that are pressed for time. The infographic can catch their attention and makes them much more likely to read the full report. It is clear that by making think tank research more visually appealing to both policymakers and the public, the likelihood of their research having the impact it was designed for, is greatly increased.

THE ROLE FOR "BIG DATA"

A significant feature of ICT is 'big data': Information that can be collected, aggregated, and analyzed by think tanks to provide quality insights into processes and human behaviors. According to the International Data Corporation, by 2025, there will be more than 150 trillion gigabytes of data to process. Big data analytics have the potential to identify efficiencies that lead to innovative new products and services, economic growth, and sustainability. They can also be very effective at showing correlation and can be harvested more quickly than traditional data.

This data is helping think tanks and their development partners reach more people in Sub-Saharan Africa. Think tanks such as the Institute of Infectious Disease and Molecular Medicine in Cape Town, South Africa, are already using big data to analyze the resilience or susceptibility of

---

[1] Deloitte University Press. Business Ecosystems Come of Age.

African populations to diseases, such as tuberculosis, HIV, and breast cancer. Coalitions such as Citi Alliances Think Tanks are using big data to contribute to the sustainability of cities. The use of GPS on increasingly affordable tablets is supporting researchers' efforts to improve the quality of their data. However, the ability of African think tanks to generate big data is challenged by high costs and low capacity.

Think tanks and civil society groups need funds to achieve their goals but also need to prove the results of their work in order to attract donors. Big data has a huge potential to optimize this cycle, and help organizations make knowledgeable decisions (Sriram 2017). A study by Every Action found that 90% of think tanks[2] collect data, but 50% of them are not fully aware of the ways data can impact their work. This is because most think tanks do not have dedicated data analytics teams. A lack of manpower, along with a shortage of systems to collect, analyze, and manage such data are challenges to most African think tanks.

An Evolving Model?

Think tanks face both political and technological challenges in the digital era that are seen as grounds for an existential crisis. There is increasing competition in the knowledge-brokerage industry, where actors such as media organizations, consulting firms, and advocacy groups are threatening the very survival of think tanks—especially in the face of rapid technological advancement. Think tanks are not yet obsolete but some of their strategies increasingly are. In recognition of this, the think tank community is undergoing a transformation designed to change funding streams, communications, and dissemination strategies, as well as research outputs for the digital era.

First, think tanks are beginning to adopt new operational frameworks. This is due, in part, to the recent pushback they have experienced as a result of external forces influenced by partisanship and the rise of populism, which limit their roles and influence in society, as well as the general public's increasing distrust in government and institutions—think tanks included.

Think tanks are shifting away from a government-based approach toward a combination of policy, practice, and activism that can mobilize public support for their work. This shift in focus implies a new

[2] Everyaction. Resource Library. https://www.everyaction.com/resource-library.

framework for the analysis of change, with some think tanks looking beyond governments as the source of change and toward other organizations that can build local support among the public, campaigners, and grassroots organizations.

In their business models, think tanks increasingly look to ensure diversity in recruitment, improve quality assurance, maintain independence and integrity of research, engage in purposeful collaborations, create innovative products and services, and work with new audiences and partners by harnessing technology and (big) data.

However, more can be done to improve transparency and accountability. Transparency around funding has become imperative to maintain the trust of citizens. Transparency is also key as governments in many African countries are increasingly attempting to delegitimize the work of think tanks and sources of their funding.

Critical to think tanks' continued relevance is the need to evolve communication techniques in order to keep the attention of key audiences—policymakers, donors, and the general public. In Africa, think tanks have to utilize the advancement of technology to disseminate research findings using multimedia, social media, online interactive forums, and infographics.

In the age of vast and instant information, think tanks need to be able to deliver analytical information in a timely and effective way. To do this, think tanks must be able to fully integrate the use of new media into their communication strategies. This entails devoting resources, both human and financial, to these ends.

References

Introduction

McGann, James G. 2019. *2018 Global Go to Think Tank Index Report*. Philadelphia: Think Tanks and Civil Societies Program, University of Pennsylvania.

Submissions

McGann, James G. 2019. 2018 Global Go to Think Tank Index Report. TTCSP Global Go to Think Tank Index Reports. https://repository.upenn.edu/think_tanks/16.

Sriram, Ramya. 12 April 2017. Nonprofit Organizations: Can They Benefit from Data Science? Kolabtree Blog. https://www.kolabtree.com/blog/nonprofit-data-science/.

Think Tanks in the Context of Africa's Development

Rose Ngugi

Abstract Rose Ngugi, Executive Director of the Kenya Institute for Public Policy Research and Analysis (KIPPRA) in Nairobi, Kenya, explores the Future of Think Tanks and Policy Advice around the World.

Keywords African think tanks · Civil society organizations · Digital platforms/Digitization · Inclusive growth · Kenya · Policy advice · Policy design · Policy formulation · Think tanks

Development blueprints in Africa, such as the Agenda 2063 for "the Africa we want," envisage a modern, prosperous continent that is poverty-free, food secure, and has educated citizens. The various blueprints envisage thriving economic activities supported by modern transportation, information, communication technology (ICT), and energy infrastructure that create decent jobs and provide economic opportunities for all. These opportunities would be in a climate-resilient and peaceful

R. Ngugi (✉)
Kenya Institute for Public Policy Research and Analysis (KIPPRA),
Nairobi, Kenya

J. McGann, *The Future of Think Tanks and Policy Advice Around the World*, https://doi.org/10.1007/978-3-030-60379-3_6

45

environment, with good governance, booming intra-African trade, and expanded democratic space.[1]

Over the last two to three decades, the continent has experienced a major transformation in economic growth, sound policies, and reforms that have improved institutions and governance. It has experienced a boom in the usage of ICT for financial services and banking services have expanded to remote regions of the continent. Despite this progress, African countries face many macroeconomic, sociocultural, political, security, and environmental challenges, and inclusive growth is still elusive. Addressing the persistent policy challenges such as burgeoning youth unemployment, developing leadership and critical skills, changing mindsets, creating an environment that enables private sector development, and building or strengthening key institutions remains a priority (African Capacity Building Foundation 2017).

African think tanks have a critical role in supporting African countries to address development challenges through evidence-based policy design, implementation and monitoring, capacity development for state and non-state actors, and provision of platforms for stakeholder engagement, dialogue, and advocacy. To deliver on their mandate, the think tanks require a conducive policy environment and transformative leadership in both state and non-state sectors.

The development of think tanks in Africa is a recent phenomenon. In Sub-Saharan Africa, the contribution of think tanks to the government policy process was especially occasioned by the need to improve governance during the structural adjustment era. Since then, the region has seen a notable increase in the number of think tanks, at over 660 currently and accounting for 8.5% of global think tanks. The growth of think tanks in Africa is further motivated by the presence of dynamic political, economic, and social reforms, which create an opportunity for think tanks to leverage. Expansion of democratic space provides African countries with a level playing field for think tanks of various inclinations to thrive, including those that are government-affiliated, nongovernmental, or private sector-led. These developments call for think tanks, networks, and policymakers to work together to strengthen the research-to-policy linkage, which is critical for Africa's development.

---

[1] African Union. 2013. Agenda 2063. https://au.int/en/agenda2063/overview.

Implementation of appropriate and timely interventions and approaches to support inclusive and sustainable growth in the continent is limited by human capacity, particularly within government institutions, coupled with limited use of evidence-based policy advice by decision-makers. To bridge this gap, think tanks in the continent are enhancing policy uptake by supporting policymakers to formulate evidence-based policies, which are important building blocks for transforming economies in Africa. They are also supporting non-state actors in enhancing participation in the policy process by convening actors with a policy mandate to debate on emerging policy and development issues; increasing awareness among key players in the policy arena through forums such as round tables, dissemination workshops, seminars and conferences; supporting the establishment and upkeep of economic policy networks; and equipping those working on policy issues through tailor-made training targeting specific stakeholders in policymaking.

Despite these efforts, think tanks also face their own challenges, including inadequate funding, a limited number of seasoned researchers, underdeveloped institutional capacity, varying levels of maturity, different country contexts, and inadequate enabling environments. Addressing these challenges is a key strategy to catalyzing the development of sound economic policy and economic development across Africa (Dalberg 2013).

Changing Competition and Technology in the Public Policymaking Arena

Policymaking has attracted various players and processes over the last couple of decades. The various players are highly interlinked and influence the speed at which policies are formulated or implemented. The various players can be categorized as those involved in the following areas: the policymaking context (including politics and institutions involved in policymaking); the evidence (research quality, researcher credibility, and the framing of messages emanating from think tanks); advocacy (between think tanks and policymaker communities either formal or informal, the role of intermediaries, civil society organizations, media, networks, and campaigning strategies); and external influences such as donor interests, international discourses, global political or economic shocks, socioeconomic and cultural.

In Africa, civil society organizations (CSOs) play an important role in providing legislators and legislative committees with expert inputs to inform legislative debates, thus providing competition to the traditional think tanks (Mandaville 2004). Therefore, think tanks of the future will need to become more informed and innovative, able to convene various actors in the public policymaking landscape, and able to package and disseminate policy products and messages (evidence) using nontraditional media (emerging media) for greater uptake. There is a need to build the capacity of researchers to learn effective communication and engagement skills for their findings to be understood by policymakers. Through effective engagement with policymakers and practitioners, think tanks will be able to identify emerging implementation gaps and make evidence-based proposals on the best way forward.

With advancements in ICT and changing tastes and preferences among consumers of "evidence," the policymaking arena has also attracted new entrants and "competitors" such as law firms, advocacy groups, public relations firms, and nontraditional media sources and companies that have transformed how policy research and advice are packaged and disseminated. There is growing use of big data worldwide, which allows the integration of various digital resources in data collection. In the public sector, this will allow governments to gather information from the internet, social media and other digital platforms, and include it in policymaking.

The potential of big data can be used in the different phases of the public policy process. For instance, in the planning phase, it is useful in the areas of agenda-setting, problem definition, policy discussion, and citizen participation, with a focus on social media data. In the design phase, it can contribute to policy formulation and information-based policy instruments. In the delivery phase, big data can be beneficial in real-time production of data and immediate feedback regarding the effectiveness of policies in order to improve future implementation processes. Finally, it will be useful for monitoring and evaluation of policies. With increasing internet penetration in Africa, successful think tanks of the future will be those that can harness the power of big data and data visualization in influencing the link between evidence and policymaking.

THE CHANGING STRUCTURE OF THINK TANKS

Over the years, the continent has become more integrated through the formation of regional blocs such as the East African Community (EAC); Common Market for Eastern and Southern Africa (COMESA); Southern African Development Community (SADC); the Economic Community of Central African States (ECCAS); the Arab Maghreb Union (AMU); the Economic Community of West African States (ECOWAS); and the new kid on the block, the African Continental Free Trade Area (ACFTA), with goals ranging from socioeconomic cooperation and integration to political and security cooperation.

At a regional level, think tanks are beginning to restructure and broaden the scope of policy research and analysis to support the Regional Economic Communities (RECs) and map out priorities at both national and regional levels. In this regard, think tanks will need to strategize to build the capacity of RECs through training and advocating for effective policy formulation and prudent management of funds. Furthermore, the future will witness restructuring of think tanks' business models through the formation of regional and inter-regional think tank partnerships and programs to support RECs.

COLLABORATION FOR GREATER IMPACT

Due to the proliferation of think tanks in Africa, with some doing the same things in the same regions, the ability of think tanks to deliver is weakened by fragmented efforts and weak collaboration. Collaboration among think tanks will help to pool skills and capacities, enhance the quality of their outputs, enhance bargaining power in the policy arena, and reduce unnecessary competition and duplication of efforts. For their voice to create impact, there is a need to institutionalize networks of think tanks and communities of practice to coordinate their activities. Furthermore, unified think tanks will find it easier to mobilize funding.

THE NEED TO REMAIN INDEPENDENT AND RELEVANT

One of the key challenges think tanks in Africa face is sustainability. Think tanks in many countries have not attracted the expected long-term funding and support from African governments, the private sector, or the donor community. Approximately 30% of think tanks are facing threat of closure and, going forward, the survival of African think tanks is pegged on their ability to remain relevant. The research will ideally be more demand-driven than supply-driven since the former has higher potential in supporting the development of Africa-led policies, programs, and strategies. Think tanks must keep abreast of current happenings to avoid making policy formulations that cannot tackle current challenges. They will be required to address the real felt needs of communities by conducting research that links policymakers and the community.

A high level of credibility of research and researchers in think tanks and among legislators can help improve research-to-legislation channels. The credibility of policy research is enhanced by the independence of a think tank as perceived by the policymaker. Achieving increased relevance and uptake will require sustained engagement with civic, public, and private sector players to develop relationships based on trust and reliability to deliver quality output that can inform and direct emerging policy debates (Jones 2011).

CONCLUSION

In conclusion, given the policy developments in Africa and all the questions raised on why implementation of the development agenda is slow in Africa, think tanks in Africa can and should play a critical role as organizations designed for and capable of long-term thinking and reflection; furthermore, they should be proactive to provide the required practical intellectual insights for Africa to tackle implementation challenges (African Capacity Building Foundation 2019).

REFERENCES

SUBMISSIONS

African Capacity Building Foundation. 2017. The ACBF Strategy for 2017–2021: Skilled People and Strong Institutions Transforming Africa.

African Capacity Building Foundation. 2019. 6th Africa Think Tank Summit: Tackling Implementation Challenges for Africa's Sustainable Development. In *Proceedings of the Summit*, 24–26 April 2019, Nairobi, Kenya.

Dalberg. 2013. *Evaluation of ACBF Supported Policy Centres and Think Tanks in Sub-Saharan Africa*. Harare: African Capacity Building Foundation.

Jones, Basil. 2011. Linking Research to Policy: The African Development Bank as Knowledge Broker. African Development Bank. Working Paper No. 131.

Mandaville, A. 2004. *Legislatures and Civil Society: Potential Partners in Poverty Reduction*. Washington, DC: NDI.

Europe Region

Western Europe

While many of the earlier think tanks in Western Europe were formed right after World War II, they have evolved and adapted to address twenty first century global issues. Among those, the 1523 total think tanks operating across the region must address the future of the EU in the wake of Brexit, new transitions and trends in climate change, and examine cyclic migration movements, as well as other issues. At the 2019 Europe Think Tank Summit, participants from various European think tanks highlighted the need for conservation, adaptation, and innovation in order for think tanks to remain relevant. The discussions not only emphasized current strategies for dealing with policy issues, but also best practices for engaging with new audiences, funding security, increasing think tank diversity, and the utilization of new technologies and communication methods.

Eastern Europe

Nearing the third decade since the dissolution of the USSR, Eastern Europe is still realigning itself from the post-Communist regional shock wave. Think tanks have come to play an immensely important role in the reconstruction process, as more than two-thirds of the region's think tanks were founded since the Soviet collapse with 159 emerging between 2011 and 2018. These 687 institutions face a host of unique challenges, from advancing reconciliation and justice efforts in the post-war former Yugoslavian nations, to addressing the war in Eastern Ukraine, and analyzing the power struggle between an expanded NATO and reemerging Russia. In this tense climate, think tanks must continue to offer insightful policy analysis and recommendations.

Artificial Intelligence: An Opportunity and a Challenge for Think Tanks

Guntram Wolff

Abstract Guntram Wolff, Director of Bruegel in Belgium, explores the Future of Think Tanks and Policy Advice around the World.

Keywords Belgium · Civil society · Policy advice · Think tanks · Transparency

How is artificial intelligence changing the nature of think tanks and what does the public expect from think tanks on the topic itself? In this chapter, I will illustrate the ways in which artificial intelligence has been changing the demand for Bruegel's research, both in terms of methods and in terms of substance.

ON THE IMPORTANCE OF A POLICY-ORIENTED AND TRUSTWORTHY RESEARCH PROGRAM

Before we explore the impact of AI, we must investigate why it is important that a think tank's research be policy oriented and based on strong values and transparency. In my view, think tanks such as Bruegel need to

G. Wolff (✉)
Bruegel, Belgium

© The Author(s) 2021   53
J. McGann, *The Future of Think Tanks and Policy Advice
Around the World*, https://doi.org/10.1007/978-3-030-60379-3_7

play an important role in translating and developing academic research into policy advice that can be understood and used by policymakers. Often, academic work is far away from political realities. It can also be unsuited in its approach if it ignores institutional, legal, and governance constraints. Therefore, think tanks can play a role in translating findings as well as practicing applied research with a more policy-oriented focus that complements more academic work.

Credibility and trustworthiness are central to that process. In an information-rich society, policymakers receive multiple inputs from many sides. But whom can they trust? In our understanding, reputation, expertise, independence, and transparency are of fundamental importance for being a trusted advisor. It starts with the scholars working for the think tank. They need to not only have an impeccable standing and be recognized academics themselves, but also need to understand policymaking and adhere to the highest principles of academic rigor. At Bruegel, they sign a statement of research integrity and have to declare all possible conflicts of interest. Scholars and managers also make an annual declaration of outside interests, which is available on the Bruegel website. These interests are not just financial; it is important for readers to be aware of other potential influences on a scholar's work. These public declarations are extensive in the areas they cover and represent the highest standard in public transparency for think tanks.

Equally important is the institutional setting. Transparency on all funding sources and governance is critical for credibility and trustworthiness. Bruegel's commitment to transparency means that we publish detailed financial statements every year. Our accounts are independently audited. We detail the origin of every cent of income, and we also report spending along nine spending lines. The financial statements clearly show what every member contributed in any given year, a level of transparency that is rare in our sector. State members of Bruegel also have the right to audit Bruegel at any time.

An important question then, is how research topics are identified and priorities are established. The process of drafting a research program combines bottom-up and top-down elements. The process always starts with suggestions by Bruegel researchers and the Director and Deputy Director, themselves researchers, give feedback and make suggestions as well. Bruegel's members then play an important role in reacting to ideas and giving suggestions for research priorities. Bruegel's scientific advisory council is consulted and Bruegel researchers and management hold numerous consultations with other stakeholders and civil society.

An important concern is the balance between long-term research capacity and short-term agility of research. Bruegel has opted for three-year cycles and a "Twin Peaks" principle, according to which long-term research investment beyond the usual annual programming cycle is combined with rapid responses to unanticipated policy developments.

Several evaluation processes are used to ensure that high standards of research, relevance, and impact are maintained. An external evaluation committee consisting of independent high-profile public figures is appointed by the general assembly to conduct a thorough review every three years. The scientific council conducts its three-year evaluation of academic and scientific standards. Beyond these external three-year evaluations, regular internal evaluations are carried out throughout the year. All Bruegel research passes through a weekly research seminar and peer review via email. Outreach reports by the communications team and regular discussions with the Bruegel scientific council complement the quality assurance process. The Director and the Deputy Director provide extensive feedback on the scholars' work. The Director has the overall editorial responsibility for Bruegel's research.

On AI in Think Tanks

Informing the drafting of the research program with multiple interactions with important stakeholders in society, business, and government can help detect important new trends early on, and thereby preemptively adjust research capacities. Artificial Intelligence is an example of a topic with rapidly gaining importance. According to Google Trends, search queries for the term "machine learning," an important part of artificial intelligence, have roughly tripled since August 2016.[1] Searches for "web scraping," a method for data collection from websites, has doubled since 2013.[2]

---

[1] Google Trends. 2020. Interest Over Time: Machine Learning. https://trends.google.com/trends/explore?date=all&q=machine%20learning. Accessed 1 February 2020.

[2] Google Trends. 2020. Interest Over Time: Web Scraping. https://trends.google.com/trends/explore?date=all&q=%2Fm%2F07ykbs. Accessed 1 February 2020.

The rise of this new technology poses at least three challenges with respective opportunities to respond.

First, the topic itself is of increasing importance to the global economy and is therefore worth studying in detail. Numerous questions arise, regarding how AI can be best integrated into business operations, as well as how some countries and companies may be put at an advantage or disadvantage because of AI. How is AI affecting productivity growth (Petropoulos et al. 2019)? What are the ethical implications of increasing use of AI? Should the state regulate the use of AI and, if so, how?[3] Last but not least, what implications will AI have on global labor markets? For example, how will AI-based pattern recognition of breast cancer impact the work of medical doctors? Bruegel has explored these questions in a recently published book (Petropoulos et al. 2019).

Second, web scraping and machine learning can be important tools for research. For example, one can use the information that large numbers of individuals put into social media feed to extract trends and new emerging topics. In a recent analysis, Bergamini (2019) explored the trends on Twitter among millions of professional economists (Bergamini 2019). Such an analysis combines web scraping techniques with machine learning tools that are necessary for text analysis. The key challenge in this space is attracting and keeping the right talent. In fact, in the EU, there is a scarcity of data scientists and programmers. The new skills needed by think tanks in order to continue to influence policies can become quickly outdated; therefore, think tanks need to invest in training and hiring new staff.

The third challenge deals with the ethical use of such methods. The way data is gathered to choose the "right" policy responses is full of political consequences. For this reason, the European Commission's 2015 Better Regulation Guidelines emphasized that impact assessment seeks to inform political decision-makers but not to supplant their political function. With the increased automation and real-time data processing promised by the AI "revolution," the discourse on evidence-based policy will inevitably change (and so will Think Tanks). We might see the automatic processing of data and an automatic proposal for the best possible way of responding to it.

---

[3] Bruegel had the pleasure of hosting the European Commission's executive vice president Magrethe Vestager for an in-depth discussion on the question of a European regulatory approach to AI.

A crucial question will be, who will own the "evidence" in the future? The data or algorithms used for machine learning might be private or common goods, according to political choices. An example of the complexity of the issue is the October 2015 decision by the European Court of Justice, which first ruled that the transatlantic Safe Harbour agreement, which let American companies use a single standard for consumer privacy and data storage in both the United States and Europe, was invalid. The framework was replaced in February 2016 by a new pact calling for companies to agree to "robust obligations" to protect European personal data and enables Europeans who feel their data has been assessed by US intelligence agencies to complain to a new ombudsman.

Conclusions

AI could change the nature of evidence-based policymaking forever by becoming an indispensable aspect of governance around the world. Think tanks like ours could quickly become irrelevant if we fail to adapt. However, even if smart policy decisions become dependent on AI, those same decisions will lack credibility if they aren't informed by the delicate standards of transparency and accountability that institutions like ours have spent decades honing and refining. Without today's expectations of checks and balances, the AI-assisted policies of tomorrow will be considered with trepidation and suspicion, and with good reason. It will require a combination of values and innovation to ensure that the policies that touch everyone are written with everyone in mind. A forward-looking, policy-oriented research program can help charter the way for any think tank. New research priorities, significant investment in staff, and high ethical standards are crucial to ensure that think tanks remain relevant and impactful in a rapidly changing world of policymaking that uses AI.

References

Submissions

Bergamini, Enrico. 19 December 2019. 2019 on #econtwitter, in a Million Tweets. Bruegel. https://bruegel.org/2019/12/2019-on-econtwitter-in-a-million-tweets/.

George Petropoulos et al. 9 July 2019. Digitalisation and European welfare states. Bruegel. https://bruegel.org/2019/07/digitalisation-and-european-welfare-states/.

Connecting Politics and Society: A Way Forward for Think Tanks

Pol Morillas

Abstract Pol Morillas, Director of Barcelona Centre for International Affairs (CIDOB) in Barcelona, Spain, explores the Future of Think Tanks and Policy Advice around the World.

Keywords Policy advice · Spain · Think tanks

For a long time, think tanks have been responsible for fostering the connection between expert knowledge and policymaking processes. Midway between academia and politics, these centers of thought have transferred rigorous studies to political praxis, both in terms of public discourse and policy. But is this link still valid at times of increased political contestation and of traditional power structures?

Distrust is also sweeping the knowledge sector and think tanks have been criticized for siding with "the elite," precisely due to the connection

---

The original version of this chapter was revised: The incorrect chapter author name has now been updated. The correction to this chapter is available at https://doi.org/10.1007/978-3-030-60379-3_43

P. Morillas (✉)
Barcelona Centre for International Affairs (CIDOB), Barcelona, Spain

between knowledge and power that they guarantee. Experts have been the target of populist attacks and, in a context of a generalized challenging of the political order, the questioning of experts and think tanks has also been exacerbated by the instruments of misinformation, "fake news" and post-truth politics. In the Brexit campaign, Leave leaders proclaimed "we have had enough of experts," while Donald Trump, Jair Bolsonaro and Boris Johnson have all casted doubts on the significance of the coronavirus, both in terms of its health consequences and disruptive impact on societies.

Another factor in the recent decline in think tanks' social relevance is the high degree of specialization in the sector. For a long time, the studies based on technical knowledge were prioritized in order to gain traction among decision-makers. "Policy recommendations" have become a near obligatory final section of think tank reports, sometimes to the detriment of these studies' broader capacity for social impact.

The trend toward linking the work of think tanks with political decisions contrasts with the difficulty of conducting detailed follow-up of public policies, as researchers are rarely able to connect to the day-to-day decision-making processes. The disjuncture between think tanks and political influence creates a double risk: irrelevance in the eyes of political decision-makers and distancing from society as a whole.

Social detachment is a problem for academia as well as for think tanks. As the academic world, particularly political science, has privileged rigor over relevance, and academicism over social needs, its social utility has diminished. Desch writes that "objectivity precludes policy engagement because the latter is inextricably linked with questions of value," and if anything prevails in the current political crisis it is debated that are deeply normative, ideologized and polarized.

Producing texts in formats that are barely digestible for the general public and of great technical complexity has not benefited the social relevance of research. Think tanks whose survival depends on the achievement and execution of research projects financed by public authorities have been more exposed to this risk than those with their own generous philanthropic financing. Another factor is the increased competition in the "expertise" sector, with a growing number of journalist-analysts and academics with a public vocation.

Adding to the process of contesting the role of think tanks is the politicization of our societies, which may be seen as an opportunity. Interest in international and European politics has been growing in recent years, largely due to the effects of the crisis in the international order in general, and European integration in particular.

The euro crisis, the refugee crisis, Brexit and the European Union's democratic deficit signal the end of a permissive consensus on European integration and the emergence of a level of dissent that restricts decision-making capacity. Exercising political leadership is also much more difficult today at both national and European levels due to the growing public scrutiny of our leaders.

Following Grande and Hutter, the international and European agendas have gained importance in the eyes of our fellow citizens. The awareness of a greater centrality of these agendas in our daily life has mobilized the electorate around issues that are not strictly national in nature. In the European case, this politicization may become an opportunity to rethink the project as a whole, along with the public policies that emerge from it. This is a healthy development for any mature and consolidated political project like today's European Union.

The effects of politicization have also increased where the links between the international (or European) and the local have been strengthened. When it comes to migration or the role of cities as global actors, the separation between the international and the domestic has faded. The same is true in the security field where, for example, the EU's Global Strategy notes the close link between internal security (civil protection, trafficking, and terrorism) and external security (deriving from international crises and conflicts). The more unity there is between the local and the international, the more likely is the politicization of political agendas.

The challenging of experts and the politicization of the agenda combine to give a new social meaning to think tanks as centers of thought. When political leaders—who used to advocate their social utility—attack them from populist positions, the response should be to regain their original purpose: to revalorize their usefulness as a public good in the face of ill-intentioned questioning of informed policy.

This does not mean falling into complacency. Think tanks today face the challenge not so much of providing policy recommendations but of presenting grand narratives and ideas to motivate and mobilize a disoriented society. They should avoid analyzing only what is politically correct or enjoys broad social consensus, because it is precisely these consensuses that have been disappearing.

Think tanks must therefore shift from acting as a link between academia and politics toward fostering a greater connection between politics and society. Faced with growing politicization, they should be centers of thought that are open to society, encourage the use of new formats, find new audiences, and return to society part of what it invests in them (especially centers that receive public funding). In times of increasing contestation and politicization, revindicating their social utility also means defending their rigor and independence within their field of specialization. The research agendas of think tanks should promote the study of issues that concern the society in which they operate, making use of the attacks they have faced to reverse the trend of generalized contestation, and thereby improve their social relevance and utility.

The growing citizen interest in European and international issues works in their favor. European politics used to be perceived by citizens as too technocratic and far away from their daily lives. This is no longer the case, as the Euro or the refugee crises demonstrated then, and as the reconstruction of European economies and societies after the coronavirus becomes part of the public debate today. European politics are increasingly perceived as domestic politics, which prompts a greater desire for the opinion and participation of citizens, also in societies like Spain where there is still a wide support for European integration. Think tanks have their part to play when it comes to connecting these political developments with societal discussions and concerns.

Think Tanks for Future—A Think Piece

Camilla Bausch and R. Andreas Kraemer

Abstract Camilla Bausch, Director and R. Andreas Kraemer, Founder & Director Emeritus of the Ecologic Institute in Berlin, Germany, explore the Future of Think Tanks and Policy Advice around the World.

Keywords China · Digital platforms/Digitization · Germany · Russia · Think tanks

THE WORLD IS FACING FUNDAMENTAL CHALLENGES

Global megatrends, like demographic changes, technological advances, increasing connectivity, and globalization have long been on the agenda of policymakers, business leaders, and scientists. Accordingly, the impact of aging societies in the West, global population growth, digitalization, artificial intelligence, robotics, and biotechnologies has been shaping the public debate for many years. New, however, is the prominence of public health as a global public good and environmental challenges such as biodiversity loss and climate change, as well as the resulting emergence of new disease vectors in such debates. These challenges are now being discussed

C. Bausch (✉) · R. Andreas Kraemer
Ecologic Institute, Berlin, Germany

at the World Economic Forum and the Munich Security Conference. Climate change and resource scarcity are among the five key megatrends identified by PWC.[1] Others, like the Zukunftsinstitut, see "neo-ecology" among the top 5,[2] and "health" among the top 12.[3] No matter which specific label or angle or group in society, environmental impacts on health, lives, and livelihoods, as well as policies, and actions in response, will shape our future in an interconnected world.

THE CRISIS

The science is clear: our way of living is overstepping the planetary boundaries. This crisis is fundamental, and urgent action is needed. The current situation reflects several interlocking and mutually aggravating crises that are eroding natural life-support systems and pushing the world beyond its limits. The impacts of global overheating, the loss of biological diversity and productive ecosystems on land and in the ocean, the disruptions in the chemical cycles of nitrogen and phosphorus, and the increasing acidification of the ocean can be observed all over the world. In key areas, we are already breaching the boundaries that define a safe and stable environment for human civilization (Rockström et al. 2009; Steffen et al. 2015; see also: IPCC 2018). The "Atlantic Lifestyle" (McGlade et al. 2016) with its energy and resource-intensive patterns of production, trade, and consumption (Kraemer 2017b) is destroying the Earth's ecosystems.

"Earth Overshoot Day" as calculated by the "Global Footprint Network" arrives earlier from year to year. This illustrative calendar date aims to mark the moment in which the yearly anthropogenic resource consumption exceeds the Earth's capacity to regenerate those resources. According to the past year's calculation, humanity had already consumed its entire annual supply of natural resources by July 29, 2019. For the subsequent five months, humankind was consuming resources that should have been protected and enhanced for the following year and for future generations (Wackernagel and Beyers 2019).

---

[1] PWC. Megatrends. https://www.pwc.co.uk/issues/megatrends.html.

[2] Gatterer, Harry. The 5 most important megatrends for companies in the 2020s. *zukunftsInstitut.* https://www.zukunftsinstitut.de/artikel/die-5-wichtigsten-meg atrends-fuer-unternehmern-in-den-2020ern/.

[3] zukunftsInstitut. Megatrends. https://www.zukunftsinstitut.de/dossier/megatrends/.

THE ENVIRONMENT–CLIMATE–HEALTH NEXUS

Public health and environmental policies were always intertwined. The density of human (and animal) populations in our cities can only be maintained—without leading to disease—through the supply of clean water in sufficient quantity, and the collection, treatment, and safe disposal of wastes and wastewaters through technical systems and networks. The COVID-19 pandemic highlights the nefarious impact of urban air pollution leading to respiratory disease that then contributes to high mortality rates among those infected with the SARS-CoV-2 virus (Wu and Nethery et al. 2020, US; Cui et al. 2003, China).

The origin of the new coronavirus itself and its transmission from animal hosts to humans is assumed to have been caused or facilitated by the destruction of natural ecosystems through industrial agriculture and humans moving into proximity with animals and hunting and eating species they did not use before, at least in dense population centers where infectious diseases are particularly dangerous (Spinney 2020). The pattern of land degradation, poverty, consumption of bushmeat, keeping animals alive in captivity close to humans, and eating exotic animals, as well as the lack of sanitary infrastructure allowing wild animals (and rodents) to come into close proximity with humans has resulted, for example, in outbreaks of Ebola (Vidal 2020) and Lassa fever (Centers for Disease Control and Prevention 2019).

While the connection between the destruction of natural ecosystems and the outbreak of diseases is being understood more and more,[4] there are also links between global overheating and the spreading of disease, from malaria[5] which is making its way back into Europe, and Chagas disease on the move from Central America to the United States (University of Vermont 2012), to the reemergence of anthrax (Walsh et al. 2018) from melting permafrost regions in Russia (Revich and Podolnaya 2011).

The short-term and urgent attention to the COVID-19 pandemic, like any pandemic, may distract from environmental and climate protection as a policy objective, but the underlying causes will come to the fore again

---

[4] For an overview and regular updates see: Geneva Environment Network. 2020. COVID-19 and the Environment. https://www.genevaenvironmentnetwork.org/covid19.html.

[5] World Health Organization. Global Environmental Change. https://www.who.int/globalchange/climate/summary/en/index5.html.

sooner or later. It is up to think tanks to serve as a memory for society and remind decision-makers so that they don't repeat past mistakes. Not many think tanks pay attention to the long-term trends—like environmental destruction—that contribute to symptoms, from disease to involuntary displacement and migration.

LACK OF ADEQUATE POLICY SOLUTIONS

The environmental crisis is a long-term challenge. It requires societies to fundamentally change course. Think tanks fit for the future, and even more so "Think Tanks for Future"—those that commit themselves to playing their part in protecting the environmental integrity of this world for current and future generations—will have to respond to this challenge.

Currently, the global community is failing to adequately react to the crises at hand. A prominent example is the failure to properly address the climate crisis. As established in the Paris Agreement (PA), the global community agreed to keep "the increase in the global average temperature to well below 2 °C above pre-industrial levels and to pursue efforts to limit the temperature increase to 1.5 °C above pre-industrial levels" (Article 2 PA). However, year after year, the UNEP Emissions Gap Report finds that greenhouse gas emissions continue to rise with no sign of peaking anytime soon. Even under the most optimistic assumptions, the current promises under the PA will lead to a 3 °C temperature increase by the end of the century (UNEP 2019). It is clear that the global community is not on track to keep to the limits they themselves have agreed upon. Such failures can be found all over the world with respect to environmental protection, be it at a regional or at a national level.

Looking at such evidence—and keeping in mind the extreme weather events already destroying livelihoods from California to Australia, from Southern Africa to Northern Europe, there can only be one conclusion: business as usual does not suffice anymore.

From a simplified perspective, the paradigm of the past 50 years for many countries, e.g., in Western Europe, was "stability" in the sense of defending and improving the status quo. Policy continuity appeared to be a key to success and prosperity. However, as a whole, this approach has now become a guarantor of failure—if not in the short term, then in the long term. Old paradigms have to shift.

On a positive note, some of the necessary shifts are slowly starting. Investment giant Blackrock—surely not known as a left-wing radical—has observed a "tectonic shift," which many have not yet realized:

> Assets under management in dedicated environmental, social and gover-nance (ESG) funds have tripled in the past decade to a little under \$1 trillion, according to IMF estimates as of June 2019. Yet we see a far bigger structural shift afoot — akin to the multi-decade impact of the post-war "baby boom." This shift is unlikely captured in today's asset prices. (Hildebrand and Donilon 2020)

THINK TANKS FOR FUTURE—REVIEW THE WAYS YOU HAVE DONE BUSINESS SO FAR

What does all this mean for think tanks? Where do think tanks have to reinvent themselves? This question is not easy to answer, as think tanks across the fields and across the globe vary greatly (McGann 2020). But it is safe to say that in the face of the fundamental urgency of the described crises and at this moment of existential threat to mankind, think tanks are challenged to review their operational assumptions and traditional modes of working. Seeing the collective failure in this crisis, think tanks are challenged to review and adapt their ways—particularly if they operate in regions or topic areas responsible for a high environmental footprint.

First, think tanks should **review their portfolios** to understand where they can and should contribute to the transformation needed in almost all areas of society. They should identify the most unsustainable policies in their field from an environmental and social angle. They should then identify those that benefit from such policies, for they might need to be convinced or helped to change their ways. Those who may be harmed by such policies and those who would benefit from policy reform should also be identified, as they might need to be given a voice. Think tanks should develop options for policy reforms and narratives with equity, poverty alleviation, and sustainability in mind. And while the transformation is a very complex project, there are easy targets, e.g., the abolition of envi-ronmentally harmful subsidies. Busting the stories and myths that have been constructed to protect the incumbents and their interests is another example.

Second, think tanks should also **review their way of engagement**. Policymakers fail at successfully implementing solutions, despite decades of warnings from science, broadly acknowledged need for urgent action, and all the known options for generating impact. Somehow, the political economy is not strong enough for the action needed.

In the face of this, think tanks have to ask themselves why their insights and advice might not have facilitated the solutions the world needs. Are the questions and findings adequate? Have the theories of change worked on by think tanks been confirmed in practice? Are the methods and audiences effective enough to trigger or at least support the change needed? A lot has changed in the world—not least because of the multiple megatrends. Along with the specific situational circumstances and opportunities, these trends should be taken into account to find the most effective way to contribute.

Some Things to Retain...

Sometimes think tanks must disrupt themselves if they do not want to be disrupted by others, as Ecologic Institute has done in a number of instances (Kraemer 2017a). However, they may not need to throw everything overboard. They should identify and keep their specific strengths.

With climate change as a prime example, policymaking must consider the long-term and long-range international impacts and consequences, and find systemic solutions off the beaten track. policymakers have the difficult task of guiding innovation, triggering change, and managing environmentally and socially sound transformations. But governments and policymakers tend to be busy addressing very current issues and shying away from the long-term challenges. They also have difficulties in inventing new approaches and tend to be reluctant to contest and debug their own policies. Therefore, they need to be supported in identifying the areas where change is most urgently needed. Think tanks can support the development of promising policy options for change and the process of thinking through policy innovations.

In this moment of crisis, think tanks can help governments move toward a systemic and long-term approach in their policymaking. This includes an improved integration of policy domains, avoiding both over-simplification and drowning in complexity. Think tanks can also help to overcome the sectoral divide, which is hard-wired into political cultures and institutions, be it government, parliament, media, or academia. That is clearly true in energy, transport, and agriculture, but it also holds for areas like research and industrial policy, or environmental, economic, and fiscal policy.

Think tanks are not bound to election cycles, they can accompany transformative processes, cooperate across borders and disciplinary boundaries, learn from each other, and tackle complexities with combined brain (and computational) power over longer periods of time. Many think tanks have exceptional networks across the globe, which can be most valuable in accelerating collective learning as well as identifying global solutions. Think tanks can support the reach beyond a domestic focus and accelerate the implementation of best policy practices. Understanding international policy coordination and governance will be important, and yes, that means strengthening multilateral agreements and institutions, for without them it is almost inconceivable how the world can redirect its economies and change lifestyles collectively, efficiently, and sufficiently. While multilateralism alone cannot solve the crisis, it will be even harder to do so without it.

... Some Things to Change

However, in this endeavor, think tanks must be able to deal with the complexity of sustainable development and policy coordination across policy domains and governance levels. This entails a broadening of the agenda for many think tanks. The policy questions would need to be addressed by multidisciplinary teams with expertise in a number of policies and geographies. This is also a challenge of internal management, which (most probably) only think tanks of a certain size can meet (Kraemer 2014). Smaller think tanks might be able to live up to the challenge by engaging in cooperative approaches.

In addition, think tanks in general appear to be uniquely placed to embrace transdisciplinary approaches, i.e., taking on board the knowledge of stakeholders to define relevant research questions and check the validity of proposed solutions (Jahn et al. 2012).

Building teams that can work effectively across geographies, languages, scientific disciplines, and policy domains in a transdisciplinary fashion remains challenging, but think tanks can do this much easier than governments or academic institutions. This holds the potential to enhance impact and acceptability in a "world in transition" (WBGU 2011).

LISTEN TO THE YOUNG

Aiming at societal change, many think tanks might have to reconsider their key audience—with the ensuing challenge to engage in new ways of communication and build up new networks. In the past, most think tanks seem to have focused mainly on policymakers. Looking at the challenges of today, broader approaches might be more effective.

Regardless, think tanks should listen to the voices of the young; many try to, some only pretend, and few succeed. Young people are politically underrepresented everywhere. Even democracies typically deny the right to vote or to be elected for roughly the first two decades after birth. However, it is the youth of today that will suffer the consequences of our collective failure to solve the environmental crises and the corresponding long-term effects.

Therefore, think tanks must as a group learn to listen to young voices and to connect with the youth so as to understand the futures they desire. As the youth are becoming more vocal—with Greta Thunberg becoming an international icon—it is a collective responsibility to provide this young generation with the knowledge they need in their quest for an inhabitable world.

THINK TANKS FOR FUTURE HELP TO IMPROVE KNOWLEDGE AND RESEARCH SYSTEMS

The COVID-19 pandemic and the lack of preparedness for a disease outbreak that was predicted and expected is a stark reminder of the failure of the knowledge systems in many countries. In its aftermath, when the origins, causes and consequences, and aggravating, as well as mitigating, factors in the pandemic are assessed, it will become clear that part of the failures was due to the isolation of scientific and policy communities, a lack of integrated or holistic thinking, and of longer-term risk assessments including environmental degradation and climate change.

Beyond the immediate policy field or topic area a think tank might work on, it is therefore also important to help shape the knowledge agenda. The knowledge systems have to be fit for the future.

First, those expected to change their ways have to receive training and education enabling them to transform their thinking, businesses, and jobs. An enabling knowledge environment is a key to supporting change and the acceptability thereof. Thus, societies do not only have to change what is taught at school and the curricula at universities, but also offer training and access to knowledge. A pertinent example here would be expanding training for farmers to ensure they have the tools and knowledge to become agents of change and develop and implement sustainable food systems solutions. Think tanks should play their part in developing and promoting such knowledge systems.

Second, relevant research funding has to flow toward solutions. For example, as climate change mitigation is an inherently social challenge, think tanks could criticize the fact that "only 0.12% of all research funding was spent on the social science of climate mitigation" (Overl and Sovacool 2020). As the authors put it:

> The funding of climate research appears to be based on the assumption that if natural scientists work out the causes, impacts, and technological remedies of climate change, then politicians, officials, and citizens will spontaneously change their behavior to tackle the problem. The past decades have shown that this assumption does not hold.

Furthermore, in many cases, think tanks tend to be evaluated based on their publications in peer-reviewed scientific journals. The structure of the "journal industry" dominantly promotes single-discipline, traditional approaches, shying away from innovative transdisciplinary approaches. In a data-driven environment, think tanks are forced to look back to where there is evidence since the future furnishes no data. However, in times of disruptive changes, this can lead down the wrong path (as many publications on the evolving renewable energy sector have shown). Facing a transformative challenge, policymakers will need forward-looking advice. Therefore, more credit needs to be given to methodologically sound, forward-looking studies, and transdisciplinary work that addresses current problems of policy or practice. This is how policies for a sustainable future can be developed, proven, and refined. This is how Think Tanks for Future can evolve.

REFERENCES

Centers for Disease Control and Prevention. 31 January 2019. Lassa Fever. https://www.cdc.gov/vhf/lassa/index.html.

Cui, et al. 2003. https://ehjournal.biomedcentral.com/articles/10.1186/1476-069X-2-15.

Hildebrand, Philipp, and Tom Donilon. 2020. Davos Brief. Black-Rock Investment Institute. https://www.blackrock.com/ch/individual/en/insights/davos-brief-2020#sustainability.

IPCC—Intergovernmental Panel on Climate Change. 2018. Global Warming of 1.5 °C. An IPCC Special Report.

Jahn, Thomas, Matthias Bergmann, and Florian Keil. 2012. Transdisciplinarity: Between Mainstreaming and Marginalization. *Ecological Economics* 79: 1–10.

Kraemer, Andreas. 2014. The Ecologic Institute and Its Influence on Policies in Germany and the EU. In *How Think Tanks Shape Social Development Policies*, ed. James G. McGann, Anna Viden, and Jillian Rafferty, 129–147. Philadelphia, PA: University of Pennsylvania Press.

Kraemer, Andreas. 2017a. Digital Disruptions and the Emergence of Virtual Think Tanks. In *Phantom Ex Machina: Digital Disruption's Role in Business Model Transformation*, ed. A. Khare, R. Schatz, and B. Steward, 281–295. Cham, New York, Heidelberg, Berlin etc.: Springer.

Kraemer, Andreas. 2017b. The Co-Transformation of Energy & Transport: Outlook for the Wider Atlantic. In *Energy and Transportation in the Atlantic Basin: Implications for the European Union and Other Atlantic Actors*, ed. Paul Isbell and Eloy Alvarez Pelegry, 3–16. Washington, DC: Brookings Institution Press.

McGann, James G. 2020. *2019 Global Go to Think Tank Index Report*. Philadelphia: Think Tanks and Civil Societies Program, University of Pennsylvania.

McGlade, Katriona, Lucy Olivia Smith, R. Andreas Kraemer, and Elizabeth Tedsen JD. 2016. Human Environmental Dynamics and Responses in the Atlantic Space. In *Atlantic Future. Shaping a New Hemisphere for the 21st century: Africa, Europe and the Americas*, ed. Jordi Bacaria and Laia Tarragona, 69–85. Barcelona: CIDOB.

Overl, lIndra, and Benjamin K. Sovacool. 2020. The Misallocation of Climate Research Funding. *Energy Research and Social Science* 62: 101349.

Revich, Boris A., and Marina A. Podolnaya. 21 November 2011. Thawing of Permafrost May Disturb Historic Cattle Burial Grounds in East Siberia. *Global Health Action*. https://doi.org/10.3402/gha.v4i0.8482.

Rockström, Johan, et al. 2009. A Safe Operating Space for Humanity. *Nature* 461 (October): 472–475. Online publication 23 September 2009.

Spinney, Laura. 28 March 2020. Is Factory Farming to Blame for Coronavirus? *The Guardian*. https://www.theguardian.com/world/2020/mar/28/is-factory-farming-to-blame-for-coronavirus.

Steffen, Will, et al. 2015. Planetary Boundaries: Guiding Human Development on a Changing Planet. *Sciences* 347 (6223): 1259855.

United Nations Environment Programme. 2019. *Emissions Gap Report 2019.* Nairobi: UNEP.

University of Vermont. 15 March 2012. With Climate Change, US Could Face Risk from Chagas Disease. *Science Daily.* https://www.sciencedaily.com/rel eases/2012/03/120315140225.htm.

Vidal, John. 2 April 2020. Don't Blame Bats or Pangolins. Human Actions Caused the Coronavirus. *Yes!* https://www.yesmagazine.org/environment/ 2020/04/02/coronavirus-destruction-environment-bats/.

Wackernagel, Mathis, and Bert Beyers. 2019. *Ecological Footprint: Managing Our Biocapacity Budget.* Gabriola Island, BC: New Society.

Walsh, Michael G., et al. 18 June 2018. Climatic Influence on Anthrax Suitability in Warming Northern Latitudes. *Scientific Reports* 8 (1): 1–9. https://doi. org/10.1038/s41598-018-27604-w.

WBGU—German Advisory Council on Global Change. 2011. World in Transi- tion—A Social Contract for Sustainability.

Wu, Xiao, and Rachel C. Nethery, et al. 2020. COVID-19 PM 2.5. Harvard University. https://projects.iq.harvard.edu/covid pm.

The Future of Think Tanks in the Western Balkans: The Old, the New, and the Upcoming

Milena Lazarevic

Abstract Milena Lazarevic, Programme Director at the European Policy Centre (CEP) in Belgrade, Serbia, explores the Future of Think Tanks and Policy Advice around the World.

Keywords Civil society · Ivory tower · NGOs · Policy advice · Policy analysis · Policy evaluation · Research centers · Serbia · Think tanks · Transparency · UK

Think tanks in the Western Balkan region[1] began to emerge following the collapse of the socialist regimes, the break up of former socialist Yugoslavia, and the ensuing democratization of the newly emerging countries. From their earliest days, they strove to replace the diminishing role of state-owned research institutes, which were particularly developed in Yugoslavia and served the central planning system of the country. Once

---

[1] The region that is nowadays commonly referred to as the "Western Balkans" comprises Albania and five countries that emerged after the breakup of Yugoslavia (Bosnia and Herzegovina, Kosovo, Montenegro, North Macedonia, and Serbia). Essentially, these are the remaining countries of Southeastern Europe that have not yet acceded to the European Union.

M. Lazarevic (✉)
European Policy Centre (CEP), Belgrade, Serbia

J. McGann, *The Future of Think Tanks and Policy Advice Around the World*, https://doi.org/10.1007/978-3-030-60379-3_10

the party apparatus was dismantled, these institutes were left with state funding to produce books and papers, but with little to no influence on the decision-making of new governments, as their "research projects bear little relevance to the agenda of the government and civil society."[2]

The newly emerging private think tanks have since grown their impact on the domestic policymaking systems, though with significant obstacles related to the deficiencies of the governments' policymaking practices and of the funding schemes. This chapter provides an overview of those challenges and proposes the ways forward for the think tanks to establish their roles as relevant policy actors and ensure their long-term financial sustainability.

THE CHALLENGING ENVIRONMENT FOR THE GROWTH OF DOMESTIC THINK TANKS IN THE WESTERN BALKANS

The Low Local Demand for Policy Advice

The efforts of the new think tanks and policy research centers—which over time became more modern and practically focused—to create policy impact has not necessarily yielded success. With the creation of new democratic institutions in the post-socialist era, one would have expected a new appetite in governments to listen to divergent voices, an openness to constructive critique and external policy advice, and for the evidence-informed formulation of policy. Yet, by and large, this has not come about. In fact, various reform monitoring reports, produced by international actors and domestic civil society alike, have repeatedly warned of the weakness and lack of openness and transparency of the region's policymaking systems (Lazarević and Đinđić 2018: 25–27). Think tanks in the Western Balkans in 2020 are still searching for new ways to influence policymaking and contribute sound analysis to the advancement of the democratic and European integration processes in their countries.

---

[2] PERFORM—Performing and Responsive Social Sciences. Serbia. http://www.per form.network/page/serbia/context.

Unstable Funding Opportunities Hindering Long-Term Development

The old and largely obsolete, state-owned research institutes are still functional in several countries of the region and the public social science research funding schemes still favor them in parts of the region (for example, Serbia). Elsewhere (such as in Albania) state funding for policy-relevant research is practically nonexistent.

Even where domestic public funding is available (for example, through support to non-governmental organizations), the persisting lack of transparency in government funding in these emerging democracies makes independent think tanks largely unwilling to pursue government funding as a path. In the absence of developed domestic private philanthropy in these countries, think tanks are largely left to fight for funding on the international development assistance market, with little security and predictability. In addition to being unpredictable, external donor support is also rarely focused on research. Instead, it usually favors activism-oriented civil society initiatives that think tanks are not best suited to implement.

This dependence on project-based funding and lack of access to core financing limits the long-term sustainability of think tanks in the Western Balkans and thwarts their prospects for engaging in more complex and longer-term research endeavors. It also negatively impacts their potential to develop internal capacities for emerging issues such as the digital economy, artificial intelligence, and others.

Development Assistance Implementing Agents as Occupants of the Think Tanks' Role

Another related problem stems from the fact that international organizations (such as the World Bank, the United Nations, the Organization for Economic Cooperation and Development, and others) and foreign consultancy companies in this region are practically occupying the role that think tanks play in most countries of the Western world. These entities are the largest beneficiaries of external aid to this region, implementing multi-million-dollar portfolios of technical assistance to governments. They receive these funds either through direct awards or through competitive tenders with requirements that make them hardly accessible to local think tanks. Although a part of this assistance goes into infrastructure-related projects, the largest share is invested into institution building, for which policy analysis and advising play a central role.

This system is convenient for the recipient governments, as international organizations are usually more compliant with governmental directions and more complacent about their actions. For the donor governments as well, the system is suitable, as it allows for a large share of invested funds to return to their countries through the high salaries of international consultants and the considerable profits for executing companies.

However, the consequence of this system is that the capacities of the local think tanks, which could (and should) perform the policy advisory role, are not systematically developed. What's more, the results and effects of such externally managed projects are often mediocre or even substandard, as international consultancies operate with little motivation to induce long-term positive change in the countries they operate in, little concern for the public interest, and are largely interested in profit maximization.

Turning Challenges into Strategies

However, these challenges have also created certain positive effects on the organizational behavior of think tanks in the Western Balkans. Moreover, within the flawed funding scene lie opportunities that think tanks could seize in order to improve their financial sustainability.

Partnerships Supporting Holistic Solutions to Policy Problems

Firstly, the difficulties in influencing policymaking and obtaining project funding have made this region's think tanks diversify and innovate in ways that are different from those in the West. Namely, think tanks in this region usually operate to some extent as hybrid organizations, as most of them are forced—by the requirements of the available funding schemes—to implement actions and initiatives that go beyond conventional policy research and analysis. Thus, they engage in advocacy and even activism, taking part in organized civil society actions, petitions, and even street actions. As classical Western think tanks are struggling to come down from the "ivory tower," reconnect with citizens, and communicate with wider audiences, the somewhat-forced model of operation of Balkan think tanks, in fact, gives them an advantage in achieving these objectives.

The struggle to win projects has thus made the think tanks in the Western Balkans more open to partnerships, more alert to the ways in which they can demonstrate their benefit to society, and more innovative in designing initiatives that can bring about policy change through combinations of methodologies and approaches. Competition for project funding has also made these think tanks engage in "unlikely" partnerships, for example, with small, local NGOs that can reach out to citizens in street markets, with investigative journalists, or with IT start-ups.

Due to the unpredictable nature of funding, initiatives that result from such partnerships do not always enjoy long-term support and are often discontinued before they reach their full potential. Yet, in numerous cases, such projects have managed to mobilize civil society for joint causes, expose deep corruption cases, build pressure to change policy, and allow citizens to voice their concerns and problems, for example, through online platforms (from which comments are systematically analyzed and presented to policymakers along with concrete policy recommendations). Seen from this angle, the "classical," Western think tanks might in fact have a lot to learn from the experience of think tanks in the Western Balkans.

Moving forward, in order to remain relevant, think tanks need to embrace new subjects such as artificial intelligence and skills such as big data analysis. Certainly, many think tankers—in the West and the East alike—will agree with this claim. Being more responsive, quicker to react, able to anticipate issues, and acquire and crunch data is all very well. But, in order to stay relevant, think tanks also need to avoid being arrogant and elitist, and become inclusive. They need to embrace their roles within civil societies in their countries, to engage in partnerships with difficult and unlikely partners, and to design joint initiatives that tackle policy and societal problems not only through top-down research and analytical perspectives, but also by bottom-up gathering of the voices of grassroots and citizens. They need to engage the youth, help citizens' concerns reach policymakers, and cooperate with those who can mobilize ordinary people for issues of the public interest.

In Serbia, for example, the Covid-19 crisis led to an unconstitutional proclamation of a state of emergency and a range of highly restrictive measures which were poorly prepared and for which people were not given enough advance notice. There have been instances of abuse of individual rights, which coupled with sometimes intimidating messaging from the country's leadership, prompted organized civil society reactions. Think tanks have been on the front lines to propose more forward-looking responses, systematic monitoring and reporting on the implementation of government's measures, and proactive action to ensure that post-crisis the government and society avoid remaining captured in the "new-normal" of increasingly authoritarian rule. For any of these actions to come to life, partnerships between think tanks and other, different civil society actors (for example, organizations providing few legal aid and social services) were necessary.

The implementation of such initiatives can be a very tedious business. Speaking from the experience of European Policy Centre (CEP) in Belgrade, it takes months of meetings and workshops to find common ground with partners who do not speak the language of policy and do not think in terms of data or indicators. Once communication barriers are broken, however, the knowledge and experience generated through such partnerships bring immense value and represent innovation in the truest sense of the word.

TOWARD LONG-TERM FINANCIAL SUSTAINABILITY

Becoming more relevant in society can also lead to think tanks becoming more recognized by donors as actors that can play a role in the provision of larger scale technical support in the Western Balkan countries. The organizations and consultancy companies providing such assistance can then be sensitized or even forced (through formal rules of the tenders) to partner up with local think tanks for the implementation of such projects. Both the donors and the implementing agents would benefit greatly from the involvement of local actors with profound understanding of the domestic policy environment, the policymaking procedures and informal practices, and system deficiencies. The local think tanks, in turn, would greatly profit from this increased funding and from gaining the opportunity to truly conduct their missions—influencing the design and implementation of public policy.

Admittedly, there are risks and potential downsides of this strategy for ensuring policy impact and financial sustainability. It brings think tanks very close to the edge of transforming into consultancies, which might entail the loss of research and analytical rigor and independence. Moreover, it risks preventing them from pursuing an independent program strategy, which is important for pushing onto the governments' policy agendas important issues that they might otherwise neglect or avoid.

Yet, if implemented with prudency, this course of action indeed does represent a solid option for achieving financial sustainability, which, at the end of the day, is better than disappearing altogether. At least two preconditions should be met in the pursuit of this strategy to mitigate the mentioned risks. First, it should not become a predominant or only source of funding for a think tank. Instead, it would need to be combined with other funding formats which allow for greater programmatic independence. Second, to the extent possible, the staff working on these technical assistance projects should be separated from the research staff engaged in the think tank's core research program.

Looking forward, Western Balkan think tanks should seek to establish dialogue with the major providers of development assistance in their countries (the EU, the USA, the UK, and others) to discuss possible revisions of the models for implementing their aid. These influential actors would benefit from an improved understanding of how their procedures tilt the level playing field for developing sound and independent policy advice in these countries.

In the long run, with a change of operational procedures, local think tanks could obtain a distinct role in the development assistance frameworks by giving them the specific task of researching and devising policy alternatives, or by performing policy evaluations for the recipient governments. Such work could be commissioned based on contracts protecting think tanks' independence. Such a format would also help educate and train the recipient governments in the Western Balkans on how to invest in rigorous policy research and analysis and become the real domestic consumers of the think tanks' products. That way, in addition to achieving their short-term objectives of supporting a specific policy, major donors in the region would also positively influence the long-term improvement of the policymaking systems in these countries.

Reference

Lazarević, Milena, and Miloš Đinđić. 2018. Western Balkan PAR Monitor 2017/2018. Think for Europe Network. European Policy Center, 25–27. https://weber-cep.s3.amazonaws.com/data/attachment_978/western_b alkan_par_monitor.pdf.

The Future of Think Tanks and the Crisis of Democracy

Roland Schmidt

Abstract Roland Schmidt, Director of the Frederick Ebert Stiftung (FES) in Bonn, Germany, explores the Future of Think Tanks and Policy Advice around the World.

Keywords Brazil · Civil society · Germany · Hungary · Policy advice · Think tanks · Transparency · Turkey

A cursory glance at present-day political advocacy would suggest that we are indeed living in a golden age of think tanks. One hundred years ago, the first think tanks, in the modern sense of the word, were envisioned in the Paris Peace Conference of 1919 and resulted in the establishment of renowned institutions such as the Royal Institute of International Affairs in 1920 and the New York City-based Council on Foreign Relations in 1921. In the decades that followed, think tanks have become an ever more prominent feature of public life across Western democracies.

Bridging the gap between academia and politics, think tanks as "a fifth estate" have contributed to public debates and have at times wielded tremendous influence in the highest echelons of political power

R. Schmidt (✉)
The Friedrich-Ebert-Stiftung (FES), Bonn, Germany

J. McGann, *The Future of Think Tanks and Policy Advice Around the World*, https://doi.org/10.1007/978-3-030-60379-3_11

(McGann 2016). Famously, both the Presidency of Ronald Reagan and the Premiership of Tony Blair were fueled by the professional input of think tanks.

Also, sheer numbers indicate a flourishing sector. Year after year, new think tanks see the light of day and join an ever-growing international marketplace of ideas—a positive trend that is meticulously documented in the annual Go-To Global Think Tank Index published by TTCSP at the University of Pennsylvania.

It is particularly noteworthy that the prosperity of think tanks is no longer confined to North America and Europe. Think tanks have expanded to all continents, where distinct centers of political expertise have emerged and continue to thrive across cultural and geographical barriers.

Despite existing challenges, year after year, think tanks publish crucial reports, outline policies, convene essential stakeholders, influence legal jurisprudence, and develop political expertise. So prominent is their role, that in democratic societies, a public debate without a contribution from think tanks has become almost unthinkable.

But despite these positive developments, the reality for think tanks at the beginning of the 2020s is more complex—and more ambiguous.

In many countries, think tanks' role as intellectually independent and as influential players is anything but guaranteed. Fundamental rights, such as freedom of expression, are increasingly questioned, and the worrisome phenomenon of shrinking spaces for civil society is well-documented.

Many of the challenges confronting think tanks are directly or indirectly related to a more general crisis of democracy. Celebrating a centennial of think tanks and reflecting on the future of these important institutions, political advocates around the world would be well-advised to consider the challenges that lie ahead.

THINK TANKS AND THE CRISIS OF DEMOCRACY

The current debate surrounding the future of think tanks occurs today in a particular political context. 2020 is the year in which the United Kingdom left the European Union following a short-sighted triumph of nativist populism. At the same time, the reelection of Donald Trump to the Presidency of the United States remains a very real and ominous possibility. These two developments are stark reminders that a growing crisis of established political institutions has fueled a global rise of populist leaders in the framework of a multifaceted backlash against globalization.

International opinion polls such as the Edelman Trust Barometer— and our own research—shows that public confidence in democratic institutions is rapidly eroding. This decline in public trust in many established Democracies includes dwindling public faith in the legal system, the media, independent journalism, political parties, trade unions, and churches.

This erosion of trust from the political center has drastic political repercussions. Populist strongmen channel public discontent and seem to emerge stronger with every election cycle, from Brazil and the Philippines to Turkey and Hungary. Worryingly, many of these leaders' ambitions are driven by a pronounced rejection of established political structures, procedures, and democratic values. Political elites are derided as detached and morally corrupted, with populist leaders masquerading as true representatives of the righteous "people."

In view of this populist fury, it is obvious that think tanks as political institutions are exposed to the very same criticism that is targeting the political system in its entirety. In view of their proximity to political power, many of the challenges confronting think tanks today, therefore, seem directly related to the general crisis of democracy.

THE WAR AGAINST EXPERTISE

One of the most infamous moments of the Brexit campaign in the United Kingdom was a television interview by the conservative MP and former education secretary Michael Gove. In an interview with Sky News on June 3, 2016, Gove made the case for Brexit by explicitly lecturing his interviewer about the limits of political expertise. Gove explained to the baffled journalist that "the people in this country have had enough of experts" and went on to lash out against "organizations with acronyms saying that they know what is best."[1]

Gove's statement became notorious because it summed up widespread disillusionment with political expertise in significant sectors of society. In this, of course, Michael Gove only mirrored a sentiment that is also too visible in the current US administration. After all, US President Donald Trump has on more than one occasion publicly expressed his distrust of experts. His stated belief that his "gut tells me more sometimes

---

[1] *Financial Times*. Britain has had enough of experts, says Gove. https://www.ft.com/content/3be49734-29cb-11e6-83e4-abc22d5d108c.

than anybody else's brain" is a frontal assault on academia and political advocacy (Le Miere 2018).

This tendency is highly problematic. Decision-makers who have "had enough of experts" are a problem not only for experts and their "organizations with acronyms," but for the wider public. Skepticism toward expertise has a habit of trickling down. Ultimately, facts and expertise are replaced by opinion, irrespective of validity or objectivity.

A public discourse, however, in which proficiency and expertise are considered subcategories of ideology is eroding the preconditions of democracy. The end of expertise and truth has resulted in unprecedented social polarization not only over what constitutes good or bad policy, but over what constitutes reality itself. The war against expertise, therefore, threatens the very fabric of a democratic society.

Perhaps unsurprisingly, the current crisis of democracy is not restricted to domestic affairs but is mirrored internationally in a full-grown crisis of multilateralism.

The international rules-based order is increasingly challenged not only from classical authoritarianism but also from within the heart of political life in established democracies themselves.

This is a tragic development given the global scope of our current political challenges from health and disarmament to climate change and migration. The world's problems are too big to face them with autistic "my country first" temper tantrums. States and in particular democratic states must cooperate, or they will fail to come up with convincing answers.

How Should We Respond? Think and Do Tanks

What do these political challenges imply for the future of think tanks? How can political advocacy make a difference in a post-factual age of misinformation and mistrust? How can think tanks stand up for truth, for rationality, for informed decision-making, and for cooperation and joint solutions? And how can they do so domestically and internationally?

Undoubtedly, the response to these questions will have to be multilayered. Trust is easily lost but hard to regain. To address existing challenges of democratic governance, think tanks would be well advised to embrace a binary role as Think and Do Tanks, combining rigorous academic analysis with strategic communication and professional campaigning.

Internationally, the crisis of multilateralism demands a coherent and consistent effort from within the think tank community. What is needed is a collective stepping up in support of the values of collaborative action: a think tank alliance of multilateralism.

In concrete terms, such an approach would comprise creating safe harbors for dialogue across political, ideological, and geographical boundaries. In a time when all too many official representatives disengage from constructive dialogue with their perceived opponents, it is up to the Think Tank community to bridge gaps where they can. In an age where the chasm between states, societies, and ideologies grows wider by the day, think tanks need to reach out across these differences and safeguard constructive political discourse in track II and official channels of communication.

A similar task applies to domestic politics. Here, think tanks are tasked with providing a broad platform for debate that is as civic as it is civilized. In times of unprecedented polarization and ideological tribalism, think tanks can and should play a crucial role in engaging marginalized, angered, and silenced parts of society.

For this to happen, however, think tanks will need to depart from their comfort zones—ideologically and physically. They will need to reach out to areas outside urban centers and attempt to broaden and diversify their geographical outreach.

In a time when perceptions are increasingly defined by feedback-loops and echo chambers, reaching beyond one's own social media bubble and widening political networks is crucial. This implies engaging in political programs outside the political centers and actively engaging the political periphery—both nationally and internationally.

None of this will be possible without the strategic use of new technologies. Think tanks, just as political decision-makers, are confronted with an ever-faster pace of political life.

Whereas political debates even a few years ago would have unfolded in weeks or even months, politics today is driven by a relentless 24-hour news cycle and a staccato of ever-changing political ad hoc crisis. The reaction span available to decision-makers has moved dangerously close to real time.

Effective think tank work will have to take these drastic changes into consideration. In view of this accelerated pace of changing discourse, expertise has to be customized and expansive. While efforts through social media and traditional communication channels should aim to shift the "Overton"-window defining the spectrum of acceptable policies in a constructive direction, social media, and face-to-face communication should be used to offer direct and personalized expertise.

At the same time, think tanks will have to continue the balancing act of surfing the wave and strategic agenda-setting. Here, organizations will need to focus much more on their particular competitive advantages. In many cases, a programmatic refocusing may be the only alternative.

None of this will be possible without a deliberate human resources strategy. Efforts to recruit political and communicative talents from a much wider social spectrum would be highly recommended. Effective think tanks of the twenty-first century will need to ensure that their hiring practices synchronize rather than isolate or detach them from society at large. This implies concerted efforts to recruit much more diverse staff members. However, this also implies widening the ideological playing field to actively fostering out-of-the-box thinking.

In all of this, think tanks would be well advised to improve their political self-presentation. In order to confront the widespread erosion of trust in many democracies, think tanks must be transparent and forthright about their ideological tendencies. This includes adopting strict transparency measures in terms of funding sources.

In politics, as in life, there is no Archimedean point from which politics can be conducted neutrally and dispassionately. For Think Tanks, debunking the myth of technocratic neutrality will go a long way to countering the erosion of public trust in democracy. In times of political upheaval, deliberate and conscious partialism is not only advisable but essentially the only course that is morally and ethically viable. Forthrightness is not a weakness, but a strategic strength.

One century ago, in Paris, international diplomats laid the groundwork to the world of think tanks as we know it. In an ever more complex and interrelated world, think tanks are well positioned to meet the existing challenges—for their sake and for the sake of democracy itself.

References

Le Miere, Jason. 27 November 2018. Donald Trump Says 'My Gut Tells Me More Sometimes Than Anybody Else's Brain Can Ever Tell Me.' *Newsweek*. https://www.newsweek.com/donald-trump-gut-brain-climate-change-fed-1234540.

McGann, James G. 2016. *The Fifth Estate: Think Tanks, Public Policy, and Governance*. Washington, DC: Brookings Institution Press.

Data Is a Powerful Assistant but the Think Tanker Is Still in Charge

Pascal Boniface

Abstract Pascal Boniface, Director of the French Institute for International and Strategic Affairs (IRIS) in Paris, France, explores the Future of Think Tanks and Policy Advice around the World.

Keywords France · NGOs · Policy advice · Think tanks

During Christmas holidays, on my way to work and passing through a little street in Paris, I saw a whole collection of Encyclopedia Universalis abandoned on the ground—31 big volumes (Fig. 1).

It was a terrifying blow for me. Indeed, for my generation, Encyclopedia Universalis was the paramount of erudition. A very expensive collection which most students or young researchers were able to get only by making a real financial sacrifice. The ones who had it were proud, the ones who did not dreamed of getting it.

I posted a picture of the collection on Twitter. In 3 days, 750,000 people had seen it, with thousands of comments. Basically, the comments revealed two opposite sides, I assume based on age differences.

P. Boniface (✉)
French Institute for International and Strategic Affairs (IRIS),
Paris, France

© The Author(s) 2021
J. McGann, *The Future of Think Tanks and Policy Advice Around the World*, https://doi.org/10.1007/978-3-030-60379-3_12

Fig. 1 Encyclopédie universalis collection relinquished in a street in Paris

For people around my age, it was considered blasphemy. How could someone dare to abandon the object of their dream or pride, the very symbol of universal culture in a Parisian street? It was not understandable. It was indefensible, a real matter of unlimited shame for the perpetrator. But, on the contrary, for many others, it was a pragmatic and wise decision. Wikipedia is nowadays available for free. If you prefer the real (and written by professionals) Encyclopedia Universalis, you can get it on the internet. This allows you to avoid having shelters occupied by these volu-minous books and, considering the price of a square meter in Paris, it appears to be a rational choice. Should the former owner have given the collection to a library? No way. It will be soon updated. I must admit that this perception is rightful, even if I could not defend it myself due to a feeling of nostalgia. As a physical book, Encyclopedia Universalis is no longer a must for an intellectual as it was in the past.

My generation must adapt itself to the new approach to knowledge and intellectual work. Technological changes have totally overwhelmed the way we work. And nostalgia set aside, let's recognize that it is for the best. When I began to work on strategic issues in the beginning of the 80s, most, if not all, of my contacts were westerners. Whoever they were, American or European, I carefully avoided having a chat on the phone with them—it was too expensive. And if I heard about an interesting book published in the United States, I would have to wait 4 or 6 weeks to get it, due to price delivery. Now, I have contacts everywhere in the world (just see the yearly report by Jim McGann and the University of Pennsylvania). I can phone for free, having time zones as my only preoccupation, and I can get most of the documentation I need in a few seconds and for free.

Time has accelerated, and the world has shrunk. Therefore, we can work faster, and we can move farther away.

The risk is losing a long-term perspective in favor of short-term views. The challenge is to take advantage of these new facilities without losing the capacity to think in a broad perspective.

Big data and data have created new challenges, but also new opportu-nities for think tanks and think tankers. There are new challenges because some think tanks, like many citizens, are not comfortable with changes, especially if they are abrupt and come from external sources and not from within the corporation.

Of course, the challenge is more important for the older generation than for the youngest. That means that the ones in a position of leadership by their status or their anteriority are more likely to be put in an awkward position. But it would be admissible for a director or senior researcher in a think tank to be able to adapt himself to changes, even if they are technological and not directly political, if they have direct implications for their jobs.

You cannot pretend to explain the world if you don't consider its most important evolutions that deeply impact your professional specialty. Therefore, addressing the subject of data and big data is not a matter of choice, but a compelling necessity. And let's look on the bright side of the issue: data and big data could help geopolitists and think tankers in their work.

Indeed, if information is more plentiful and easier to find, we will spend less time getting it and will have more time to think and to write. Big data and data can be considered a (free and available 24/7) performant assistant, which gathers facts, information, and so on, quicker than anybody, including yourself. If we have immediate and easy access to the figures we need to understand and explain strategic issues, we will be cleverer. In a sense, we will have more time to think. In our organization, we now use a monitoring software, or "webmining" software, which searches, gathers, and selects information according to our needs.

Some could fear that big data will put an end to their (most of the time self-described) monopoly on knowledge. If the knowledge is widely diffused and therefore accessible to people with less experience, would the status of some experts be questioned and contested? Once again, this thought is a misconception. The expert—the real one—will still make a difference. If the information is the same for everybody, the way you use it will be different according to your expertise.

One particular challenge for French and European think tanks with big data is the financial and human resources required. Data models need to be built from scratch and we are competing with the so-called Start-up Nation when it comes to recruiting talent that might be able to develop these tools. This is a financial battle that we cannot win. While interesting work is currently being done internally by American think tanks, in Europe, lack of financing means we need to be creative and united to start complex big data projects. Think tanks, universities, and other organizations need to work together in order to muster the required resources for such projects. For example, we are currently leading a study on energetic flows across the world, and the use of big data on such a study is essential. But, we, as a think tank, don't and cannot have the means to compile and create an efficient database. So we had to externalize these parts of the work to a specialized company. With a compiled database on this subject, we can produce our geopolitical analysis and bring our expertise. This is a relevant example of our need for data for the studies we produce. Each study today starts with a data analysis, and this becomes the first step of our work. This is an area in which we are lagging and where we need to take quick action.

It is not only in the realm of studies and research that data is useful to our organization. Think tanks need to speak to the right people and the right organizations in order to achieve their purpose as policy influencers. This creates an endless need to expand our network of contacts beyond our researcher's rolodex. Technology and data now allow us to achieve this. Our institute organizes over 50 events a year that are open to the public. This open-door policy means our events are popular, but it also makes it difficult to understand who is walking through our door and why. We have therefore invested in software to collect this information and better know our audience. Is a VP of compliance from Total coming to all my events on climate change? Is a member of parliament from the foreign affairs commission coming to an event tomorrow? This is all information that was complicated to gather and then share inside our organization. We are now able to be proactive in reaching out to key stakeholders that might share an interest in our work and mission.

Beside think tanks, there are other organizations which may appear to be working in the same field (geopolitics, international relations) but that are doing a very different job. Our job is to make the world in which we live easier to understand and to give a better understanding of it. We could—and this is the very essence of intellectual debate—have different interpretations, divergent thoughts, contradictory opinions. But all of them must be based on our own experience and our own understanding.

Law firms, advocacy groups, and public relations firms don't have the main goal of enlightening citizens; rather, their goal is convincing them. Their goals could be legitimate, but we could not put a public relations firm working to improve the image of a state run by a dictator and an NGO like Amnesty International or Doctors Without Borders into the same basket. Basically, our methods, our goals, must be different.

For sure, a think tanker may try several times to convince his public. We could in fact advocate for or against a military intervention or a diplomatic move. But it must be based on a serious study of the issues and situations. A think tanker must be able to change his mind if new facts, new arguments are found which change the intellectual framework.

An advocacy group, in the case of new arguments, will react not by changing its mind, but by continuing to argue for the same thesis.

Firms or advocacy groups have a premade choice, and their work consists in adapting their narrative to their goal. The challenge for think tank credibility is to be able to work with other actors (states, business groups, NGOs, and so on) while keeping their autonomy and independence. We must avoid being out of focus and becoming someone else's spokesperson.

Think Tanks, Covid-19, and Internationalism

Diego López Garrido

Abstract Diego López Garrido, Executive Vice-President of Fundación Alternativas in Madrid, Spain, explores the Future of Think Tanks and Policy Advice around the World.

Keywords China · India · Multilateral organizations · Policy advice · Russia · Spain · Think tanks

Living as we are in the midst of this global crisis, I will start by briefly mentioning what are, from my perspective as a Spaniard and a European, the major economic, social, and political trends that may follow the pandemic:

1. **Economic**: A huge depression is emerging in all economies (mainly in Western countries) while the technological revolution not only continues, but is exacerbated—dominated by the five big digital multinationals and driven by the United States and China, with Europe lagging behind.

D. L. Garrido (✉)
Fundación Alternativas, Madrid, Spain

2. **Social**: Increasing inequality—the legacy of the Great Recession (2008)—and a weakening of the European Welfare State due to two main factors: the growing burden on public health expenditures (without enough public revenue to sustain these) and the reduction of wages in these countries.

3. **Political**: The Covid-19 crisis will push a more multipolar system and a surge of national populist movements all over the Western world against a political order built around the EU, the United Nations, and other multilateral organizations, as a reaction to the failures of economic globalization and the explosion of the pandemic crisis.

A part of the European population (mainly corresponding to the declining middle class) choose a closed nation against a supposed failure of the internationalism that originated against nationalism and protectionism after the Second World War. This is what Brexit represented, and it is also what Trump defends in the United States: promoting walls, protectionism, and isolation. This shadow of doubt that is cast over internationalism is also what contributes to a fragile EU (divisions between northern countries and southern countries, the Visegrad Group, etc.) and feeds the problems within NATO to address threats coming from Russia.

Is there an answer to these challenges? Is it possible, after coronavirus, to see a new internationalism, which has been at the core of progressive ideology for decades and has contributed to the creation of the EU?

In my opinion, a new internationalism based on international law, human rights, and equality is possible. We are talking about a modern internationalism based on the necessity of international cooperation to fight climate change, jihadist terrorism, and nuclear weapons proliferation; an internationalism to reach agreements in the area of taxation—which is the only policy that can effectively combat the rising inequality and recover a strong Welfare State—through tax harmonization; the creation of digital taxes; and a fight against tax havens, tax evasion, and tax elusion.

All of these challenges are impossible to solve successfully without internationalism.

We see a big contradiction: states, individually, can't address the most relevant crisis of our lives, yet many people could turn ideologically toward nationalism, against immigration, against free trade, and against free movement of people. Before the coronavirus outbreak, George

Friedman said that the political divide has ceased to be between the left and the right. The new fault line is between internationalists and nationalists; between those who regard the system of alliances, mutual responsibility, and transcultural life built in the past seventy-five years as essential, and those who regard a globalist perspective as incapable of addressing the complexities inherent to challenges that touch upon different nations, cultures, and classes.

Fundación Alternativas believes in internationalism, in order to complete the system of states born in Westphalia and organized now around the United Nations. Europeans have another political tool: the European Union, its member states, its institutions, its budget, and its citizens. Without enhancing the European project, Europe will be irrelevant as a global actor, stuck in between the G-2: United States and China, and behind Russia and India.

But to build a new and open internationalism, we should project the progressive culture, the Keynesian strategy, to an upper level: the international level. This is a real challenge after Covid-19. Because of that, we should coordinate think tank action to devise the best public policies.

European think tanks should embody internationalism in a renewed transatlantic link based on enduring values, the most important being the rule of law, democracy, and the protection of fundamental rights (social rights, data protection, etc.). These are the real priorities of our populations, not the exclusive and rigid identity promoted by populism. It will be very difficult to achieve our objectives and provide a real alternative to illiberal capitalism without a structured think tank network and trade union participation.

I am aware that the Covid-19 crisis makes such a project of integration based on internationalism even more difficult than it previously was, but I believe at the same time that European think tanks will be an influential force in addressing the deep recession we have ahead of us.

Widening and Deepening: Partnership and Multidisciplinarity in Challenging Times

Paolo Magri

Abstract Paolo Magri, Executive Vice President and Director of the Italian Institute for International Political Studies in Milan, Italy, explores the Future of Think Tanks and Policy Advice around the World.

Keywords Brazil · China · Civil society · France · Fundraising · Italy · Nigeria · Policy advice · Policy making · Russia · Think tanks · Turkey

CURRENT CHALLENGES FACING THINK TANKS

Today's world is marked by turmoil, uncertainty, and—to some extent—unpredictability. This was true even before the coronavirus pandemic took the world by storm, expanding at light speed across continents, forcing countries to close down business, and ushering in the worst recession since 1929. At the same time, both policymakers and the wider public seem to have grown "fed up with experts," thus raising the question of whether think tanks and policy advice are still relevant. The answer is yes, provided that think tanks are able to navigate uncertainty and adapt to the "perfect storm" they face.

P. Magri (✉)
Italian Institute for International Political Studies, Milan, Italy

J. McGann, *The Future of Think Tanks and Policy Advice Around the World*, https://doi.org/10.1007/978-3-030-60379-3_14

101

Upon closer inspection, uncertainty is anything but new and has always shaped the work of think tanks. It has pushed them to reassess their mission and rethink their own decision-making, activities, fields of analysis, fundraising, and staffing policies. Already four decades ago, in 1977, John Kenneth Galbraith chose to title his book *The Age of Uncertainty*. At that time, the Cold War was raging, a wide part of the world was still under dictatorships or non-democratic regimes, and the West was going through one of the worst stagflation crisis ever. Indeed, scholars and experts have always labeled their own times as profoundly uncertain, oftentimes with good reason. So how and why is today's uncertainty different?

It is unprecedented as it is more comprehensive, faster, and involves a wider range of countries at the same time and everywhere in the world. It is more comprehensive because it abounds at the international, national, and social level alike. During the Cold War, the bipolar international system implied stable and clear alliances and, almost invariably, democracy went hand in hand with well-being. Additionally, the multilateral system was still holding steady, upheld by the main beneficiaries of the post-WWII order (the United States, above all else). Today, all these certainties risk being shattered, with the G20 (so far) achieving only limited coordination of national policy responses, which were adopted by political leaders with the main purpose of protecting their own citizens and business, rather than supporting global growth. At the national level, just a few decades ago, traditional parties were competing for votes, but even at their worst performance at the ballot box, their survival was not in question. Today, the rise of nontraditional, nationalist/populist parties is threatening the very existence of traditional parties. At the social level, growing inequalities are undermining citizens' confidence in the future. In addition, instead of empowering people, the speed at which information moves around these days risks spreading feelings of chaos and uncertainty.

Speed is indeed another major feature of today's uncertainty. Change occurs much faster due to the rise of new technologies, digital communication, and the ensuing spread of social media. People live in a 24/7 news cycle, which is also becoming highly reactive: news calls for immediate comment and swift action, which ever more frequently comes at the expense of expertise and in-depth analysis. At the same time, "knowledge producers" must come to grips with the fact that consumers have a shrinking attention span, making it harder to keep an audience interested in more than a few minutes (or even seconds) at a time. Finally, in bringing the world's knowledge to the tips of our fingers, near-universal web access has also made information more contested. Fake news and false beliefs are abundant, freely available, and hosted by websites that can be much more easily mistaken for credible, respectable outlets. In this context, experts are not necessarily perceived as the legitimate gatekeepers of valuable advice. The spread of the coronavirus emergency provides plenty of examples, from the alleged origin of the virus in military laboratories to the deadly consequences of self-medication after unreliable medical advice.

In the face of all the above, are think tanks equipped to understand these all-encompassing, multifaceted uncertainties? And can they adapt to the needs of a world that asks for information that is faster, more comprehensive, down-to-earth, and easily actionable by policymakers and the public alike?

THINK TANKS AND TODAY'S WORLD: WHICH WAYS FORWARD?

Apart from a few notable exceptions, today's think tanks tend to be relatively small and heavily specialized along with specific policy areas (energy, development, education, healthcare, etc.) or regions of the world. Think tanks continue to be biased toward selecting their research staff for heavily specialized, highly skilled experts who are certainly adept at delving deeper into a single topic, but might struggle to put all the pieces together in today's complex and fast-changing world. To cope with this problem, most think tanks tend to foster multidisciplinary exchanges by encouraging dialogue among experts; for instance, when discussing Libya, they may ask experts on Russia, Turkey, terrorism, migration, and (nowadays) even epidemiology to pitch in and join forces, possibly by also involving international peers.

These efforts definitely add new pieces to the puzzle, but they still risk losing sight of the big picture. Approaching a complex issue from multiple sides is key, but think tank experts still tend to be focused on their own (traditional) areas of expertise. Even collaboration among peers may not suffice to grasp the many dynamics at work in novel areas that are growing more and more interconnected. This is probably what many small-to-medium-sized think tanks lack the most: the capacity to analyze current trends and developments from a bird's eye view and across old and new fields of analysis, and to then offer effective and timely views both to policymakers and the wider public.

Against this background, think tanks need to be ambitious and aim at increasing diversity in two respects. First, they have to reconsider their own staffing policies and scale up "internal diversity." To use a metaphor, they need to look for their own Leonardo da Vinci. Dozens of painters died in 1519, but Leonardo is still a worldwide celebrated painter five centuries later, even though he actually made only a few paintings. This is because he was, at the same time, an outstanding painter, sculptor, architect, inventor, botanist, cartographer, and so on. In a nutshell, he was "polyvalent" as opposed to "highly specialized."

Needless to say, think tanks cannot hire Leonardo. But they can increase internal diversity by injecting new figures into their staff of highly specialized experts. These new experts need to be solid, but also versatile and eager to move from one topic to another and from one region to another in order to connect the dots. In a nutshell, think tank managers need to find and cultivate their own polymaths. These experts can be a twenty-first-century "Leonardo of policy making" only to the extent that they are able to move freely from the WhatsApp revolution in Lebanon to the paralysis of the WTO, from Huawei and 5G to climate change.

Second, think tanks have to nourish "external diversity" by pushing the boundaries of their partnerships well beyond the comfort zone of peer-to-peer collaboration. To be honest, think tanks often lack at least some expertise they need to make novel, useful and effective contributions to understanding today's world and managing uncertainty, and the coronavirus pandemic has served as a glaring example of this: who would have thought that foreign policy think tanks would need to come to terms with disease modeling so fast? And yet, this is all the more evidence that think tanks need to become acquainted with far-flung topics as diverse as epidemiology, global cities and urbanization, infrastructure, artificial intelligence, cyberspace and warfare, illicit trafficking, demography, social and traditional media, and many more. Those who already do so are at an advantage, and can act as an example for those who follow. However, they too risk embracing an approach that is too narrow, not in the breadth of the topics they cover, but in the way they do so, so long as their experts continue to look at the policy level with little interaction with business and civil society approaches. For midsize think tanks, it is hard to widen these skills by simply asking peers elsewhere on the planet to fill in the blanks once in a while, be they think tankers from France, Nigeria, China, or Brazil. Thus, while widening their internal diversity, think tanks also need to work on their external diversity, by broadening the range and scope of their partnerships and acquiring talent with valuable expertise.

Granted, this is no easy feat. Multidisciplinary collaboration among experts from contiguous fields, such as economists and political scientists, is already fraught with difficulties, let alone those from apparently distant fields such as foreign policy and epidemiology. In fact, it is a highly complex and time-consuming task, which requires constant attention to preserve think tanks' independence vis-à-vis larger and powerful actors. But it is also a feasible and an unavoidable task.

At the Italian Institute for International Political Studies (ISPI), we are trying hard to move in this direction by launching and cultivating knowledge partnerships with a wide array of companies. For instance, over the last two years we have started knowledge partnerships with McKinsey on global cities and infrastructure, BCG on young leaders, KPMG and Deloitte on new technologies, Google on AI, ENI and ENEL on energy transition, and PMI on illicit trafficking. This, I believe, is the direction that our peers could follow: while preserving integrity and impartiality, never be intimidated by reaching out to big partners; you may find that what you do neatly complements what they need, and vice versa. Another lesson is that we should always strive to include donors within our work streams and research projects rather than having them only as financial backers so that they are more aware of the research and engaged in it from day one. This raises each partner's interest in our research, and it may also lead them to an increased ownership of the results.

At the same time, it should be acknowledged that it is always hard to balance the need to transform an organization, making it fit for the challenges of the next decade, with the simultaneous need to offer the classical services that think tanks attach to their fundraising activities, such as public events, workshops and roundtables, executive briefings, etc. In order to avoid creating a "substitution effect" between old but well-funded activities, and new but fledgling projects, fundraising partners need to be involved in designing, planning, and launching of new products. In my experience as Director of a medium-sized think tank, it is refreshing to see how many of our funders appear eager to take the less beaten path and attempt something new. It is all the more needed today, when the pandemic forces us to reconsider our activities, in particular those that imply large gatherings and direct social interaction.

In today's fast-changing world, small-and-medium-sized think tanks risk being left behind, especially when the worst recession of our times is fast approaching, leading many to question whether to continue to provide think tanks with vital financial support. But it does not need to be so. Our access to policymakers and our capacity to provide valuable and accurate analysis to a wider public should not go to waste. To the contrary, we should leverage these strengths and embrace change, so as to make think tanks fit for a post-pandemic world. We can achieve this by being humble, acknowledging our limits, and embarking in a quest for discovery. We can do this by looking for a more diverse and versatile staff, even at the cost of sacrificing specialization. And we can also do this by aiming at wider partnerships, in which we do not only engage our peers, but also move further from our comfort zone: out, and into the world.

Tackling Global Challenges in an Era of Disruption and Contradiction—The Changing Role of Think Tanks

Melissa Leach

Abstract Melissa Leach, Director of the Institute of Development Studies (IDS) in Brighton, UK, explores the Future of Think Tanks and Policy Advice around the World.

Keywords Civil society · Policy advice · Policy capacity · Think tanks · UK

Introduction

Think tanks are currently caught in a paradox. From environmental and climate injustice, to extreme inequalities and global pandemics, the world faces an extraordinary set of challenges that think tanks can contribute significantly to addressing. Yet, they must do this at a time when profound disruptions such as rapid technological advances, shifting centers of global power, decreasing levels of trust in experts, democratic disorders, and fake news are providing a myriad of new threats and opportunities that challenge the ways in which they currently operate.

M. Leach (✉)
Institute of Development Studies (IDS), Brighton, UK

© The Author(s) 2021
J. McGann, *The Future of Think Tanks and Policy Advice Around the World*, https://doi.org/10.1007/978-3-030-60379-3_15

For those organizations, like the Institute of Development Studies (IDS), that are focused on global development, there is a growing need to respond to global challenges such as pandemics, climate change, and extreme inequities in ways that recognize these as universal issues requiring solutions that cut across the traditional divides of country borders, academic disciplines, government departments, and sectors such as health, education, and technology. The global pandemic of COVID-19 has starkly underlined the depth of these challenges. A health crisis of massive proportions, both the disease and public health responses have major social, economic, and political impacts—exposing and widening cracks in the systems all people and countries depend on. Addressing these, requires multiple forms of expertise, mobilized across boundaries. There are needs not just to mitigate negative impacts, but also to seize new opportunities for transformative change.

IDS has a unique perspective as a research and postgraduate teaching institution based at a university that shares some attributes with the higher education sector, but also performs much of the same role as other university-linked think tanks internationally. Based on our experience, we would argue that think tanks are well-placed to make a tangible contribution to tackling the world's most pressing challenges and to overcoming traditional divides, bringing an understanding of people's lived experiences and the political, social, and economic realities that shape these, to inform policy and practice.

THE ROLE OF THINK TANKS

The world has set itself an ambitious agenda in the United Nations Global Goals for Sustainable Development (Global Goals) to be met by 2030. Thinks tanks have an important role in shaping the innovative and agile policy and practice approaches needed to meet this agenda, while taking into consideration the threats and opportunities inherent in the disruptions and contradictions that the world faces, and how they play out locally, nationally, and globally.

The role of think tanks in different contexts is multifaceted. As well as the generation of viable policy options, this role also relates to research capacity, convening and facilitation, and the promotion of internationalism. It is worth looking at each of these in turn and the implications for think tanks themselves, their research and policy partners, and those that fund them.

One of the overriding challenges we face in seeking a fairer and more sustainable world is the more equitable and inclusive generation of research and evidence. Despite transformations in geopolitics, northern universities, and research organizations still dominate the production of academic research in both the natural and social sciences (Fransman and Newman 2019). A broad movement has emerged to build research capacity in low- and- middle-income countries, but this has focused far more on the university sector than on think tanks. Despite some notable exceptions, including the ten-year Think Tank Initiative supporting over 40 think tanks in 20 countries of the Global South, many of the large donor-driven initiatives to grow research intermediaries' capacities have disappeared. Part of the problem is that research capacity and policy capacity are frequently separated. Investments, such as those made by the UK Government in the Global Challenges Research Fund (GCRF), have helped promote the building of more equitable partnerships between UK universities and Southern researchers to work together to address the Global Goals. Yet, some have argued that this overseas development assistance funding has been awarded in a way that disproportionately benefits UK universities (Ritchie and Kenny 2019). Although efforts have been made to help strengthen the capacity of non-academic research policy organizations that are doing important work,—that both generates evidence and connects it with policy (Barnes-Huggins 2019)—much more attention is still needed. Research-policy partnerships require bringing together policy-focused change agents with academic researchers (Georgalakis and Rose 2019). However, to persuade donors they are a legitimate part of this research ecosystem, think tanks must also demonstrate their independence from political and private influence. With more policy relevance and less reliance on individual researcher's interests, comes the risk of ideological and donor-driven bias (Mendizabal 2020).

Think tanks have a crucial role to play in convening and facilitating evidence-informed debate. It is dangerous to focus exclusively on the promotion of specific policy instruments. Too often, think tanks measure their success in terms of the uptake of their own policy recommendations and engagement with their reports. With donors driven more and more by a highly instrumentalist understanding of research impact—direct changes to policy and practice—think tanks can be viewed solely as advocates for particular solutions. However, given their intermediary role, which they share to some extent with the media, think tanks are in an excellent position to help open spaces for informed debate. We need think tanks that can champion knowledge as a global public good and that fight the tide of corporatization of this sector. One way to achieve this is to partner with like-minded independent research organizations. Indeed, think tanks in the Global South are already collectivizing and working together for positive change by combining their perspectives while grounding their work in their own contexts (Ordonez, A 2019)

Of course, think tanks must also help generate viable policy options. One of the hardest lessons to learn for academic institutions is that research can be epistemologically robust, without being policy ready. This has been demonstrated more powerfully in climate science than in any other sector. Producing and communicating good science and speaking truth to power have, to a large extent, failed. This is far more than a matter of accessible research and strong communications. Decision-makers look to research, not unreasonably, to reduce their policy uncertainty (Nutley and Nutley 2007). In order to do so, research has to provide answers to their dilemmas. This does not preclude think tanks from seeking to influence policy actors' understanding of the problem, steering them toward asking a different question, or rethink the ways they conceptualize and address uncertainty itself. With their access to multiple research studies, rather than focusing on promoting a single project or program's learning, think tanks are ideally positioned to help. They are also generally much better at framing research for policy or even reframing policy discourse long term. This is about far more than just synthesis and research dissemination.

It is in this area where we see the greatest potential for think tanks to help address the huge global challenges we face. Transformative change comes about as a result of multiple perspectives and wider bodies of knowledge. Whereas universities tend to be supply-driven in their production and dissemination of their research, think tanks more often seem to appreciate the interactive nature of evidence-informed policy (Cairney 2016). When their funders and their governments allow them to do so, they can operate very effectively at the interface between research and policy. For example, the Social Science in Humanitarian Action Platform (SSHAP; www.socialscienceinaction.org), hosted by IDS with key partners, brings research evidence about the social and political-economic contexts of disasters and emergencies into the hands of policymakers and practitioners, helping their responses to be more effective, sensitive, and community-engaged. The model of mobilizing academic networks and rigorous research through on-demand briefings developed during the

2014–16 West African Ebola outbreak has been successful in 2020 as applied to help responses to the COVID-19 pandemic and to demonstrate the value of social science perspectives, integrated with those from medical and epidemiological science in addressing disease challenges. Such instances show how think tanks—if they can overcome their tendency to promote themselves and their brand and concentrate on brokering evidence from diverse perspectives—may truly transform knowledge.

Finally, think tanks can also play an important role in promoting internationalism and transdisciplinarity by facilitating mutual learning across countries and sectors. This is critical if we are to counter historically and politically embedded knowledge hierarchies around whose knowledge counts, and that undermine abilities to identify, define, and implement solutions to the world's most pressing challenges. The COVID-19 pandemic has underlined the shared nature of global challenges—viruses know no borders—as well as opportunities for Europe and North America to learn from preparedness and response in Asian and African countries, thoroughly undermining outdated, yet tenacious, assumptions about knowledge flows between so-called "developed" and "developing" countries. It is clear that for this and other challenges, we need global networks that co-generate and exchange knowledge and learning, and shape global development agendas together. Current disruptions in the global knowledge landscape—including populist politics, the marginalization of expertise and evidence, and shrinking space for civil society and critical research—create new challenges around engaging research with policy and practice and defining and evaluating impact. We need approaches that address the politics of knowledge and power asymmetries in the generation and use of evidence. Think tanks can challenge orthodoxy around engaging research with policy and practice and contribute new learning around research and development impact in the context of challenge-driven research.

CONCLUSIONS

Think tanks must seek to strengthen their partnerships, capacities, and capabilities to generate and champion evidence that is grounded in people's lives and informed by the social, economic, and political realities that shape these. They must also work with others and funders to champion this approach and help develop innovative and cutting-edge research agendas that are adequately resourced, deliver value for money and most importantly, are contributing to global development that is equitable and sustainable. At IDS, we see ourselves as part of an emerging international movement of progressive think tanks, universities, and independent research organizations that seek to challenge linear and instrumental views of evidence uptake and rigid evaluation methods and criteria that are no longer fit for purpose.

In a world of ever more complex challenges in which the kind of knowledge and influence conventionally associated with think tanks is under threat, either from dominant monopoly players, "post-truth" narratives, or shrinking spaces, we must continue to push the value of independent evidence produced and brokered by national and international think tanks that can operate across government, academia, and civil society.

Reference

Ordonez, Andrea. 2019. Development Effectiveness from Within: Emerging Issues from Recipient Countries. Southern Voice. http://southernvoice.org/development-effectiveness-from-within-emerging-issues-from-recipient-countries/.

Mendizabal, Enrique. 2020. Reclaiming the Think Tank Space in the 2020s. On Think Tanks.

Nutley, and Nutley. 2007. https://www.jstor.org/stable/j.ctt9qgwt1.

Ritchie, Euan, and Charles Kenny. 2019. *The UK Needs a New Formula for ODA-Funded Research*. Center for Global Development. https://www.cgdev.org/blog/uk-needs-new-formula-oda-funded-research.

Georgalakis, James, and Pauline Rose. 2019. Introduction: Identifying the Qualities of Research-Policy Partnerships in International Development—A New Analytical Framework. *IDS Bulletin* 50: 1–20.

Fransman, Jude, and Kate Newman. 2019. Rethinking Research Partnerships: Evidence and the Politics of Participation in Academic-INGO Research Partnerships for International Development. *Journal of International Development* (advance online publication).

Cairney, Paul. 2016. *The Politics of Evidence-Based Policy Making*. London: Springer.

Barnes-Huggins, Tiffany. 2019. New Knowledge Briefs on Lessons from the Think Tank Initiative. Think Tank Initiative. http://www.thinktankinitiative.org/blog/new-knowledge-briefs-lessons-think-tank-initiative.

Scientific Approach, Objective Analysis, and National Interests of Russia: IMEMO Traditions are Always In Demand, Always Valued.

Alexander A. Dynkin

Abstract Alexander A. Dynkin, Director of the Institute of World Economy and International Relations in Moscow, Russia, explores the Future of Think Tanks and Policy Advice around the World.

Keywords China · Policy advice · Russia · Think tanks

These are turbulent times—a kaleidoscope of events, irresponsible and unpredictable politicians, conflicting streams of information, popularity of incompetent, and consistently biased bloggers—all of this makes even more acute the need for deep academic knowledge, scientific approaches, and objective analysis. These are the basic principles of IMEMO's work, and thus, they are our value foundation. This is how we have worked for more than 60 years.

The information you receive from Google is appealing due to its accessibility and simplicity. However, Google cannot answer the following questions: what will happen in the future? How will these events occur?

A. A. Dynkin (✉)
Institute of World Economy and International Relations, Moscow, Russia

© The Author(s) 2021
J. McGann, *The Future of Think Tanks and Policy Advice Around the World*, https://doi.org/10.1007/978-3-030-60379-3_16

What are the chances of these scenarios and their consequences? Moreover, it will not be able to answer the question: what can we do in these situations?. Perhaps artificial intelligence will be able to answer these questions due to big data processing, but this is also created by people.

Therefore, the need for think tanks will not disappear in the foreseeable future, it may even increase. At least that is what the IMEMO experience shows. For more than 60 years, our think tank has never experienced as much demand as it is now; never before have our scientists worked in such a stressful period of time. State authorities and Russian business are interested in our analysis, assessments, and recommendations. Russian and foreign media are interested in our investigations and comments. Colleagues and politicians abroad are interested in our findings and opinions. IMEMO scientists continuously participate in various international conferences, seminars, and projects.

IMEMO is a classic interdisciplinary, nonpartisan think tank. This is a difficult task, as being unbiased these days has become extremely difficult and only a few can manage it. But IMEMO, thanks to its sufficient budget financing, grants, and contracts, is able to stick to this principle. This is further confirmed by well-known western colleagues, who hardly represent pro-Russian sentiment. For instance, in the discussion about IMEMO's annual forecast "Russia and the World"—which is regularly published by the "New Perspectives" magazine—popular western scholar Mark Galeotti notes: "IMEMO's latest forecast … is, one should first note, a sensible and judicious document, downbeat and realistic, that manages to reflect the official perspective without being blinded by it." This is the very definition of IMEMO's position in Russian politics and society. The works of IMEMO not only reflect Russia's perspective but also influences the process of shaping "official" policies and political decision-making in the country.

However, the influence and authority of the Institute are not based on conformism or "serving" political leadership—that is the fault of think tanks and political technology centers serving political parties around the world and in Russia. The position and goal of IMEMO is primarily to analyze what is happening in terms of the country's national interests and it is from this position that IMEMO scientists often criticize official decisions on a variety of economic and political issues. They criticize but at the same time they also propose solutions that are in line with the long-term national interests of the country. I must stress that, although it was difficult, IMEMO took the same position during the Soviet era. It is with this position that IMEMO has earned its authority and respect in expert circles at home and abroad, as well as in the country's leadership.

We work according to the standards of classic think tanks, including primarily American think tanks such as the Council on Foreign Relations. Their influence and strength consisted, among other things, in the tradition of rotation: TT experts went to quite high positions in the State Department, worked in Congress, and then returned to TT. Such rotation not only improves the quality of state bodies' work, it gives the experts an understanding of how and to what extent it is possible and necessary to implement the decisions optimal for the country into real policy. After all, there are no ideal solutions. Politics is the art of the possible, not ideal solutions but practical recommendations. This is what politicians expect from think tank experts.

Classic think tanks are those most in line with these expectations, as is IMEMO. The Institute's scientists have, at various times, participated in negotiations on key arms control treaties and worked in the Ministry of Foreign Affairs, the Russian Government, and Russian embassies abroad. Experts with the ranks of generals and ambassadors work at IMEMO. Their experience and knowledge are invaluable, and in some cases simply indispensable. It's about the so-called "second track."

It seems that politicians now often live in parallel worlds. Personal ambitions have overshadowed national security interests. However, the breakdown of dialogue at the official level is often fraught with extremely negative consequences. Therefore, dialogue on the "second track" becomes especially important. This is where the knowledge and experience of our experts help, as well as their authority among foreign colleagues. These qualities have become an acute deficit in world politics and international relations, often even between allies. It is trust that underlies such a non-public format as the "second track," and makes it possible to seek mutually acceptable solutions and compromises on the most difficult issues—without interference of the media and conscious distortion of the dialogue. These formats are very efficient. They bear real fruit, even if not immediately, when favorable circumstances arise for making decisions proposed by experts. In this respect, IMEMO's authority in Russia is very high and indisputable.

There are now 300 scholars at IMEMO. Among them there are many venerable individuals, whose names are known and respected all over the world. These are experts in a wide range of issues including:

security (military, environmental, energy, economic, and food), international relations, economics and finance, innovation and new technologies, sociology, culture, and ethno-religious issues.

We respond flexibly to emerging gaps in expertise. Anticipating the emergence and deepening of social imbalances in the world, we have significantly expanded this area of research in advance. Over the past few years, the Institute has also established centers for post-Soviet and Middle East studies. IMEMO has brilliant specialists in China and Asia-Pacific, which is also an expanding sphere. The Arctic research team is also growing stronger with younger staff and we will probably have to deal with the African continent more as well.

We are adjusting the structure of our centers, adapting them for the emerging challenges in the world economy and international relations which require expert assessment. It is clear that in the coming years we will have to increasingly deal with issues related to climate change and cybersecurity. That does not mean that the Institute will change its focus—we will remain the institute of the world economy and international relations. However, in order to assess the scale of these global challenges and threats on the world economy and international relations, we will work closely with our colleagues at the Academy of Sciences and also invite the best brains from hard science, space research, cyber, and defense to work on our projects.

We also carry out project work—temporary research groups are created, financed by public and private foundations and business. 15% of revenues from IMEMO contracts are allocated to basic research in a wide range of areas and problems. This is how we practice deep history analysis and search for the sources of different policy and strategic decisions in different regions of the world.

IMEMO's authority is largely based on our forecasting work, which we have been doing for decades. We have unique forecasting techniques and methods of verification for our forecasts. In the expert community, as well as among politicians, economists, and business circles in Russia and abroad, our forecasts are well known and have acquired a high reputation. IMEMO prepares and publishes long-term strategic forecasts. Now we can confidently say that much of what we presented in our work "World 2035. Global Forecast" has occurred. We are now preparing a forecast for 2040. Our forecasts have been translated into several languages and have become, in a sense, points of reference for social science experts in the world.

The annual forecasts of IMEMO "Russia and the World: Economy and Foreign Policy" also attract great attention. Our work has been increasingly published abroad for several years in the "New Perspectives" magazine. Using well-known foreign forecasting methods, we are constantly supplementing them with new and technologically advanced findings. In preparation of strategic forecasts, we also use the results of situation analyses which are regularly held by IMEMO, in which we conduct interdisciplinary brain-storming on a given relevant problem. This is completed by elements of the Delphi method through anonymous questionnaires and the Foresight method, as well as SWOT-analysis.

Forecasting the development of the international situation at the current stage is extremely difficult, primarily due to factors such as:

- Sharp acceleration of world processes and reactivity of participants' behavior; growth in the number of players, including non-state actors, and stakeholders in world politics; growth of influence and conflict potential in relations between local human civilizations;
- The fragmentation and degradation of the old system of world relations and the transition to a new, not yet defined stage;
- The impact of information and technological factors which significantly change the social and economic basis of life and values of both individual states and the relations between them;
- The lability and polarization of public sentiment around the world and the use of foreign policy as a domestic policy becoming normative.

In any forecast exercise, the key parameter remains to be time: short, medium, and long term. Thus, a positive short-term forecast is sometimes combined with a negative long-term forecast in one study, and vice versa.

Despite these challenges, forecasting in all time horizons is IMEMO's top priority and also its main achievement. Prognostic work is also of great importance to best utilize our distinguished scientists and their joint work with young experts. After all, we know the "A.Clarke's rule"— "if an outstanding but elderly scientist claims that something is possible, he is very likely right; but if he claims that something is impossible, he is very likely wrong."

These are tough times for think tanks. Our competence is judged by millions of people in our own countries and around the world. We are active on Twitter and Facebook, with more than 2,000 daily visitors on our website. Thousands of people want to attend our forums, such as the Primakov Readings, and we don't have halls big enough to accommodate them. The interest is clear—IMEMO's authority allows us to gather the world's most famous scientists and politicians on these forums.

Previously, in our writings we said that the next global crisis will stem not from economic or financial domain, but rather geopolitical, or other unexpected spheres, from the "wild cards" including pandemics. As the COVID-19 global shock is demonstrating, scholars are not fully able to predict all dramatic challenges, their scope or consequences for the world. This pandemic is a threat to the world, it has appeared unexpectedly and makes the global security and economic balance even more fragile. However, on a fundamentally scientific and interdisciplinary basis, think tanks can elaborate scenarios and optimal recommendations for stabilizing the socioeconomic, financial, and political situation. Cooperation of think tanks in such situations cannot be overstated. I am absolutely sure that the more complex our world becomes, the more complex challenges and security threats there will be, the more classic think tanks will be in demand, such as IMEMO and our close partners—Carnegie Endowment, IFRI, SIPRI.

The Future of Think Tanks Around the World

Laurent Bigorgne and Francis Verillaud

Abstract Laurent Bigorgne, Director and Francis Verillaud, Special Advisor at the Institut Montaigne in Paris, France, explore the Future of Think Tanks and Policy Advice around the World.

Keywords China · Civil society · Digital platforms/Digitization · France · NGOs · Policy advice · Russia · Social cohesion · Think tanks

Since the turn of the century, Institut Montaigne and its peers across the globe have been evolving within a dramatically changing environment. This year, the coronavirus brought to the forefront numerous policy challenges for all countries and exacerbated the underlying tensions that were already present.

New Challenges for Think Tanks

These challenges echo the massive shifts that have been occurring since the end of the last century. They are mostly ideological, ecological, and technological. There is an urgent need to rethink how we act, in order

L. Bigorgne (✉) · F. Verillaud
Institut Montaigne, Paris, France

to adapt the world's economies and societies to an intelligible and operational framework. This is why think tanks are particularly relevant today. They can rapidly mobilize high-level expertise to tackle our new collective challenges.

In the twenty-first century, we are experiencing at least two main transformations that are impacting the world order (or disorder), the world economy, and the social landscape:

The first transformation is the ecological challenge, which we can certainly grasp through the effects of climate change, but is not limited to this sphere. The ecological challenge is fueling a major debate at the global level between international organizations, NGOs, and many national governments. It has now also become a concern for citizens, consumers, producers, companies, and their shareholders. There is little debate that the environment and the future of our planet are at stake.

The second transformation is the digital revolution. Its effects are still not fully known, yet it has already profoundly modified our relation to space and time. It has become a fundamental issue for economic competitiveness and security. However, as they become central to our well-being, digitalization, and artificial intelligence are putting into question our fundamental rights and freedoms.

Simultaneously, the world is experiencing both a rapid transformation of the geopolitical status quo as well as a deep crisis of democracy and its core values. We are now facing a reversal of globalization, and the distress of the institutions that were created to regulate it. Western powers, under the ailing leadership of the United States, are now struggling to keep up with the competition that is emerging with nondemocratic States like China and Russia. Unfortunately, Europe has not yet found its voice in the new geopolitical game.

The weakening of the Western democracies has made room for the development of populism and for authoritarian regimes, both outside and inside the European space.

These challenges are also visible in the changes within our societies. The tools that policymakers and think tanks previously applied to public policy issues appear increasingly incapable of bringing solutions to the problems of citizens. The specific analysis may be different from one country to another, yet everywhere we can observe the polarization of our societies along the political spectrum and increasing social fragmentation.

Inequality is on the rise, and can be observed along income, educational and social lines, as well as in relation to economic globalization.

There is competition for trust among political parties, unions, and traditional media, which has led to citizens increasingly rallying around their authorities. Most importantly for our purposes, there is also room for improvement for universities, think tanks, and experts to rise up to the challenge of producing relevant knowledge and making it available to everyone.

THE STRENGTHS AND WEAKNESSES OF THINK TANKS

One may ask: what is the core mission of a think tank in 2020? How can think tanks become more useful? How can they influence decision-making in the best interest of our societies, while respecting the values of impartiality and independence according to which they were designed?

The landscape in which think tanks have evolved since their creation has been totally disrupted in recent years. All the elements central to the success of think tanks are being redefined:

- Digital technology is reshaping communication strategies and practices, and research dissemination can now use new tools and channels.
- The revolution of big data and AI is offering think tanks new, powerful, analytical capacities.
- The complexity of issues and their level of technicality are increasing the need for specialization.
- Fast growing competition in the policy advice landscape is multiplying the number of actors and their diversity. Think tanks have to act not only alongside universities, but also alongside a growing jungle of new actors such as advocacy groups.
- One direct effect of these changes is the rising costs of think tanks' operations. Thus, many cannot raise the economic resources needed to handle the competition. Their survival often comes at the price of their independence. Funding is now more crucial to the existence of think tanks then it has ever been.
- Last but not least, the extension of their outreach through social media, and at the same time the fragmentation and polarization of the political spectrum, mostly in democratic states, have exposed think tanks to very violent attacks. These have threatened their integrity and even their *"raison d'être"* as sources of independent expertise and knowledge.

The task may seem overwhelming, but it may just be a matter of "going back to the basics." This can be synthetized into 3 recommendations.

1. Think tanks are designed to build qualitative and complex answers to concrete policy issues. The task of a think tank is not to predict the future, but to understand causes and consequences of complex issues in order to dissect the potential challenges that undermine our societies. To do so, think tanks must have the capacity to mobilize relevant expertise and confront decision-makers and civil society with concrete facts.

2. Think tanks, as they grow and integrate new norms and standards, need to avoid rigid habits and allow their intellectual framework to evolve constantly. Most of the concepts and tools used by think tanks are becoming outdated or obsolete and are losing their relevance.
   As previously noted, there has been a surge of new questions and challenges that think tanks must tackle. How can the competitiveness of our economies and sustainability of the environment be reconciled? How can we ensure the full development of the digital revolution and simultaneously guarantee social cohesion and respect for individual rights? How can we reinvent an effective and coherent public policy framework? How can we reconcile the need for globalization and the geopolitical fragmentation linked to demands for sovereignty?

3. Think tanks must reassemble their key assets to address the transformation of the world. Of course, organizations need to focus on their own strengths and define who and what they are. Whatever the diversity within the think tank community, there is a set of elements that are almost compulsory to all of them:

   - Building a strong identity for each think tank, which must not be confused with their brand, is a powerful move to ensure its resilience in a changing environment. No real strategy can be set for an organization without a strong identity.
   - Quality of expertise is of course indispensable. Yet we all know that expertise becomes rapidly obsolete and outdated. The key issue is to ensure access to the best expertise at all times. This might question the need for a permanent, costly, expertise. The present pandemic demonstrated that a broad expertise has

been much more relevant in tackling the numerous issues the crisis brought up. Interdisciplinarity seems to be an important feature for the think tank of our time.

- Choices for think tanks have to be made seriously in terms of the dissemination of findings and solutions. All depends on the quality and the efficiency of their networks among decision-makers, both public and private. On the other hand, it also depends on their communication capacity and positive media coverage.

At the end of the day, much of the response is tied to the organization itself, its leadership, its identity, and certainly its flexibility.

Focusing on these areas can help think tanks build independent and focused responses to the challenges highlighted earlier.

VALUES AND GUIDELINES

The present task for think tanks is enormous. On the one hand, think tanks must respond to the complexity and diversity of the new challenges of our societies, on the other hand they must constantly reinvent themselves. They need to acquire new skills, knowledge, and practices in order to become legitimate actors in the public debate.

Without a solid compass, this task will be difficult. Think tanks need to build a strong strategy to be efficient. And strategies, in turn, are always tied to a set of values. This compass is essential to preserving strong guidelines for the think tank, even amidst the worst storms.

Think tanks cannot limit themselves to the "production of new ideas and solutions"; they also have to respond to the vast movement of distrust and fear that is constantly generated within our societies.

It is therefore urgent for think tanks and their community to invent new instruments, to change the way they address the public, and to increase their aptitude to feed the public debate. Since they can be stronger together, they also need to develop new, effective coalitions to carry and promote the values of democracy.

Caught in the Firing Line—How Think Tanks Stay Relevant in Times of Global Transition and Turmoil

Peter Fischer-Bollin

Abstract Peter Fischer-Bollin, Head of the Division Analysis and Consulting at Konrad Adenauer Foundation (KAS) in Berlin, Germany, explores the Future of Think Tanks and Policy Advice around the World.

Keywords China · Civil society · Civil society organizations · Germany · Policy advice · Think tanks · Transparency

A globally networked world of ever-closer connections between people, goods, capital, and services makes it crucial to identify new trends and challenges at an early stage. This is essential to lay the groundwork for policymaking with a systematic, forward-looking approach that will positively shape conditions for freedom and democracy, innovation, economic competitiveness, and both internal and external security. Political decision-making at the national, regional, and global level is currently being impacted by a number of trends and developments:

P. Fischer-Bollin (✉)
Konrad Adenauer Foundation (KAS),
Berlin, Germany

© The Author(s) 2021
J. McGann, *The Future of Think Tanks and Policy Advice
Around the World*, https://doi.org/10.1007/978-3-030-60379-3_18

The **growing bipolarity between the United States and China** is felt all over the world. Under President Trump, the United States is withdrawing from regional and global organizations and treaties, and seeking direct, bilateral confrontation with China and other powers. China, on the other hand, is expanding its economic, military, and political influence by wielding soft power across the globe such that it is, at the very least, perceived as a carefully planned strategy. The impression of global competition between the democratic free market economy and the system of state capitalism, as run by the communist party (CPC), is largely undisputed albeit not completely dominant; hence, leaving room for multipolar constellations.

At the same time, we can observe the **increasing dysfunctionality of multilateral systems**, as major powers regularly block each other's policies. The present crisis of multilateralism is accompanied by global conflicts over the **safeguarding of natural resources**. This, in turn, is leading to new alliances being forged involving contracts, financing, technology, and infrastructure. It concerns resources such as fossil fuels, raw materials required for state-of-the-art technology (including 'rare earths'), lithium, foodstuffs, drinking water, and also data—the "oil of the future." This explains why in addition to regions that have been embroiled in geopolitical rivalries in the past, such as Central Asia and North Africa, new areas, such as the global data space, the Arctic, Antarctic, and outer space are now also increasingly implicated. There is evidence of increased friction between the major world powers in all these areas. In some cases, this has become a race and involves circumvention or even blatant violation of international law. The anticipated **growth of the world's population** to nearly ten billion by 2050 will increase pressure on natural resources. Furthermore, the consequences of climate change are making resources even scarcer and further fueling the return of geopolitics to a question of borders, power, and access to territories.

In order to stay relevant, think tanks have to provide a holistic analysis, whereby interdependencies between various issues are investigated more thoroughly, while also exploring opportunities for cooperation and new alliances. In times of increased connectivity, it will also be essential for a sound analysis **to move beyond the circle of typical viewpoints** and sufficiently incorporate international perspectives. In this context, KAS has been developing strong networks in many countries and regions where the foundation is active. This includes people from various backgrounds and expertise. Cooperation and exchange with think tanks worldwide is one central aspect of our international work. Particularly in the context of weak governance structures, think tanks play a critical role as policy advisors promoting more informed policymaking and as credible mediators between the political sphere and civil society. Building partnerships between think tanks and working together in networks is a promising strategy to gain more attention among political decision-makers. In Sub-Saharan Africa, KAS is supporting two networks of think tanks who have joined forces in order to strengthen their voice in the political discourse by developing and promoting common positions. This engagement reflects our efforts to promote the development and good governance by strengthening think tanks and civil society organizations worldwide.

Thanks to our **values-based approach, we have established trust with many stakeholders** while giving KAS the opportunity to work context-specific. As a political foundation, collaboration with democratic political parties as well as many other partners from civil society, academia, business, and the justice sector has always been integral to KAS. There are no doubt constraints and limits to such collaboration in countries ruled under nondemocratic regimes, those struggling with conflicts, and/or experiencing an authoritarian roll-back in the political system.

At the same time, think tanks must increasingly vocalize the benefits of international cooperation among the wider public. The debate's international dimension must be extended to include both citizens and national as well as local political parties. In view of growing expectations toward Germany's foreign policy by our allies and other countries worldwide, KAS—as one of the intermediaries in this realm—will reinforce its efforts to utilize the foundation's broad networks to enrich this essential debate at home and abroad. The contribution of think tanks and civil society organizations through the development of policy solutions is highly requested and appreciated in the German political landscape. The number of inclusive participatory processes of policy development in different policy areas attests to this culture. It is also an integral part of the German development cooperation to strengthen and build partnerships with civil society organizations around the globe.

In this context, communication is key for succeeding in this issue. By providing cheap, fast, and direct access to information and communication, social media and other electronic media have deeply impacted **political communication within democratic societies**. This has afforded citizens more opportunities for participation but also created less reliable information. Rational, factual debate has given way to emotional arguments in which facts and political processes are relativized—a trend clearly visible in many countries worldwide.

This increasing polarization and loss of confidence in traditional political institutions—such as parties, parliaments, governments, courts, and also traditional media—are challenging our basic structures of freedom and democracy. Strong pillars of a pluralistic society such as associations, clubs, and churches are in retreat in many Western countries. Transparency of decisions regarding both arguments and procedures seems to be the order of the day. For think tanks, the changing methods of communication are both a challenge and an opportunity: Against the backdrop of the increasing spread of fake news, alternative facts, and the emotionalization of political debates, the role of think tanks—whose work contributes to objectify discussions—becomes increasingly important. However, in order to be heard in the concert of different opinions and analysis, think tanks must adapt their communication strategies and find new, innovative ways to reach their target groups. In a situation of increased competition over the interpretation of facts and narratives, they must carefully reconsider how to best position themselves in their environments.

In many open societies, political leaders find it increasingly difficult to reach out to **young people** in particular. In part, this is due to changing means of communication, and to today's youth being less connected to their milieu. This also affects more established ties to political parties. It applies even more to Africa and Latin America, where young people often constitute a large proportion or even the majority of the population. It is therefore indispensable to identify young leaders at an early stage and to motivate them to become actively engaged in politics, business, culture, or other areas of public life. Here, outreach will increasingly rely on innovative and inclusive ways of communication, while providing inspiring opportunities at the national and international level. The foundation's worldwide alumni network serves exactly this purpose by representing a broad reservoir of talented young people from different backgrounds and areas of interest.

Demographic change, be it as youth bulge in Africa, or the opposite as an aging population in many European and East Asian countries, is likely to present a global challenge on two fronts. In particular, the expected doubling of the African population by 2050, e.g., in a single generation, will increasingly have an impact upon Germany and Europe. The younger generation expects more opportunities, in part fueled by the images and stories seen on the internet that seem to promise a better life in Europe and North America. Economic development, freedom, social security, education, health, and political participation are the only ways to improve their prospects at home. Yet, this is precisely what is lacking in these countries, some of which are ruled by dictators, others riddled with corruption, and others under the influence of foreign governments. They have become a playing field in the global competition for resources, often resulting in violent conflict, habitat loss due to climate change and land use, as well as religious fundamentalism. Some states may collapse, creating dire consequences for the security of neighboring countries and beyond. Hence, young people believe that a bright future can only be found elsewhere. At the same time, their migration creates a brain drain that negatively impacts a potentially bright future for their countries of origin.

The belief that it is imperative to leave their home countries is also fueled by advancing global warming which represents an enormous challenge in regards to providing for the world's rapidly expanding population. Its largely negative impact on **habitats**, and hence also on agriculture for food production, combined with more frequent extreme weather events and natural disasters, exacerbates the risk of civil and inter-state wars and associated **migratory movements**. This applies especially, albeit not only, to Africa. On this continent, as well as in Asia and Latin America, many cities are becoming megacities of ten or 20 million inhabitants or more. Unlike the experience of Europe, city life is no longer synonymous with improved standards of living in terms of income, education, housing, and services. Instead, it is often a daily battle for survival in extremely polluted neighborhoods with a lack of public utilities and services such as water, energy, security, education, and health care.

We cannot overstate the interconnected nature of these challenges if we are to effectively address the complexity of our tasks. Think tanks have to be ready to leave inefficient structures behind and to break up the silo mentality still prevalent in many research areas and projects. Developing new approaches of collaboration within the organization itself will be just as important as creating new entry points for analysis by identifying unforeseen trends. As such, KAS has recently started a reform process. By creating a new think tank division within the foundation, important steps have been taken in this respect. This new division interlinks the work on domestic, European, and global issues and prepares the ground for new approaches and closer cooperation with relevant stakeholders. However, further moves will be needed to deal with the full scale of the transition and turmoil as well as new opportunities accompanying those major changes. Although ad hoc international cooperation is undoubtedly on the rise to confront a global system in crisis, we have to stay the course on our values, beliefs, and underlying ethics—the significance of which will become increasingly important for our societies in the turbulent times to come.

Think Tanks Today and Tomorrow: A View from Ukraine

Anatoliy Rachok and Yuriy Yakymenko

Abstract Anatoliy Rachok, Adviser to the President and Yuriy Yaky-menko, Director of Economic Programmes at the Razumkov Centre in Kyiv, Ukraine, explore the Future of Think Tanks and Policy Advice around the World.

Keywords Analytical centers · Civil society · Policy advice · Policy analysis · Russia · Think tanks · Ukraine

Think tanks have become an integral part of the political and intellectual environments of countries in the modern world. Remarkably, they exist in different sociopolitical systems, attesting to their societal significance, and ability to adapt to different functional settings. Quantitative changes in think tanks in different regions of the world over the last decade point to their stability in developed nations and the rapid growth in emerging economies. This trend persists despite recent profound changes in global politics and the economy, and especially in technology. Therefore, the initial conclusion and forecast is that think tanks will not disappear; think tanks will have their place in the future societies, just like universities.

A. Rachok (✉) · Y. Yakymenko
Razumkov Centre, Kyiv, Ukraine

© The Author(s) 2021   131
J. McGann, *The Future of Think Tanks and Policy Advice Around the World*, https://doi.org/10.1007/978-3-030-60379-3_19

But this does not mean that think tanks themselves won't change. The surrounding changes already have had an impact and will affect think tanks. Their development in Ukraine further confirms this thesis.

Independent policy analysis institutions, globally known as think tanks, started to emerge shortly after Ukraine gained independence and began to rebuild as a democracy with a market economy. Here we refer to think tanks as civil society institutions that are nonprofit making (non-commercial) and independent from the state (government bodies, universities, etc.). In Ukraine, they mainly used the US think tanks as prototypes. The most prominent domestically and internationally Ukrainian analytical centers were established in the first half of the 1990s. By the mid-2000s, Ukraine was already among the European leaders by the number of independent think tanks.

Ukraine's peculiarity is that non-governmental think tanks which do not receive state funding on a regular basis, are in fact the leaders among policy analysis institutions. According to experts, the activities of state-run analytical structures, as well as the specialized institutes of the National Academy of Sciences with budget funding, are less effective. Party-affiliated think tanks could not develop in Ukraine due to the weakness of the political party system. Lone attempts by Ukrainian businesses to create public think tanks have also failed. For-profit or commercial think tanks currently act more like consulting firms and are generally unknown to the public.

Over the years of their existence, non-governmental think tanks have accomplished many missions that arose from particularities of specific periods in the country's history. In early years of independence, their efforts largely focused on facilitating post-Soviet transformations, creating new state institutions, and building the market economy. At that time, think tanks have done a lot to familiarize government officials and politicians with lessons of other countries' democratic reforms and their adaptation to the Ukrainian context, also promoting relevant models among the public.

At the same time, think tanks shouldered a mission of political enlightenment, contributing to better understanding of political processes in a multiparty system, differences between competing ideologies and practical implications of their realization in different spheres. Think tanks have consistently helped voters recognize the differences between political programs of candidates and parties in presidential, parliamentary, and local elections. With increasing social attention and confidence, think tanks have gradually emerged as the "public tuning fork" for assessing the government by monitoring, analyzing, and evaluating its actions from the viewpoint of public interest. It is clear that not every government welcomed such activities—at times think tanks came under pressure and even suffered persecution.

Since their establishment, most of Ukraine's independent analytical centers positioned themselves as based on democratic values, supporting the country's path of democratic reform and its European and Euro-Atlantic integration. Also, a smaller number of analytical structures supported the Eurasian integration and an alliance with Russia. The differences in geopolitical orientation became particularly radicalized during the periods of political confrontation in Ukrainian society, such as the 2004 Orange Revolution and the Revolution of Dignity in 2013–2014. Stronger voice in favor of the European, democratic path of development, expressed by the majority of think tanks, played a role in the formation of pro-European position in larger parts of society.

At the same time, exploring the most critical problems of domestic and foreign policy, national security, and defense as well as developing recommendations for policymakers have been the main functions of think tanks. The primary mission of the think tank's identity is the research and generation of new knowledge, whereas interpretation of the existing knowledge, along with clarification and explanation of political processes and decisions as well as advocacy of own (or others) ideas and proposals are the supplementary features. For example, at different times non-governmental think tanks in Ukraine played a significant role in developing conceptual state documents in different spheres, including strategies, concepts, and political programs. Sociological research has become an important and unique tool for studying various processes in society. For the Razumkov Centre, one of the few think tanks in the world that runs its own sociological service, a capability to monitor public opinion regularly provides both great research possibilities and competitive advantages.

Think tanks play a crucial role in the time of crisis. When Russia used the "disability" of Ukrainian government institutions for launching its aggression and putting Ukraine at risk of losing its statehood, think tanks, and their experts arranged "external" analytical support for higher state institutions, especially in the area of national security and defense, in repulsing the Russian aggression.

Ukrainian think tanks took an active part in elaborating Parliamentary Coalition agreements, action plans for several Cabinets, dozens of bills, strategies, and other papers. At the same time, the experts actively contributed to the implementation of the EU–Ukraine Association Agreement by participating in the development of relevant regulatory acts, in advocacy and monitoring of their implementation. Think tanks helped to spread accurate and truthful information across the world about the reforms in Ukraine and the consequences of Russian aggression, also contributing to the formation and strengthening of the international coalition in support of our country. Finding ways to end the Russian-Ukrainian armed conflict, overcoming its consequences and restoring sovereignty and territorial integrity is one of the priority areas for the national think tanks' activities.

Since their foundation, the leading think tanks have gradually proven their proficiency and earned public credibility. Their research work is highly appreciated by the national government, the academics, and society. They serve as a source of objective and unbiased information about Ukraine for international organizations, foreign governments, corporations, scientists, experts, media representatives all over the world. Ukrainian think tanks are represented in more than 30 different nominations in the TTCSP rating. They are members of international expert networks and have bilateral partnerships with renowned colleagues from around the world. This, however, does not mean that their development is trouble-free, and the future is cloudless.

The first and foremost problem is the financial one. Only a few think tanks in Ukraine have supervisory boards or panels that work to ensure their ongoing financial provision. As for others, funding is the concern of CEOs or development officers. Funding sources are also limited. In Ukraine, there is no market of analytical services for government structures, where non-state and state analytical centers could have competed on equal ground. Stable budget funding is usually available only to the state-run analytical structures with very few exceptions to the rule.

The national legislation on nonprofit and non-governmental organizations—with think tanks also falling under these regulations—permits them to make a profit and use it for statutory activities, but restrictions on its size do not allow sustainable functioning of even smaller think tanks. The traditions of Ukrainian business philanthropy are still in infancy. Moreover, businesses do not have proper financial incentives to support research, while conditions of philanthropy are far from perfect.

Under these circumstances, most think tanks seek funding for their research from external donors either in Ukraine or abroad. In recent years, the reliance on external support has increased significantly. At the same time, donor funding is often linked to limitations on the choice of research topics by the donor's mandate. The tasks that donors assign to think tanks increasingly include advocacy for certain policies, communication with stakeholders in the process of advocacy, as well as various educational programs and training. In these processes, the research itself recedes into the background, which may result in gradual loss of expert qualifications, while the fight for donor funding sometimes goes beyond professional ethics.

Even if think tanks do find money for research, it is about project financing at best, whereas very few donors provide institutional funding and for only certain think tanks. Moreover, the task of drafting bills and advocating for policies predetermined by external donors may come into conflict with the need for impartial analysis and critical assessment of all existing policy alternatives. For Ukrainian think tanks, the problem of dependence on external funding is particularly relevant, given the possible outflow of international aid projects—for some, this will become a matter of survival.

The situation, however, does not appear hopeless and there are several ways to improve it. Above all, think tanks should agree with government agencies on true opening of the market of analytical services based on the principle of mutual benefit and interest, using the best international practices. Nowadays government agencies willingly invite individual experts to perform external expert reviews or to draft policy documents— this is mainly done through the experts' membership in various advisory and consultative bodies within government agencies. Such work is mostly unpaid. At best, an expert may get some reward, but not the think tank he or she belongs to. When government agencies start concluding contracts for expert services directly with think tanks on a competitive basis, this would become a powerful drive for their development.

Adjusting the legal status of think tanks as for-profit and socially beneficial organizations would allow them to earn more and spend more on their activities and development. Decentralization—that is currently underway in Ukraine—may offer additional opportunities for local think tanks to get funding for research commissioned by local communities. Efforts to support local business research also look promising, but think tanks need to have proper expertise in relevant fields and develop clear analytical products. It is possible that crowdfunding for specific, socially important research in some "uncharted" spheres may eventually become a reality for Ukrainian think tanks as well.

While anticipating the problem with external funding, the Razumkov Centre has set a goal of diversifying its sources as much as possible, particularly focusing on internal sources, attracting donor pools for large projects, and working directly with the clients in the person of international organizations.

The funding problem is key for determining the directions of further development of think tanks, for discovering new and promising research areas, and for addressing the issue of recruiting young talents. After all, human resources are core assets that need sustainable development. As nonprofit organizations, think tanks can hardly compete with consulting and lobbying agencies in terms of remuneration.

At the same time, think tanks hold the edge in attracting specialists who value their own intellectual freedom and opportunities for professional self-fulfillment in public policy analysis and development without being employed in the civil service. Work in a think tank is usually associated with lower reputational risks, compared to the public or business sectors. Ukraine's leading think tanks today are quite attractive employers for university graduates and young professionals not only from Ukraine but also from abroad. However, it is difficult to guarantee the stability of job and competitive pay. The process of employing foreigners is also complicated.

The scarcity of funds narrows the possibility for ongoing advanced training of personnel, which is a must in the modern world. Yet there are positive trends in this aspect as well, as in recent years many universities have become more active in supporting their own think tanks. Moreover, some curricula already include courses that are essential for political analysts working in new contexts, such as quantitative research methods in political science.

Activities of think tanks in Ukraine are certainly affected by the environment in which they operate. This environment becomes increasingly more intense and competitive due to the presence of new actors specializing in consulting, lobbying, advocacy, or monitoring, as well as 24/7 media. Real-time access to large volumes of information and research, simplified data search and systematization have greatly eased the work of mass media in the preparation of "analytical" materials on political, economic, and other topics, and somewhat "sidelined" the think tank experts.

Still, this mainly concerns the materials for "general consumption." The particular value of think tanks' products is that they offer primary, unique knowledge generated by their own research. Regrettably, in the age of general simplification and even primitivization of the content of the information sphere, such studies are often ignored by the media. As for government agencies or politicians, the research, analysis, and policy recommendations by think tanks remain perfectly relevant, although time-saving principles, new information technologies, and arrival of the new generation of specialists to civil service require more lapidary presentation of materials, visualizations, and the like.

Another advantage of the leading Ukrainian think tanks is their ability to attract the best experts (including international on ad hoc basis) in their respective fields, as well as years-long system of contacts with current and former officials and policymakers, which goes along with a deep understanding of the real mechanisms behind policymaking and implementation. Also, think tanks play an important role as discussion platforms for experts, government officials, members of the public and other stakeholders. The Razumkov Centre's experience suggests that non-governmental think tanks may serve as forums for composed and equal exchange of views on complex international issues. All this allows think tanks to compete against other actors in the area of political expertise and consulting.

This does not mean that think tank analysts should limit their communication to colleagues, academia, and policymakers. Instead, they must remain competitive in reaching wider audiences through their presence in media—both traditional and new, including social networks. This is particularly important in the environment of post-truth, fake news, and alternative facts, where think tanks remain the ones that pursue evidence-based knowledge. Unfortunately, the expert opinions in real life are often devalued through "formatting" of discussions in online and social media, active participation of "bots" and the general trend of dominance of public sentiment over fact-based knowledge. For some experts, commenting on various events in the media turns into their primary activity (and the source of income), while the frequency of appearing on TV becomes a major assessment criterion for donors.

Obviously, each think tank builds its own information strategies. Nowadays it is hard to imagine a respectable Ukrainian think tank without at least one page in social media, recorded audio and video commentaries of experts and infographics. However, all these activities require considerable human and financial resources. Moreover, while a form is important, the question of content and research should be a priority. Otherwise the think tank risks becoming a "packer" of other people's views in a beautiful wrapper.

Analytical work is essentially the work with information. Therefore, innovation in information technology (IT) dramatically expands the "nutrient medium," in which think tanks exist and develop. Particularly important in this regard is open data policy that not only increases transparency of management processes, but also creates a competitive market of analytical services that is accessible to each participant regardless of its relationship with the government (or specific data manager).

Rapid development of data science—the accumulation of big data, the application of machine learning technologies, and the expansion of data-driven approach to decision-making—offers plenty of new opportunities to think tanks, while ignoring these innovations and lacking expertise in data science will lead to a loss of competitive advantage. Thanks to greater flexibility and adaptability to new forms of work compared to government analytical structures, it is the non-governmental think tanks that can pioneer such research.

Another challenge that think tanks need to address is the changing nature of politics, the increasing fragmentation and polarization of political space. On the one hand, the public becomes increasingly more sensitive to populist rhetoric. The focus is on sentiments and preferences, rather than on facts and objective research, which leads to weakening or even eradication of any opportunities for rational argumentation/counter-argumentation in public political discourse.

On the other hand, due to generational changes in politics and the spread of anti-elitist tendencies in societies, people who have no idea about politics altogether or who lack systematic knowledge in any sphere, let alone the managerial experience, may come to power. Social elevators become social catapults that do not entail gradual development of competences as these people move upwards. Instead of effective policy, they suggest effective action—as a result, the quality of policy decisions is no longer measured by the GDP growth or the level of income, but by the number of views and likes under a president's last video address or his Twitter message.

The accuracy of these conclusions for Ukraine was clearly confirmed by the results of the most recent presidential and parliamentary elections, where the victory was claimed by a comedian with no political experience and his virtual party, named after the popular TV show, in which he starred. The fragmentation and polarization of the political field further complicate the process of policymaking and the search for compromises endorsed by the majority of stakeholders and public opinion. Along with the destruction of the reputation of independent media, there is less noticeable but equally important problem of distrust toward any holders of expert knowledge. The spread of anti-elitist sentiment and conspiracy theories poses a potential threat to the reputation of think tanks, and hence to the effective fulfillment of their sociopolitical role.

Nonetheless, the new shape of society and the emergence of a new political elite are by no means an excuse for think tanks to withdraw from the process of rational and critical policy analysis. However, in such settings, the importance of quality of expert advice and the reputation of their developer increase significantly, especially when it comes to formulating public policies involving serious political contradictions.

The lack of professionalism in politicians and the gullibility of voters must be counterbalanced by the proficiency, dedication, and integrity of political analysts, who accept part of responsibility for the content of policy implemented by its "traditional" subjects. Public confidence in think tanks amidst total distrust toward political institutions may become an important factor for legitimizing the actions of a government that takes heed of the recommendations of reputable think tanks. The latter, in turn, must learn how to deal with new, "unconventional" political forces, at least within traditional, representative political systems.

So, Ukraine's example proves that think tanks have many things to think about and plenty of work to do. It is obvious that the relevance of specific problems or their correlation for think tanks across countries may vary, but their list is identical. This reaffirms the importance of broad international communication between members of the global analytical community, with TTCSP-led global and regional forums playing an important role. Constant sharing of best practices and experiences in addressing the existing problems is decisive for think tanks to be able to adapt to ever-changing conditions of their existence and to respond to multiple challenges induced by changes in today's world.

Middle East and North Africa Region

Although the Middle East has the fewest total number of think tanks of any region, at 464, the sector is expanding at a greater rate than any other region. Between 2011 and 2018 the Middle Eastern think tank industry grew by over 33%, with the number of new institutions founded expanding by a factor of more than nine compared to the previous decade. This enormous growth is for good reason, as the region must address the policy issues surrounding the ongoing Syrian civil war, Israel–Palestine conflict, Qatar diplomatic crisis, increased tensions between Iran and the United States, and more.

To Survive, Think Tanks Must Be Part of the Change

Ezzeddine Abdelmoula

Abstract Ezzeddine Abdelmoula, Manager of Research at Al Jazeera Center for Studies in Doha, Qatar, explores the Future of Think Tanks and Policy Advice around the World.

Keywords Latin American think tanks · Policy advice · Qatar · Saudi Arabia · Think tanks · UAE

CHALLENGES THINK TANKS FACE TODAY

The environment in which think tanks operate is fast-changing and becoming more complex. Among the various drivers leading these changes and shaping this transforming environment is technology. Communication technology, and continuous technological innovations in particular, have had a crucial impact on the way institutions function, communicate, and exert influence. Think tanks are no exception in this regard. The role they play in disseminating relevant information, assessing and analyzing situations, and providing policy advice is

E. Abdelmoula (✉)
Al Jazeera Center for Studies, Doha, Qatar

© The Author(s) 2021
J. McGann, *The Future of Think Tanks and Policy Advice Around the World*, https://doi.org/10.1007/978-3-030-60379-3_20

143

increasingly being challenged. Their effectiveness and sometimes relevance, is also being questioned, especially with the coming of new types of competitors, including public relations agencies and giant information providers. Open sources, big data, and artificial intelligence have created new dynamics and transformed the global marketplace of ideas in terms of information creation, packaging, and dissemination. These new dynamics have made the mission of think tanks even more challenging.

Besides these challenges, which are common among think tanks at a global level, regional and local think tanks are faced with challenges specific to their own geopolitical and socioeconomic contexts. Think tanks based in democratic polities deal with sets of challenges different from those existing in authoritarian political systems. The Middle East region is a good example of how difficult it is for think tanks to work independently from economic and political pressures. In many cases, these institutions find themselves caught between the lack of local funding and the prohibition—and sometimes criminalization—of foreign support. In cases where government funding is available, it often comes with conditions and pressures compromising the integrity of policy advice and the quality and independence of research output.

For decades, the Middle East has also been a fertile ground for instability, protracted crises, and conflicts of various forms. The Gulf crisis, which erupted in June 2017 when Saudi Arabia, the United Arab Emirates, and Bahrain decided to impose a land, sea, and air blockade on Qatar, presents a good example of how volatile regional politics affect the work of think tanks. Since the outbreak of the crisis, contributions from these three countries decreased dramatically. Researchers and analysts, who were actively involved in our work prior to the crisis, started to decline our assignments. It has become extremely hard to invite participants from Saudi Arabia, the UAE, and Bahrain to take part in our Doha-based events. In such circumstances, bringing in different views and different sides of the story becomes very challenging, whether in written analyzes or in conferences and debates.

Additionally, populist politics and political polarization along ethnic, religious, and sectarian lines have been on the rise. The media and the use of new communication technologies have made it easier for disruptive discourses to maximize their influence and gain ground among various segments of society. Alongside this growing trend, trust in states, political parties, and institutions in general is declining. Anger and grievances are being translated into popular uprisings and protest movements across the

MENA region. Similar developments, albeit on a smaller scale, are taking place in other parts of the world, including Sub-Saharan Africa and Latin America.

Against this backdrop of turbulence and disruptions, think tanks can still play significant roles. They need to interact dynamically with these ongoing changes to turn challenges into opportunities. They need to reposition themselves within this unstable order to assert their relevance and continue to provide adequate services. The need for informed and independent policy advice will always exist, and the demand for providers of such advice increases especially in times of uncertainty. The more trust in governments and political institutions declines, the more the need of policymakers for reliable sources of information and analysis rises. However, to be able to fill in this widening gap, think tanks need to adapt both in structure and in strategy. In short, they, too, have no choice but to embrace change and be part of its dynamics.

Required Changes in a Changing Environment

To remain valuable and continue to play influential roles, think tanks are required to effect a number of changes at different levels:

1) Adaptability and flexibility: In this highly competitive environment, where roles, business models, ideas, and human expertise increasingly overlap, it has become hard for institutions to survive and provide services in the traditional way. The fast rhythm of global and regional geostrategic, political, and economic developments, coupled with the ongoing information revolution and overwhelming technological innovations, cannot be met without a great deal of adaptability and flexibility. Flexibility in structure, agenda-setting, product diversification, communication strategies, recruitment, and staffing is key, not only to institutional survival but also to compete and excel. Adaptability to this new environment is crucial for think tanks to continue delivering their message to the right people at the right time in the right format.

2) Multidisciplinary approaches: The complex nature of issues facing policymakers and policymaking processes in general requires complex approaches. This is required to understand, analyze, and give relevant recommendations about the best way to deal with these issues and face their possible consequences. Domestic issues

are increasingly regionalized and sometimes globalized, especially in parts of the world like the Middle East. Social issues are best understood if their economic, political, and educational dimensions are considered: what happens in the market cannot be separated from what happens in other areas such as the university, the technology sector, the transport system, the political sphere, and even the climate. It may not be easy for all think tanks to apply multidisciplinary approaches, especially those with limited financial and human resources. Partnerships and mutual cooperation among think tanks can facilitate this task and reduce its cost. Working through partnerships is undoubtedly a win–win situation for all parties.

3) Continuous learning and training: Whatever the skills and quality of staff think tanks might have, the fast-changing world we live in requires continuous learning and training. Working together and exchanging experience and expertise between think tanks is certainly one of the most effective ways to transfer knowledge, innovative ideas, and best practices. Collective learning through direct contacts and joint projects provides invaluable opportunities for analysts and researchers to sharpen their skills and keep themselves abreast of the latest developments in their field. Learning from the practical experience of other institutions does not necessarily occur through exposure to their success stories only, but also through knowing their problems. Knowing the problems of others helps us know our own.

4) Embrace technological advances: Technology is the domain where the fastest changes are taking place worldwide. It is also the cause of many disruptions in our social and political systems, as well as in the work of our institutions. Dealing with technology has become inevitable, because it is increasingly shaping our lifestyle and affecting the smallest details of our daily lives, especially the way we communicate. However, technology is also providing unprecedented solutions to many of our problems. This, for example, can be seen in distance working during times of disruptions. The most recent case is the 2019 coronavirus pandemic, which forced institutions to change the way they work. With the help of technology, many institutions managed to keep their workflow unaffected as they began to work remotely. Since the outbreak of the virus, my institution evacuated its headquarters and all staff members were

able to carry out their jobs from home. Technology provided us with the necessary means to meet virtually, communicate, plan, and execute all of our tasks to keep business going on, uninterrupted, although in different forms.

Institutions that have openly embraced technology have achieved dramatic advances in meeting their goals and objectives. Much of the structural, operational, and financial challenges facing think tanks can be effectively dealt with by employing technological solutions. Technology is no longer simply a tool; it has become a business model and a way of thinking. It is the way forward for think tanks to sustain themselves and depart from their traditional cubicles.

5) Empowering younger generations: Among the most disruptive effects of technology is the creation of a widening generational gap in the work of tank tanks. This is most visible in the field of human resources and recruiting policies. Compared to the older generations, the younger generations are generally better equipped to deal with technology and related innovative concepts and ideas. They may lack experience when it comes to running think tanks or producing research and policy recommendations, but the responsibility to bridge this generational gap lies on the shoulders of the current think tanks' leadership. In this technology-driven environment, it is vital to involve the youth and enable them to play influential roles and move up to leadership positions. Empowering future generations is not only a pragmatic move to benefit from their skills and fresh perspectives, but also—and more importantly—an opportunity to extend a bridge to the future.

The Credibility-Funding Nexus and Its Impact on Research Quality in Middle East Think Tanks

Shaikh Abdulla Alkhalifa

Abstract Shaikh Abdulla Al-khalifa, Chairman of the Board of Trustees at the Bahrain Centre for Strategic, International and Energy Studies in Awali, Bahrain, explores the Future of Think Tanks and Policy Advice around the World.

Keywords Bahrain · Digital platforms/Digitization · Government-funded/Privately-funded · Policy advice · Policy analysis · Research centers · Think tanks

Think tanks in the Arab world, and in the Gulf in particular, share much in common with their counterparts across the world. However, there are several challenges that are more salient in the region, and merit elucidation.

The first is the issue of funding. Like think tanks in western countries, think tanks in the Arab world must allocate significant human and financial resources to the task of securing funding for their activities. However, unlike their western counterparts, Arab think tanks must do so in an

S. A. Alkhalifa (✉)
Bahrain Centre for Strategic, International and Energy Studies, Awali, Bahrain

J. McGann, *The Future of Think Tanks and Policy Advice Around the World*, https://doi.org/10.1007/978-3-030-60379-3_21

149

environment where many stakeholders are unaware of the existence of think tanks, let alone what their responsibilities are or whether they merit financial support. Even highly educated locals would struggle to provide a cogent response to the question: "What is the difference between a think tank, a consultancy, and a university?"

In the Gulf region, this is a somewhat inevitable consequence of the relative youth of our educational systems, since research centers are a natural outgrowth of mature universities and other knowledge institutions. The University of Oxford was founded in 1096, but it took until 1831 for the Royal United Services Institute, the world's oldest think tank, to be established. In 2019, the Kingdom of Bahrain celebrated the centenary of its educational system—the oldest in the Gulf region—and the role of learning and knowledge in our society continues to rise. Part of the mission of Derasat, which simultaneously celebrated 10 years since its establishment, is to raise awareness about how think tanks can contribute to developing Bahraini society.

The second idiosyncratic challenge is a corollary of the first. The dearth of public awareness about think tanks means that governments account for the lion's share of funding. In the eyes of Western observers, this undermines the credibility of the output of Arab think tanks, making it much more difficult for us to influence perceptions beyond our shores.

There are some notable exceptions within the region, such as the King Abdulla Petroleum Studies and Research Center (KAPSARC), which is both administratively and financially independent, as it has been granted a sizable endowment to fund its operations. But this highly expensive solution is not scalable, which is why the majority of think tanks within the region remain dependent upon direct funding from the government, such as the Emirates Center for Strategic Studies and Research in the UAE, the King Faisal Center for Research and Islamic Studies in Saudi Arabia, and the think tank that I chair, Derasat, in Bahrain. All of these think tanks, and others in the region, such as the Kuwait Institute for Scientific Research, engage in some measure of contract-based research following the RAND model; but this is rarely enough to fund operations completely. Moreover, those procuring the research are invariably ministries and other organizations in their home government, making them forms of indirect government funding.

We understand the role that financial independence can play in improving the quality of research. However, within Western countries, observers underestimate the inaccuracies that emerge when independent Western think tanks produce research relating to the Arab world without having a presence within the countries that they are studying, and without employing citizens and residents of those countries. No amount of visits by foreign delegations can substitute for the intimate knowledge of local conditions that only locals possess. This misperception creates self-sustaining cycles of inaccurate analysis of the Arab world, whereby attempts by publicly funded Arab think tanks to contest the views put forward by independent Western think tanks are erroneously dismissed as being propaganda, with little effort expended to evaluate the research output of Arab think tanks based on its intellectual merit—a violation of the fundamental mission of any research organization.

At Derasat, this challenge is reflected in the difficulty that our researchers face when submitting their op-eds to leading global media outlets. Such publications tend to favor either a high-ranking govern-ment official for the government's view—and such a person typically does not have the training to produce an analytical op-ed—or these publica-tions opt for the opinion of an individual affiliated with an organization that is both administratively and financially independent of a Middle Eastern government, even if that person resides outside the Middle East. Government-funded think tanks in the Middle East face an uphill struggle to convince editors of the value of their opinion.

Fortunately, there are reasons for optimism. The Arab region actually has a rich history of private funding of research and public understanding of the role of knowledge in society. Many of the scientific advances that arose during the Golden Era, from 750–1250, were the result of the private patronage of science, with wealthy merchants sharing the govern-ment's appreciation of advancing knowledge in all fields, including those with and without commercial relevance. The economic visions of the Gulf countries are attempts to reactivate society's latent thirst for knowledge, and to recreate the effective public-private partnerships that previously drove our region to the cutting-edge of science.

Globally, there are serious questions regarding the future of think tanks, and many of the contributions to this volume reflect these growing concerns. However, in the Arab world—and especially the Gulf region—several factors point to an expanding rather than shrinking role for research centers, especially homegrown think tanks, by which I mean organizations that are established locally and staffed primarily by locals, including research corps.

The first reason relates to national security concerns. Due to a combi-nation of the history of colonialism and a desire to realize high rates of economic development, foreign experts have featured prominently in policymaking in the Arab world, often in the form of advisors and consultants. Moreover, the historically limited levels of homegrown talent in areas such as international relations and economic development have meant that the think tanks operating in the region, especially the Gulf, have research corps composed primarily of foreign scholars. These foreign experts in government and research circles have made invaluable contributions to policymaking, and will continue to do so throughout the coming years.

However, during the last decade, the nature of the Great Powers' interests in Arab societies has evolved, and Gulf societies in particular have begun to appreciate the importance of homegrown talent to complement and balance foreign advice in critical areas such as international relations and economic development. The economic visions of the Gulf countries, for example, are nominally economic strategies, but this belies their importance to national security. Consequently, it is critical that a highly knowledgeable corps of citizens emerge to provide objective analysis in a manner that serves the national interest. Therefore, we should expect to see growth in the volume and quality of homegrown policy analysis.

An intermediate and likely transient attempt at addressing the concern about the lack of homegrown talent has been the establishment of Middle Eastern branches of major global think tanks. In some cases, such as Carnegie Beirut, they have been partially successful at hiring local researchers, and combining the traditions and resources of the mother think tank with the locals' expertise. However, in the Gulf, the rate of success in nurturing homegrown talent has been lower, and it is likely that there will be greater efforts at hiring and developing local researchers in the coming period. For this reason, Derasat requires junior hires in the research department to be Bahrainis, and partially bases the evaluation of its senior researchers on their demonstrated impact on the development of the junior researchers working under their purview.

Naturally, this will be a positive development for local think tanks; but there is an additional reason to expect growth. As mentioned above, policymakers in the Gulf region have come to appreciate the importance of independent organizations in influencing policy in the western world. From the perspective of Western media, think tanks, academic organizations, and the general public, independent think tanks—be they administratively or financially independent—possess a unique form of credibility that plays a significant role in shaping Western policy toward the region. In critical issues such as climate change, global security, and international trade, for the Gulf countries, they can no longer rely exclusively on overtly government-led efforts to articulate and protect national interests. Think tanks need to play a larger role, and a societal consensus regarding this is slowly forming.

Consequently, we expect the Gulf societies—led by their governments in this regard—to increase their investment in homegrown think tanks, both in the form of private and public funding. We expect to see a larger proportion of high school graduates pursuing academic qualifications that suit think tank work, and greater societal prestige conferred upon those who manage and work in think tanks.

Despite this generally positive message regarding the future of think tanks in the Gulf region, the mounting pressure of funding that think tanks all across the world are facing will need to be confronted here, too. In this regard, we expect a continuation of the digitization of think tanks that started in the 1990s with the spread of the internet.

We have all become accustomed to reading research papers in electronic form, or attending seminars remotely via web-streaming technology. Looking forward, we expect this process to become more radical, with think tanks becoming virtual in an attempt to economize on the significant operating costs of traditional brick-and-mortar operations. One of the first think tanks to head in this direction was the Gulf Labor Markets, Migration and Population Program (GLMM), which was jointly established by a number of knowledge institutions including the Gulf Research Center, which is based in Saudi Arabia. Such a development would also be consistent with the growing attention being paid to environmental concerns, as virtual think tanks with researchers working remotely will decrease the carbon footprint of these organizations.

As an illustration, the Kingdom of Bahrain has recently launched a teleworking system for public sector employees as part of the Kingdom's efforts to realize the UN Sustainable Development Goals. In many senses, think tanks are better placed to take advantage of virtual structures than traditional organizations such as businesses or ministries, because research in the social sciences rarely requires more than a laptop and an internet connection.

In conclusion, despite the clouds that have gathered over the international system over the course of the last decade, this remains an exciting time to be a part of the think tank community in the Gulf region. Young scholars can look forward to making a growing contribution to policy and society more generally, and we will all be beneficiaries.

How to Reduce the Gap Between Think Tanks and Policymakers—The Experience of the Egyptian Center for Economic Studies (ECES)

Abla Abdel Latif

Abstract Abla Abdel Latif, Executive Director and Director of Research at the Egyptian Center for Economic Studies ECES in Cairo, Egypt, explores the Future of Think Tanks and Policy Advice around the World.

Keywords Egypt · Policy advice · Policy community · Social justice · Think tanks

Technology is advancing extremely fast, climatic changes are threatening the whole world, poverty and social injustice are increasingly threatening sustainable development efforts, and political conflicts are impeding developmental efforts not only in the countries involved, but also extending beyond their borders, to regional and international levels. All of these challenges call for close collaboration between think tanks and policymakers. In fact, the only way policymakers can keep up with these challenges is by associating themselves with think tanks, specifically those that perform the thinking for them.

A. A. Latif (✉)
Egyptian Center for Economic Studies, Cairo, Egypt

© The Author(s) 2021
J. McGann, *The Future of Think Tanks and Policy Advice Around the World*, https://doi.org/10.1007/978-3-030-60379-3_22

Yet there seems to be a widening gap between policymakers and think tanks. Policymakers more often than not make their decisions without regard for think tanks. More often than not, they don't consult them at all, and when they do, they take their recommendations very cautiously as supporting evidence, seldom as a main source. We often hear expressions like, "you do not understand the situation," "your analysis is too theoretical," or "your suggestions are not realistic." We often also hear frustrated, sometimes even hurt, comments on the part of think tanks as they feel no appreciation for their efforts. The incredible solutions they provide to policymakers who do not want to use them, and instead opt for mediocre solutions that they feel comfortable with, insults their effort and expertise.

Closing the gap between think tanks and policymakers is becoming more and more important for all of these reasons, but this cannot be realized unless the nature of the gap is analyzed and dissected. Only close and detailed analysis of the problem can lead to a conclusive and sustainable solution.

Many resources go to think tanks, primarily to guide policymakers—if not directly and immediately, at least indirectly and eventually. The existence of such a gap between think tanks and policymakers means that scarce resources are going to research that does not find its way to its beneficiary, thus resulting in a waste of resources.

The purpose of this article is to closely analyze the nature of this gap between think tanks and policymakers and identify solutions to make a tangible impact. To do so, this article focuses primarily on economic and strategic planning interests of think tanks. Supportive examples from Egypt, specifically from the experience of the Egyptian Center of Economic Studies (ECES), which I currently manage, are presented. The article also attempts to answer the question of why the gap between policymakers and think tanks in the Arab world might be even wider than that of the Western world.

The gap between think tanks and policymakers can be broken down into five types: an information gap, a time frame gap, a language gap, a communication gap, and a trust gap. While each seems to be dealing with a separate issue, the reality is that they are all interlinked and feed into the last item: the trust gap.

The time frame gap deals with the different pace of action between policymakers and think tanks. Policymakers are under a lot of pressure to make decisions. They have questions about alternative solutions to problems, and they want the answers now, or even yesterday, if possible. Think tanks, on the other hand, want to take their time with research. More often than not, by the time they are done, their research is useless because the issue is no longer relevant and decisions have already been made. This gap exists to different degrees depending on the topic and time frame.

The time frame gap is further emphasized by the information gap. In order for think tanks to act quickly, they need updated and reliable information. This is in itself a big problem, especially in developing countries such as those within the Arab world. When the work of think tanks is assessed by policymakers, they hardly ever remember this problem.

The language gap is equally important, policymakers need simple language that they understand and can use to defend their policies. Think tanks often use economic, social, and political jargon that sounds alien to policymakers. Policymakers often feel intimidated when confronted with complex language, and they are often more comfortable using alternative, mediocre analysis and conclusions simply because they understand it better.

The communication gap is another major problem. Outcomes of research and policy recommendations are typically presented in seminars and published journal articles. This channel of communication is used more by academia than policymakers. A deeper communication problem lies in reaching out to policymakers. Policymakers are typically involved after the research has been completed and policy results are presented; they are hardly ever involved in the process of research, choice of methodology, or decision on assumptions. Policymakers typically just see results. Moreover, their "what if" questions are not answered because research is already completed. "What if" scenarios deal with changing the assumptions of an analysis and results/policy recommendations, and policymakers want to know these scenarios to be able to make decisions. It is a sort of sensitivity analysis for the policy recommendations out of the research. While policymakers need these scenarios now, think tanks typically need to rerun models to get the needed answers. This takes time, which is another technical constraint leading to a wider communication gap.

Another aspect of the communication problem, closely related to information and time frame gaps, is accessibility of the "stock and flow" of research on a certain topic. By "stock and flow" of research of any topic, I mean all the accumulated research—measured at any point in time—on any topic, versus ongoing research on the same topic and policy briefs that attempt to do quick analysis of a situation. While the first might be accessible to all, the flow is often much less accessible not only to policymakers, but also to other researchers, whether they are part of think tanks or independent. This leads to older policy recommendations prevailing, as well as missed opportunities for capitalizing on new research.

Finally, keeping aside commissioned research, think tanks choose the topics they want to work on. Whether or not policymakers have similar priorities is a major question.

All of the above gaps feed into a lack of trust in think tanks. Policymakers do not trust think tanks especially if they are not "theirs" i.e., governmental in nature. They see think tanks as specifying policies for which they will not pay the price. Should the policy recommendations be inappropriate, the blame falls on the policymaker not the think tank.

All think tanks try to narrow the gap in different ways. At ECES, we have developed a few techniques to help address the problem. We present three of them below:

1) *Involving policymakers in the research process from the beginning, even when the research involves economic modelling. This is achieved through forming, for each project, a steering committee including relevant policymakers as well as representatives from the business community.*

This technique has helped ECES narrow all gaps addressed above. Involvement of policymakers from the very beginning contributes to better mutual understanding of the problem at hand. It sets expectations on what can and what can't be done, the necessary assumptions that need to be adopted, not to mention the needed input information and data to do it. It also allows for continuous communication between the three stakeholders: Policymakers, the business community and ECES, thus bringing to the table latest updates concerning research progress, new developments of relevance, and timely solving of research problems that might emerge in the process. These steering committees also significantly help address the language gap. Since they are managed by ECES, it is our team's responsibility to listen to the other two stakeholders and "translate" their language into that of research and also translate research results into language they understand and appreciate.

2) *ECES has also developed an innovative technique of publishing, on a daily basis, simple language economic commentary on pieces of economic news, to make policymakers and the business community feel that we are keeping up with changes in the economy, explaining what is going on and its implications, and correcting wrong decisions before the government gets deep into implementation. We call this daily publication "Views On News". Through monitoring the reaction of both policy makers and the business community, interest in this daily publication is increasing at an accelerating rate and is taken very seriously by all.*

In response to the COVID-19 situation, our "Views on News" became "Views on the Crisis" and three short, yet very deep, reports were published on the 16th, 17th, 18th of March 2020 to address the impact of the crisis on key sectors and macro variables through the crisis cycle (WWW.ECES.ORG.EG). According to feedback from policymakers, these reports are helping the government in real time.

3) *Collaborating with other think tanks is also a key technique used by ECES to improve the quality of research as well as access to policymakers.*

Two specific examples are presented here: collaboration with the Cairo Office of (IFPRI) and collaboration with (ERF). In the first case, IFPRI is developing a new tool that contributes to narrowing the timeframe gap. It is running economic models with different scenarios in advance so as to address the timely needs of policymakers. The COVID-19 scenarios we detailed in our reports at ECES are currently being used by IFPRI to develop different assumptions for their model, which means richer research for both think tanks. In the second case, ECES has agreed with ERF to be allocated a special session in their annual conference, where ECES's policy-oriented research will be presented to the regional community attending the annual conference. This is also an enriching experience for both institutions, and policymakers also benefit.

These are a few of the techniques we use. We try as much as possible to put ourselves in the shoes of the policymakers while remaining research-oriented. We continue to learn through experience in order to both grow our institution and benefit the larger policy community.

Evolving with the Marketplace of Ideas: How Think Tanks Can Thrive in the Era of Twitter

Amos Yadlin

Abstract Amos Yadlin, Executive Director of the Institute for National Security Studies in Tel Aviv-Yafo, Israel, explores the Future of Think Tanks and Policy Advice around the World.

Keywords China · Israel · Policy advice · Research institutions · Think tanks · Transparency

BACKGROUND

Following Israel's failure to foresee the outbreak of the 1973 Yom Kippur War, Maj. Gen. Aharon "Ahrele" Yariv founded the Institute for National Security Studies (INSS) in 1977. In the leadup to the war, Israeli academics and government analysts failed to read the Egyptian strategy and the media failed to thoroughly question their working assumptions. Yariv established the Institute within academia in order to challenge and support the government of Israel by providing a second opinion and out-of-the-box thinking. Since then, we have grown more ambitious by becoming independent of academia, a shaper of policy rather than a

A. Yadlin (✉)
Institute for National Security Studies, Tel Aviv-Yafo, Israel

© The Author(s) 2021 161
J. McGann, *The Future of Think Tanks and Policy Advice Around the World*, https://doi.org/10.1007/978-3-030-60379-3_23

second opinion, and a source of expertise for the media. My slogan as the head of the Institute is: Aim for the precision and depth of academia, the speed and appeal of media, and the responsibility and actionability of the bureaucracy.

Think tanks have been accused of many different things, from serving the Illuminati (Fagan 1966) to providing poor policy advice (Taleb 2016), but I remain convinced that they are valuable assets for the public as well as for decision-makers. To serve their intended audiences, they must provide concise and professional reports that explain the implications of recent developments within the context of the strategic environment, followed by actionable recommendations to achieve desired outcomes. While the current political and social climates pose considerable challenges to our efforts to inform the public discourse and provide decision-makers with high-quality advice, at the INSS we have sought to adapt to the current moment while staying true to our professional values.

In general terms, the think tank culture in Israel and the broader Middle East appears to be growing, as new organizations sprout up and seek to identify and fill gaps left by established institutions. However, the region-specific challenges facing new and established organizations alike remain considerable. Except for Israel, many states in the region limit freedom of speech, and so policy recommendations with implicit critiques of current policy may not only be ignored by autocratic governments, but even punished by them, leading to self-censorship by important voices. In addition, the hostility between different religious, ethnic, and national groups is a tragic reality of the Middle East and places significant limitations on the level of cooperation between institutions. This is particularly regrettable since many of the most pressing issues are not confined to any particular state but have an impact on the broader region, and, though it is often not forthcoming, greater cooperation could greatly benefit efforts to cope with them.

Think Tanks in a Changing Environment

The Information Revolution was expected to put endless amounts of information at the fingertips of the public, leading them to become more informed about what is happening around the world. But that is only a partial description of how things have played out over the last few decades, as the internet has also been discovered by those with malicious intent, who use it for the transmission of propaganda and disinformation (not to mention espionage and theft). More recently, social media sites like Twitter have created echo chambers that contribute to the polarization of politics and the decline of political moderation. Social media has created a generation of readers who consume their news in 144 or 288 characters rather than through extensive in-depth reports.

Because of the tectonic societal shift taking place, INSS has understood that continuing to focus the bulk of our efforts on producing books or detailed reports of over 3000 words would risk losing our central role in the national security discourse in Israel. Politicians and common citizens alike no longer have time to read dozens of pages leading up to a conclusion and policy recommendation—like it or not, we are living in a world where people demand immediate results. However, at the same time, as professionals committed to advancing the national interest and the public good, we could not and would not sink to emulate the oversimplified and radical discourse of the day.

How have we managed the tension between popular appeal and professionalism?

First, we concluded that there was a need to re-evaluate our media strategy. Connections with traditional newspapers and television stations were no longer adequate by themselves to reach our target audience, which includes not only senior decision-makers but also young adults (people 18–35 years old). Therefore, we directed resources toward building a presence on Twitter, Facebook, and Youtube in order to reach this latter demographic, which we consider important given that it contains both young voters and future decision-makers. Ultimately, though it was not identified as such at the time, the strategic shift presented INSS with a major opportunity to both expand its global reach and receive feedback from those who consume its research. Not only do we now operate social media accounts presenting our research materials in three languages (Hebrew, English, and Arabic, with expansion to additional languages under consideration), but we are able to conduct a dialogue that allows us to see how the English-speaking world or the Arab world responds to our work.

Second, an executive decision was made to focus less on historical background in our writings and more on actionable recommendations. To be clear, any and all research we produce must have a strong historical basis and should be built upon extensive research. However, we are also aware that writing for an audience that values its finite amount of time and likely has a limited attention span means prioritizing, and we are more interested in conveying our message about what should be done in the future than that about how to see the past. We believe that our publication titled the *INSS Insight,* which is capped at 1200 words and should ideally allocate the last one-third of the text to present policy recommendations, is well-balanced between professionalism, relevance, and accessibility. As a research institution, we have not ceased to produce long-form research products, but there has been an undeniable shift in focus from weightier pieces to more current and concise publications.

Third, INSS has invested greater resources in bringing onboard young researchers at the beginning of their careers. The more senior members of the organization have decades of experience in academia, the diplomatic corps, or the defense establishment, which—though certainly valuableis no substitute for being a member of these new generations, which have distinct worldviews from their predecessors. The Institute's combination of early career professionals and accomplished experts serves two important purposes: first, our young researchers are mentored by knowledgeable professionals who can help them navigate the difficulties of starting a career in a highly competitive field; and second, the younger generation can look at long-standing issues with a "fresh set of eyes," to question prevailing assumptions and develop innovative solutions to protracted problems. This synergy has proved invaluable to the INSS, which seeks to harness the wisdom of experience without ignoring the importance of forward-thinking innovation.

Fourth, because security studies have traditionally been a male-dominated field, INSS takes great pride in the fact that over 40% of its research staff is female. On a purely practical level, we have found that diversity of experience and opinion can bring new ideas to the table and allows for fruitful discussions and debates. In addition, because around fifty percent of the Israeli population (the primary consumers of our research products) is female, we consider it imperative that women be well-represented on our research team. The Institute sees its role as a venue for women to advance their careers in national security as important for the success of the organization and the country.

Fifth, INSS has broadened the scope of its research to include areas of growing interest to Israel, including the rise of China, the perils of fake news/disinformation, and potentially existential threats. Oftentimes, the reaction of the government bureaucracy to newly identified trends can lag behind those of more nimble organizations, like think tanks, and that is why decision-makers and security officials now approach our new programs for advice on how to deal with these complex issues. Our ability to adapt quickly and focus on emerging issues provides us with a unique advantage from the perspective of decision-makers, which I think is evident from the fact that INSS research on the abovementioned subjects continues to be read by decision-makers at the highest levels

Sixth, the INSS has broadened its partnerships with colleagues in the region and with the private sector. Slowly warming ties between Israel and other states in the region have allowed for low-profile meetings and discussions with counterparts from Middle Eastern countries about how to better advance collective security from shared threats. Given that no official diplomatic ties exist between Israel and some of these countries, think tanks can play an important role in transmitting and receiving messages. In parallel, partnerships with the Israeli private sector have added value to the Institute's research products. Colleagues at the Center for Strategic and International Studies have done a superb job at integrating geospatial intelligence (Asia Maritime Transparency Initiative 2018) into their policy reports, and the INSS aims to follow suit (Orion and Yadlin 2018), as providing visible evidence is especially important in an era in which the general public has become skeptical of expertise.

Finally, looking to the future, the Institute is not only working with the government of Israel to design an "exit strategy" from the combined health, economic, and social crises caused by the global outbreak of the Coronavirus (COVID-19), but is also developing mechanisms that would make think tank work and activities more resilient to disruption. The 2020 pandemic, which has hampered international travel and large gatherings, has provided a strong impetus to consider such a contingency. Shifting to virtual conferences, in which experts discuss subject matter (as per a usual public event), but the audience watches from behind their computer screens at home rather than crowded event halls, is one new practice that has been adopted. In addition to being more friendly to the environment, this approach could prove beneficial in a variety of conceivable circumstances: inclement weather, participation of high-level officials demanding extreme security measures, and time conflicts. Through weekly brainstorming sessions with the Institute's senior staff, I am hopeful that we will yet develop and implement many more ideas to cope with the Coronavirus that will far outlive the disease.

Democracies depend on the ability of their citizens and elected officials to make informed decisions, which is growing considerably more difficult in an era when it can be a challenge to do "basic" tasks like separating fact from fiction. If they can adapt to cope with current challenges while maintaining the principles of professionalism, think tanks may not only survive but will in fact help to shape a brighter future. I hope that sharing my experiences and assessments will prove useful to my esteemed colleagues, as their insights on everything from operating a think tank to the state of global affairs have been invaluable to me.

REFERENCE

Asia Maritime Transparency Initiative. 9 May 2018. An Accounting of China's Deployments to the Spratly Islands. The Center for Strategic and International Studies. https://amti.csis.org/accounting-chinas-deployments-spratly-islands/.

Fagan, Myron C. December 1966. CFR Completely Unmasked as "Illuminati" in U.S. No. 123. Cinema Educational Guild, Inc. https://www.amazon.com/CFR-Completely-Unmasked-Illuminati-US/dp/B005J1P0QE.

Orion, Assaf, and Amos Yadlin. 14 May 2018. *Iran in the Nuclear Realm and Iran in Syria: A New State of Play*. The Institute for National Security Studies. https://www.inss.org.il/publication/iran-nuclear-realm-iran-syria-new-state-play/?fbclid=IwAR0BQmTvWywAHNoSooPXW6IpsXgDWHq1W3820V7o0O7NrTmwGrxZhhA8fL0.

Taleb, Nassim Nicholas. 16 September 2016. The Intellectual Yet Idiot. Medium. https://medium.com/incerto/the-intellectual-yet-idiot-13211e2d0577.

Think Tanks Have Stories to Tell…

Slim Bahrini

Abstract Slim Bahrini, Executive Director of the Maghreb Economic Forum in Maghreb, Tunisia, explores the Future of Think Tanks and Policy Advice around the World.

Keywords Fundraising · Policy advice · Think tanks · Tunisia

No one should doubt the vital role that think tanks play in shaping policy agendas and introducing new ideas, as they ignite a fundamental debate between the research and the policymaking worlds. However, at the same time, no one would doubt that think tanks have been facing numerous, serious challenges throughout the last several years which may be fatal to many think tanks around the world and are particularly felt in the Maghreb region and African continent.

Without doubt, the most common and prominent challenge that think tanks face is fundraising. To be more specific: access to sustainable and long-term funding. Indeed, many think tanks in the Maghreb rely on small and short term project-based funding. This allows them to survive for a couple of years but requires them to constantly search for different

S. Bahrini (✉)
Maghreb Economic Forum, Maghreb, Tunisia

J. McGann, *The Future of Think Tanks and Policy Advice Around the World*, https://doi.org/10.1007/978-3-030-60379-3_24

sources of funding. This process requires a substantial amount of time, and it makes the work difficult as it distracts think tanks from their main mission.

This challenge has resulted in the incapacity of think tanks to recruit and/or keep the brightest minds because they cannot offer them the best salaries. This has affected the rigorous work of think tanks.

This issue creates a dilemma around think tanks' independence. Indeed, how can a think tank guarantee its independence—and more precisely, its intellectual independence—if it fails to develop its own research agenda and ideas due to the fact that it is chasing short-term project-based funding? How can a think tank stay true to its DNA if it has to actively seek funding to stay operational; funding that does not necessarily serve and fit the mission of the think tank?

In the particular phase of transitional democracy that the region of the Maghreb is currently witnessing, it has been exhilarating to see the rise of think tanks throughout the last decade. They have played an important role in: (1) providing the audience with sound analysis on local/regional events; (2) studying the root causes that led to the changes in the region; and (3) trying to explain the projections of these changes in order to ensure positive impacts. Now, it is sad to see that most think tanks are at the tough end of a quick natural business cycle.

Another major challenge that think tanks are facing is how to deal with the proliferation of information. The number of platforms feeding different types of audiences a near-infinite amount of information simply cannot be measured anymore.

Think tanks are ideally placed to play an important role in using this amount of information and data in order to determine what is significant and what is not. This has contributed to making them a distinguished source of information. Throughout this process, think tanks should consider expanding to reach a wider audience, and for that they need to be flexible and progressive. To be progressive, they need to review the entire think tank business model and adjust it for the digital age. This can only happen if think tanks equip themselves with the skills and knowledge required to thrive in a digitally charged future.

No longer is the question about whether going digital means think tanks need to simply make small and quick adjustments to adapt to new technologies. It is clear that there needs to be a much bigger change. Indeed, being digital for the sake of just having a presence on social media channels is not enough—as believed and practiced among many think tanks. Think tanks must reshape their entire business model.

The greatest challenge for think tanks is that this shift requires serious organizational changes which could be hard to achieve, particularly in academic institutions. Scholars, and specifically the older generation of scholars, pose a challenge with their fear of change and their way of leading their think tanks. Thus, if we are to talk about organizational changes, we must talk about implementing new practices that scholars, and specifically the older generation of scholars, have yet to master. Many may be resistant to this change, as they tend to like how things were always done. Yet, things are not what that used to be; globalization and the expansion of information and communication technology have opened up knowledge and empowered people to access and demand it at a snap of their fingers.

This increased access to information has also resulted in further demand for democratic participation in: (1) knowledge production and (2) public debate. These can no longer be restricted to the political elite and decision-makers; today, it needs to include everyone. If think tanks fail to include a diversity of voices and interests, the recommendations they make to policymakers will have gaps and disconnections, resulting in resistance and opposition from the wider audience. That wider audience can balance the decision-making power, (sometimes described as the rise of populism, which is considered, in my opinion, a tool that has not been mastered by elites and think tanks) and ultimately can lead to the ineffectiveness of policies or the opposition of them.

Technology, communications, big data and data visualizations have not only changed the work of think tanks, but also affected the traditional practice of think tanks, from data collection to the way they communicate and engage. Embracing these new practices will make think tanks grow like never before, as they will have to constantly reinvent themselves, improve, be smarter, and be faster.

This is the origin of the fear that the older generations' "same old, same old" thinking will hold back think tanks. This is the concern they always raise, the speed versus credibility concern, waving the argument that if think tanks embrace new practices and start moving quickly, it will affect their credibility. Such credibility is what should distinguish the work of professional scholars, who are trained to put accuracy ahead of speed in order to create credibility and impact. This is not correct (at least not anymore) in this digital era we live in, where having an impact and building your credibility requires both accuracy and speed at the same time. Not only how but when our audience and public response is extremely important to our work.

While scholars' focus on the concern of think tank credibility, they miss out on what should have been the best use of technology for think tanks: technology, communications, and data visualization have turned everything into a conversation and/or a debate. This aligns with one of the central goals of think tanks. Are we, as think tanks, not contributing to create space for debates, nurturing them and encouraging stakeholders to engage, and at the same time offering alternative analyzes and views in these same platforms?

Let us explore this idea further: that social media has had a significant effect on think tanks, moving studies and research from papers, books, and analysis to Facebook, Snapchat, and Twitter. By creating a new and exciting advocacy ecosystem (in which even a small voice can participate in the debate), social media can be turned into a promoter of the work of think tanks and can support the advocacy of the think tank itself—leveraging and influencing decision-making.

Think tanks are missing this big window of opportunity because they are too reluctant and stubborn to change, evolve and upgrade their business model. It is no longer about hundreds and thousands of study pages with technicity and complex analysis and recommendations, and it is no longer about only reaching the elite and the people in power, either to educate or influence them. These methods stand in the way of starting a conversation and in the way of how we communicate. It is reduced to storytelling—and think tanks have stories to tell!

Think tanks must make a better case for what they do and why they do it. This is why I believe that scholars are no longer the guardians of the think tank industry. They now need to cede this role to communicators.

It is essential to reach out to a wider range of audiences, as well as to engage new key players (and especially to those who were traditionally outside the policy-related bubble). Outreach is often understood as offering platforms for a large number of actors and as improving communication strategies; as mentioned before, the small and quick changes to adapt to new technologies are not sufficient. These advancements signal a much bigger change and a more radical approach instead. This approach must combine both the change of the business model and the redesign of research methods.

Reinventing the role of think tanks means moving out of think tanks' self-centered bubbles, engaging critically with power, and rethinking responsibilities toward society at large. This does not divert from the original mission of think tanks—to provide research on policy issues for government and centers of decision-making—and it would help give them more relevance, speed, accuracy, integrity, and autonomy from power.

For think tanks, this is an opportunity to hear more voices and to engage with society in new ways that shape the progress of our work. We, as think tanks, have a tendency to forget that our job is to help shape progress for the future so that everyone benefits from it. How can we be able to do that if we cannot shape the progress of our work?

Central and South America Region

In the context of the diverse political, economic, social, and cultural landscape of the 30+ countries that comprise Central and South America, there are several transnational issues that think tanks must address. Environmental changes, persistent inequality, systematic corruption, and increasing violence force millions of people throughout the region to live in a constant state of uncertainty. The 1023 think tanks in the region, seek to explain the social, political, and economic situation of their home countries, as well as address the aforementioned issues, in a commitment to the search for change in the policies and practices of several public and private actors.

Think Tanks Toward the Future: Challenges and Opportunities

*Adalberto Rodriguez Giavarini, Gustavo Martínez,
Juan Battaleme, and Guillermo García*

Abstract Adalberto Rodriguez Giavarini, President; Gustavo Martínez, Managing Director and Public Affaires; Juan Battaleme, Academic Secretary; and Guillermo García, of the Consejo Argentino para las Relaciones Internacionales in Buenos Aires, Argentina, explore the Future of Think Tanks and Policy Advice around the World.

Keywords Argentina · Chile · Civil society · Civil society organizations · Latin American think tanks · Policy advice · Think tanks · Uruguay

The increasing turbulence in domestic and international affairs makes this a propitious moment to review how think tanks influence societal knowledge and government policy. Nowadays, rapid dispersion and proliferation of knowledge in a sprawling ecosystem of overlapping agencies and funding streams tangle the absorption of information by political and policy actors toward an opaque decision-making scenario. This governance challenge in a "post-truth politics" world offers think tanks the opportunity to concentrate this knowledge and take on a role as reliable information curators. This is so because it is related to an "epistemic

A. R. Giavarini (✉) · G. Martínez · J. Battaleme · G. García
Consejo Argentino para las Relaciones Internacionales, Buenos Aires, Argentina

© The Author(s) 2021
J. McGann, *The Future of Think Tanks and Policy Advice
Around the World*, https://doi.org/10.1007/978-3-030-60379-3_25

crisis"[1] which is evidenced by a growing distrust in those profession-
ally responsible for creating the knowledge that underpins public policy.
However, at the same time, "experts" and "technocrats" were and are
expected by the public and political decision-makers to provide ideas to
end crises and to ensure they "never happen again." As for what the
expert's paradox reveals, in times of crisis, policy advice is still required to
justify policy decisions, and policymakers seem to urge, more than ever,
strong policy advisors for which Latin American think tanks retain some
potential competitive advantages.

Think tanks have a long history in Latin America and have been present
since 1790 (Mendizabal 2013), when the *Sociedad Académica Amantes
del País* was established in Lima. From that point onwards, think tanks
have played various roles in Latin American societies, according to the
social and political context of each country and period. In the Southern
Cone countries, the development of think tanks began during the military regimes of the late twentieth century, and was further expanded after
the transition to democratic governments. Think tanks played an important political role in the economic and political transformation which
took place in the last decades of the twentieth century, replacing state
intellectuals and public experts and establishing important links with
international institutions.[2] Some experts have even shown that more
recently countries with relatively strong institutions have more think tanks
(Mendizabal 2013). Given their importance, what challenges do think
tanks face in the region and specifically in the Southern Cone?

First, the region must continue its efforts to address prevailing
inequality and diminish the gap between diverse sectors of its population. Gender, age, and ethnicity are persistent factors that determine
the inequality of opportunities that citizens of the Southern Cone face.
Another emerging trend in the Southern Cone is migration. Wide
migratory flows originate in other South American States, particularly

---

[1] We may relate this to the digital revolution. These crises are framed in a paradigm
shift that requires reconsidering social indicators; for example the GDP. The following
WEF article may be useful:
  Roy, Katica. 26 November 2019. How is the Fourth Industrial Revolution changing
our economy?. *World Economic Forum.* https://www.weforum.org/agenda/2019/11/
the-fourth-industrial-revolution-is-redefining-the-economy-as-we-know-it/.

[2] Chile has 13 internal think tanks, compared to the six of Argentina, five of Mexico,
three of Peru, and zero of Bolivia.

Venezuela and Colombia, especially in recent years. This great migration was partially absorbed by Argentina, Chile, and Uruguay, the first two being the countries with the biggest percentage of immigrants in South America. Acknowledging all the benefits that immigration represents, such as the increase in the economically active population, it also creates challenges for these societies, especially in terms of pluralism and equal rights. These challenges cannot be ignored by think tanks and must be faced with seriousness and commitment.

Another important challenge is the impact of new technologies which have profoundly transformed societies' access to information and present both new problems and capabilities for think tanks. Evidence-based research needs time but, in a fast-changing world, objective analysis, and ideas are urged. Traditional methods of communication used by think tanks, which exclusively target political elites and decision-makers, need to be joined by new methods based on virtual means if these organizations desire to maintain relevance in the twenty-first century, as stated in the Think Tanks and Civil Societies Program's *2018 Latin America Think Tank Summit Report* (McGann 2018).

It is unlikely a think tank in the global south, more specifically in Latin America, approaches the endeavor of influencing international policy alone (Ordoñez 2013). Rather, they must coordinate with other think tanks to face the challenge. The diverse nature of Latin American think tanks, their regional diversity and the competing interests among them are a challenge for coordination. Seeking to make this needed cooperation more possible, the Argentine Council for International Relations (CARI), has sought to foster international cooperation and peace through its diverse activities since 1985. To do so, CARI has signed various cooperation agreements with more than 60 civil societies all across the world which contribute relevant experience and knowledge.

There are few centers that can take their research to international venues and, as a result, knowledge prepared by international organizations or think tanks based in the north, tends to dominate the international debate. Policies in developing countries could enrich the international debate with a fresh perspective based on the academic and practical knowledge of politics. In this regard, if independent think tanks work together around converging principles, then they will be able to contribute to the emergence of an inclusive international society and thus confirm their normative as well as practical value. The growth in the number of think tanks within developing countries in recent years, and their increasing role in influencing policy and practice, suggests that they could be an untapped resource for sustainable social change. Reducing the rate of policy failures and increasing aid effectiveness will require more adaptive, flexible, and politically savvy approaches. In many contexts think tanks—operating as they do at the nexus between politics and policy change—can make a major contribution. They must also be open to experimentation and unafraid to employ new ways of working. In addition to getting the basics right, traditional think tanks must be intellectually innovative and act entrepreneurially to be truly impactful organizations in the coming years.

Although there is little systematic data available, anecdotal accounts suggest that fiscal austerity has entailed leaner times for think tanks (Hernando, Pautz, Stone 2018). Foreign funds from international organizations have recently moved toward less developed areas of Africa. This constitutes one of the most pressing challenges for Latin American think tanks. Despite their advantages compared to their less fortunate neighbors, Southern Cone countries are also affected by this situation. Some experts believe this presents an opportunity for a more national research agenda with increased public funding. However, what little foreign funding still remains is saddled with conditions and limitations, harming think tanks' capability for independent research.

According to the 2017 Latin America Think Tank Summit Report from the University of Pennsylvania, public funding has not increased enough to replace the missing international funds (McGann 2017). Government agencies and ministries have less funding available to support what can sometimes be considered a luxury—non-state sources of policy research, analysis, and advice. Private sources of funding are unlikely to make up shortfalls other than in exceptional cases and circumstances. Financial means are, therefore, a major challenge.

Think tanks are often better placed to influence policy than traditional civil society organizations because their research tends to be more politically informed than that of academics. Yet CSOs and academic institutions tend to be more prominent on donor radars than think tanks. In a competitive knowledge-based global economy, donor funding is always condition-based and thus undermines autonomy. As such, think tanks should rely on one of their strongest assets: flexibility. Since they are not bound to stronger structures as other institutions are, they have the capacity to analyze the best ways to balance funding availability and sustainability to avoid becoming consulting firms.

Nowadays, think tanks are often called to recommend suitable and coordinated actions in the policymaking process. Coordinated actions can help societies provide a forum that fosters dialogue and pluralistic debate between officials, civil society, and business leaders—both domestically and internationally. These spaces for open debate hold an utmost relevance. Think tanks are unique for their intersection of evidence-based research and policymaking, and their multidisciplinary audiences (governments, policy specialists and the wider society) allow them to be a powerful force for ideas in a challenging region.

References

Hernando, Marcos Gonzalez, Hartwig Pautz, and Diane Stone. 2018. Think Tanks in 'Hard Times'—The Global Financial Crisis and Economic Advice. *Policy and Society* 37 (2): 125–139.

McGann, James G. 2017. 2017 Latin America Think Tank Summit Report: Global Challenges from a Regional Perspective: The Role of Think Tanks in Latin America. TTCSP Global and Regional Think Tanks Summit Reports. https://repository.upenn.edu/cgi/viewcontent.cgi?article=1020&context=ttcsp_summitreports.

McGann, James G. 2018. 2018 Latin America Think Tank Summit Report: Think Tanks: A Bridge over Troubled Waters and Turbulent Times. TTCSP Global and Regional Think Tanks Summit Reports. https://repository.upenn.edu/cgi/viewcontent.cgi?article=1022&context=ttcsp_summitreports.

Mendizabal, Enrique. 28 January 2013. Think tanks in Latin America: What Are They and What Drives Them? On Think Tanks. https://onthinktanks.org/articles/think-tanks-in-latin-america-what-are-they-and-what-drives-them/.

Ordoñez, Andrea. 29 August 2013. Five Challenges Think Tanks Face to Influence International Policy. *On Think Tanks*. https://onthinktanks.org/articles/five-challenges-think-tanks-face-to-influence-international-policy/.

Roy, Katica. 26 November 2019. How Is the Fourth Industrial Revolution Changing our Economy? World Economic Forum. https://www.weforum.org/agenda/2019/11/the-fourth-industrial-revolution-is-redefining-the-economy-as-we-know-it/.

The Digital Transformation in Think Tanks: Moving Forward in the Use of Technology

Elaine Ford

Abstract Elaine Ford, Founding Director of D&D Internacional - Democracia Digital in Magdalena del Mar, Peru, explores the Future of Think Tanks and Policy Advice around the World.

Keywords Civil society organizations · Fundraising · NGOs · Peru · Policy advice · Think tanks

In Peru, there is much talk today about digital transformation, but always from a corporate approach, at the level of private enterprise. Undoubtedly, this effort is vital to improve the organizational environment and adopt the advances in technology to offer greater services and thus favor users. It is a job that is already responding very well in certain companies, and they will be the ones that will set the tone in front of the rest.

But what can we say about think tanks? Innovation and digitalization processes have not fully reached this type of organization that seeks to contribute in public policies, in research, and in the dissemination of knowledge. The way in which think tanks work and are organized in Peru is due, in most cases, to traditional models where technology has not

E. Ford (✉)
D&D Internacional - Democracia Digital, Magdalena del Mar, Peru

© The Author(s) 2021   181
J. McGann, *The Future of Think Tanks and Policy Advice
Around the World*, https://doi.org/10.1007/978-3-030-60379-3_26

yet become a fundamental component to boost management. This goes through issues from organizational culture, fundraising management, agenda issues, external communication tools, and interaction with stakeholders. We want think tanks of the twenty-first century with practices and attitudes according to modern times.

In this article, I want to give some guidelines to be able to implement a digital transformation from think tanks in various areas where technology can serve as a great tool. To do this, I dare to identify the 5 M's that must be taken into account in any reform of this nature, these are:

1. **Mindset.** As a starting point, we must consider that all change comes from people. Changing the mindset means changing the set of attitudes and behaviors that may already be established or conventionally acquired behaviors. In this case, it is necessary that think tanks break old molds and be able to adopt, in the most efficient way, the tools and ways of interacting in the technological age. For this, the will is a key element, because without it the desired changes will not be achieved. This must come from the highest management, who will define the guidelines, but the various organizational teams must also exercise it. Without the will, it is difficult to undertake change.

2. **Management.** The management of think tanks and civil society organizations in Peru have different characteristics according to the size of the institution, which depends directly on the level of funds they manage to raise for administrative-institutional functioning. Something that is increasingly difficult, considering that in the country there is less international cooperation available and there are more institutions that compete for these funds. For over a decade, Peru has ceased to be a recipient of cooperation due to the growth achieved and the increase in GDP. Consequently, the search for financing is a permanent challenge for medium and small-sized institutions. In this sense, leadership and vision are relevant aspects in management, since it allows identifying new forms of financing, new sources, strategies, projects, and even self-management so that the financing of the organization can be sustainable over time. Crowdfunding is an increasingly used modality, as well as the creation of alliances for the development of a specific project. Therefore, leadership and innovation strategy will be crucial for management, project development, and fundraising.

3. **Matter.** This issue is very important because it is related to the thematic agenda addressed by the various organizations, NGOs, or think tanks in Peru. Over the last decades, we have seen institutions that have led the field with great studies and initiatives. These same institutions have managed an agenda according to the political, economic, and social situation both in Peru and globally. But, unfortunately, they have not been able to adapt to the new agendas or themes that begin to be a trend and priority in the local and international scene. For example, in Peru, many organizations focused on human rights or democratic transition remained anchored in the past, without the ability to visualize the future and address those same issues from another perspective. Consequently, the product of their research or publications ceases to have the brightness and interest of yesteryear. The new generations of young people will have more interest to better understand other areas with an impact on their real or future life, according to current times.

It can be said that today there are many issues that are being neglected in Peru, which require more research, field-work, reflection; however, they are displaced by an outdated agenda over time. This point is related to the previous one because it will be the one who leads the management of the organization who must decide which issues to prioritize and attend to, in keeping with the institutional mission. In that sense, venturing into new innovative themes and projects with new actors are positive attitudes that will give a new air to the think tank. For example, COVID-19 reached Peru and nothing was done about it, so we decided rapidly, a few days after the lockdown, to launch the #Covid19TechChallenge to allow people to participate with digital solutions and show how technology can serve the health crisis. This is a way to react fast to the main trends and global matters with a national perspective.

4. **Message.** Possibly, this point is the most important. It is the way we communicate the work that the organization does. These are the formats that are delivered to the public, to the press, and to different audiences. In the case of a think tank, one must think not only of the speed of information and scope, but also of how it is delivered so that it is better digested and understood. The traditional format is completely valid, but considering that technology is a permanent companion of the individual, we must also think about other presentations and ways of communicating. Simply, it will be

necessary to define which is the most appropriate platform in the web 2.0 to communicate, according to the content and according to the expected result. We see communities on Facebook, specialized blogs, video channels, and podcasts, among others. Email through tools such as Mailchimp is very useful for mass communications that allow you to link the content to a website or other platform.

The message must reach the desired audience in a timely manner and also periodically. The online user expects to receive information constantly, without being overwhelmed. It could be a post, a fact, a statistic, with a certain periodicity, that allows us to maintain the relationship online over time. For us, communication is one of our priorities. We use, at the same time, several online channels to let our audience know about any new initiative, inviting them to participate in our activities, workshops, and conferences, among others. In these years, we have built a wide audience in Lima and different regions in Peru.

5. **Mechanisms of interaction and collaboration.** I refer to the ability to interact with other stakeholders and citizens who can contribute in the definition of topics, in the elaboration of proposals, identifying the needs and priorities of their community, contributing in the debate, and in the construction of ideas. Co-creation processes must also be considered in think tanks, as they will serve a lot in the internal organization to define the areas and topics of intervention. Likewise, the Internet and new technologies offer the possibility of interacting online with citizens through deliberation; gathering their feedback, opinions, and points of view; applying small surveys on certain topics; disseminating content and information prepared by the think tank; and sharing the material with people and new audiences, among other multiple forms. The work of a think tank could have greater notoriety and influence through the strategic work that is designed for the transmission of the message and the collaboration processes that are established as mechanisms of interaction with its digital audiences.

Technology empowers people, and that's the main reason why it is important to give them the possibility to participate. In Peru, we have identified that citizens have adapted very well to digitalization. Now, we talk about "digital citizens," and our program is focused on creating awareness and educating about the need to be "responsible digital citizens." So, in that way, part of this transformation in think tanks should include new mechanisms of co-creation and collaboration.

Technology empowers people and that's the main reason why it is important to give them the possibility to participate. In Peru we have identified that citizens have adapted very well to digitalization. Now we talk about "digital citizens," and our program is focused on creating awareness and educating about the need to be "responsible digital citizens." So, in that way, part of this transformation in think tanks should include new mechanisms of co-creation and collaboration.

Think tanks are a great support for deliberation, for the information society, for the construction of citizenship, and for the strengthening of democratic governance. The processes of digital transformation should also be considered within them, since innovation will inject them with the modernity that is required in contemporary times. It is important that think tanks have the ability to renew themselves internally at the organizational level, in their day-to-day work, and in their contact with individuals and the outside world. The 5 M's described in this article try to be adviced to take into account in order to invigorate and strengthen the valuable work undertaken.

The Future of Think Tanks: A Brazilian Perspective

Carlos Ivan Simonsen Leal and Marlos Correia de Lima

Abstract Carlos Ivan Simonsen Leal, President and Marlos Correia de Lima , Executive Director of Fundação Getúlio Vargas in Rio de Janeiro, Brazil, explores the Future of Think Tanks and Policy Advice around the World.

Keywords Brazil · Fundraising · Policy advice · Think tanks

Think tanks exist to help society move forward by providing evidence-based recommendations in order to enhance public and private decisions. Such institutions help policymakers design, implement, and oversee solutions to problems and understand the issues affecting social–economic wellness. Also, they propose questions and methodologies to address society's most significant challenges. Helping develop society more sustainably is their ultimate goal. So, in order to accomplish that, think tanks need to engage different stakeholders in building these solutions—they cannot achieve their goals on society's sidelines.

In the next few years, think tanks will have to address many challenges to survive and thrive in their role of policy aide de camp to society. This

C. I. S. Leal (✉) · M. C. de Lima
Fundação Getúlio Vargas, Rio de Janeiro, Brazil

© The Author(s) 2021
J. McGann, *The Future of Think Tanks and Policy Advice Around the World*, https://doi.org/10.1007/978-3-030-60379-3_27

187

essay briefly considers four of them. Although they are viewed through a Brazilian lens, some of the challenges can be easily recognized worldwide. The main challenges are the following:

a. **Financial sustainability**. Though think tanks were already facing a revenue crisis, the coronavirus pandemic's impact on how think tanks pay their bills is devastating. The local economy's contraction hit donors, and funding from institutional research partners is at risk as companies suffer the consequences of a strong recession. This scenario will last into the near future, since economic recovery is not immediate, nor is it assured. Even after it occurs, funding will take time to trickle back towards think tanks. Governments, who already contributed little to think tanks in Brazil, will also decrease funding as budgets are stretched thin, and challenging policy choices are made. Simultaneously, competition will increase as small and large consulting companies, alongside media, diversify their products and services.

In order to survive, think tanks will have to become lean and mean without affecting policy-relevant research and its incidence on the decision-making process. Hence, it's time to review expenditure not related to performing analysis, communicating findings, and working on policy. Investment and research into innovation will help these areas to improve, and digitalization may provide substantial operational gains on efficiency. Fundraising efforts will also have to increase, and this will require a deeper connection to the communities think tanks operate in, and more robust compliance policies to minimize the risk of jeopardizing independence and reputation. A new business model is still under construction.

b. **Influencing policy**. How do think tanks keep the capacity to impact in times of skepticism toward science? Political polarization is a threat to think tanks' ability to influence policy choices, as it tries to take rationality out of the public debate. It also affects think tanks' credibility: "opinionism" dominates public debate online and offline and policymakers increasingly consider evidence-based research non-essential when proposing policy solutions to complex problems. This situation directly affects think tanks, as their primary *raison d 'être* becomes impractical.

As part of this phenomenon, traditional approaches to influencing policymakers may no longer work. It is now necessary to think of new ways to reach decision-makers. One alternative is to have the public sway politicians toward think tanks research and proposals. In other words, be where the public is: social media, free-to-air TV, podcasts, and—we hope soon—major events.

In order to face the challenge to engage with the broader public to influence policymakers, establishing clear lines of communication and information between research teams and society will be critical. In this context, applying the command, communications, control, intelligence, and interoperability methodology (usually called "C^3I^2") may have an essential role in internal governance as well as in achieving external objectives.

Alongside the use of artificial intelligence, think tanks can create strengthened and targeted processes to reach out to people and, as a result, impact policymakers who respond to their constituents. Translating societies' aims and what drives their decisions to policymakers may be a different way of helping them in their policy choices.

One way or another think tanks will only be able to generate impact if their evidence-based research reputation remains intact—and they must do it on the public's playing field.

c. Maintaining a long-term focus. Time constraints on research have never been more publicly visible: partners and leadership expect think tanks to provide fast and ready-to-use solutions for immediate problems as the environment becomes unstable. It is a short-term trap for think tanks, as they feel the pressure to swiftly research and propose policy recommendations on multifaceted problems that have multiple side effects and causal factors. Complex issues are hardly diagnosed in a short timeframe and continuously change. However, society currently lacks the patience needed to allow research to mature, and daily issues tend to pull experts and resources out of long-term research on structural problems, focusing on the "today's crisis."

In order to perform their role, think tanks count on leadership's abilities to navigate short-term demands and, at the same time, sustain long-term research programs, providing vision regarding essential research topics that might not yet be in vogue. It's not a matter of only responding to present challenges, but mainly to drive tomorrow's decisions.

d. Innovation. Innovation is the key to determining the survival of think tanks: innovation in searching for revenue sources, innovation in engaging with society and influencing policymakers, and innovation to maintain a focus on long-term research while dealing with short-term opportunities.

Innovation will come out of the management processes of the challenges mentioned above. Investing in technology means operating through the cloud, using artificial intelligence in research and management, and applying C^3I^2 to day-to-day operations, goals, and research. Think tanks need to become comfortable with these concepts, their application, and their functionality to survive. They also need to apply them and their necessary infrastructure to areas as diverse as anthropology and applied mathematics—while using multidisciplinary approaches for solutions and policy-relevant research.

Think tanks must prioritize. A methodological choice should be made considering the availability of data, the viability of a study, and how much time robust research needs. Investments in technology and methodological tools can help think tanks go through this process and make correct choices that will provide focus and sustainability. Amidst the current conditions, producing reputable knowledge and communicating it in an understandable and time-sensitive way to society, governments, and donors, is paramount for long-term survival.

Think tanks in Brazil are currently pressured by the four challenges outlined in this essay, as are probably most in the global think tank community. Due to their commitment to society, they must face the task at hand and consider how to survive best the next years and beyond.

It is our firm belief that the preeminent way to do this is to fully commit to technological innovation that helps to further the exposure of the think tank community's bedrocks: evidence-based research and impact. Focus our efforts and expenses on research and provide findings and recommendations to the public in an increasingly innovative way. If think tanks do not innovate, they will not last. And without think tanks, society will lose a crucial source of informed fact-based policy research and decision-making—thus, we will all be worse off in the long run.

North America Region

Because of its economic vibrancy, the continued cooperation, interconnection, and integration of the North American countries is fundamental to their shared success. Even though only three countries make up the region, it comprises 25 percent of the total think tanks globally with a total of 2058 think tanks, of which 1872 are located in the United States. From growing concerns over immigration to a newly-revised NAFTA trade deal, think tanks in the region face the challenge of addressing these issues and must continue to offer insightful policy analysis. (For more information on the future of U.S. think tanks, please refer to Future of U.S. Think Tanks book, also written by Dr. McGann).

Fit for the Future: Enhancing the Capacity Think Tanks

Aaron Shull

Abstract Aaron Shull, Managing Director and General Counsel of the Centre for International Governance Innovation (CIGI) in Waterloo, Canada, explores the Future of Think Tanks and Policy Advice around the World.

Keywords Canada · Civil society · Fundraising · Policy advice · Policy evaluation · Think tanks

Author's Note: I wrote this chapter before the outbreak of COVID-19. When offered the chance to amend the chapter by the editor, I opted to treat it as a thought experiment to read the chapter and see if the recommendations advanced still hold. The essence of those recommendations is that think tanks must become interdisciplinary or transdisciplinary in their work, be more serious about partnering with one another, and show results, not simply write more papers or policy briefs but real, tangible policy results that impact people's lives for the better. The only amendment that I would make, considering what has transpired, is to add an exclamation point. The challenges that the think tank industry is facing

A. Shull (✉)
Centre for International Governance Innovation (CIGI), Waterloo, Canada

© The Author(s) 2021   193
J. McGann, *The Future of Think Tanks and Policy Advice Around the World*, https://doi.org/10.1007/978-3-030-60379-3_28

are existential. But, if we can bring together the world's best experts across a range of disciplines from health, security, economics, international trade, and global supply chains; work together with the best of our peer institutions; and advance ideas that can create a real, lasting, and beneficial impact, we will have realized the promise and power of good ideas.

Institutions that focus on public policy research, colloquially referred to as "think tanks," face a number of challenges in the contemporary operating environment.[1] These come from a range of vectors, including those inherent within the industry, as well as tidal waves crashing from the outside.

When addressing those challenges originating from outside the industry, perhaps the biggest one to consider is the rise of political populism in states the world over. At its essence, this political doctrine is premised on mass appeal to "ordinary people" and a distrust of "elites." But it is also important to look at the genesis of this growing trend, which is driven by the fact that the economic benefits of globalization have not been evenly distributed and by huge disruptions in national labor markets and domestic industries; this is compounded by the fact that the "elites" almost melted down the global financial system in 2008. If the think tank industry is to be introspective, we will need to admit that we all missed the coming of a worldwide economic crisis and failed to provide policymakers with the sound ideas needed to subvert it.

There is also a convergence of traditionally discrete policy areas. Take climate change, for example. Climate change is a horizontal governance challenge because it touches on almost all areas of political governance, which include energy, transportation, infrastructure, forestry, health, taxes, and agriculture. At the same time, climate change poses a vertical integration problem because there are international governance dimensions—most notably, the United Nations Framework Convention on Climate Change. There are also subnational governments that are deeply impacted, including municipalities. So, while think tanks have previously undertaken deep assessments of one distinct policy area or distinguished themselves by doing either international or domestic work, it seems that those days are over.

---

[1] The author would like to thank both France Mathewson and Kailee Hilt at CIGI for their thoughtful contribution to many of the ideas in this chapter.

Likewise, policymaking in this era is complicated by the fact that big data and artificial intelligence (AI) cut across traditional governmental verticals and have implications for the quality of the economy, society, and democracy. Governance of big data and AI is in its infancy in countries and in global cooperation processes—and so the prospect of the digital era looms large.

There is also a disturbing trend toward what Yale Law professor Amy Chua calls political tribalism. This thrust toward identity politics has buttressed deep political divisions and created an "us" versus "them" mentality—both among elected leaders and the people who voted for them. At the same time, this trend has led to an erosion of civility in politics and to a seething disdain for the "others." This reality compounds the challenge for think tanks to remain nonpartisan. If an organization is nonaligned, then it may expose an instinct among policymakers to seek advice or ideas from those think tanks aligned with their political "tribe." Or worse, if a think tank is perceived to be associated with a minority or opposing opinion, they could produce the most cutting-edge research available but still be passed over or ignored.

This trend toward "tribalism" is magnified by two aspects of social media: filter bubbles and mis/disinformation. Filter bubbles are created when content is selected based on an algorithmic assessment of the user; typically, this is done to drive user engagement and to keep the user on the platform for as long as possible to enhance advertising revenue for the platform in question. In practice, this usually equates to content being served that aligns with the user's interests and supports their beliefs. In short, the public square has moved online—but it is no longer the place of reasoned political discourse and debate, weighing all sides of complex policy issues. Now, users are served only one side of a debate, further cementing their political positions.

The even darker side of this phenomenon is the rise of misinformation and disinformation on these same platforms. Often used interchangeably, there is a pointed difference between the two terms—which rests on intent. With misinformation, false or misleading content is shared but there is no purposeful intent to deceive. The opposite is true with disinformation. However, the end result remains the same: the audience in question receives factually inaccurate information. This is to say nothing of the sheer volume of information being shared daily. Each day there are 682 million tweets; more than 4 million hours of content uploaded to YouTube; 67,305,600 Instagram posts; and 4.3 billion Facebook messages (Schultz 2019).

The Global Survey on Internet Security and Trust conducted by Ipsos on behalf of the Centre for International Governance Innovation (CIGI), in partnership with the Internet Society (ISOC) and the United Nations Conference on Trade and Development (UNCTAD) is an example of not only the growing fragility of the Internet but also netizens' growing discomfort with social media and the power these corporations have over netizens' daily lives. This work is the first of its kind and is the world's largest and most comprehensive survey of internet security and trust, involving more than 25,000 internet users in over two dozen countries across North America, Latin America, Europe, the Middle East, Africa, and the Asia-Pacific region. The results are telling as "social media companies emerged as the leading source of user distrust in the internet surpassed only by cyber criminals -with 75% of those surveyed who distrust the internet citing Facebook, Twitter and other social media platforms as contributing to their lack of trust" (Centre for International Governance Innovation 2019).

This is the environment in which think tanks are trying to disseminate their message, making the omnipresent challenge of trying to cut through the noise, and to deliver unbiased analytical work to the right audience, at the right time, through the right medium. In short, think tanks need to plan for impact from the inception of research projects, identifying the audience early and engaging with them in tangible ways.

These extrinsic challenges are mirrored by those found within the industry itself. There are the perennial challenges of fundraising, and the concomitant question of how to best maintain credible research independence from the interests of donors and funders. There is also competition with other think tanks and nontraditional research sources such as law firms and consultancies. This competition not only rests on who can deliver the best research or analytical product, or who can court the greatest amount of donor or foundation dollars. It also relates to talent, especially where labor markets are tight such as in the fields of data science, web and software development, and graphic design.

Think tanks are also facing an increasing push to be both *wide* (covering a range of topics) and *deep* (honing a well of professional substantive expertise). At the same time, there is also the challenge to be timely and topical, following the news of the day, while also maintaining a rigorous research program which provides the intellectual heft and credibility that the best think tanks are known for.

Finally, think tanks must also be mindful to cultivate talent, creating career ladders for growth, and increasing both diversity and inclusion. If think tanks want to remain an effective voice in political society, then they should reflect the diversity of the societies they wish to inform. This is especially true, given that many of the challenges currently being addressed—like climate change or digital governance—will come to define how people live generations from now.

Found in these challenges are also the seeds of opportunity. The future of the industry can be bright, but there are critical steps required to realize that promise.

First, think tanks need to become interdisciplinary or transdisciplinary in their work. In the same way that the major public policy challenges have become horizontal, think tanks need to be able to marshal and integrate a range of expertise in order to holistically assess and recommend mechanisms for addressing complex issues. Indeed, think tanks more than any other organization have the best chance of achieving this holy grail of research. The incentive structures within most academic settings are still deeply disciplinary, with many of the best experts publishing in focused journals. Likewise, governments present a large bureaucracy, structured in departments with all the dependency paths which that entails. In short, the ship of state turns slowly. To achieve this interdisciplinary goal, think tanks will need to be nimble, creating consultative and collaborative research environments, and fostering incentive structures that reward teamwork and co-creation.

CIGI's partnership with the International Development Research Centre (IDRC) on a project centered on Online Gender-based Violence is an example of how collaboration between institutes can facilitate a pool of knowledge and resources through the convening of global experts with a shared aim. The project seeks to conduct a globally significant survey of women's/LGBTQI + online experiences in the Global South. With this data, it is hoped that development, private sector, and government actors can better design responses to online gender-based violence through regulation of online social media platforms, education programs, or legal recourse.

CIGI will facilitate the convening of this knowledge-sharing network that will serve as a collaborative space to form meaningful partnerships and foster interaction among those who are already working in this space to enhance learning and collective knowledge. Ultimately, this network will help to accelerate productivity and agility in the realm of tool development and skills necessary to better equip policymakers, communities, and organizations alike. In addition, the opportunity to meet and work with experts across disciplines and at other institutions will build relationships and professional networks that will continue well beyond the life of the foundation grant.

Second, think tanks need to get more serious about partnering with one another. The complexity of the problems that policy communities are facing, combined with a limited set of resources, almost necessitates working in tandem—though the industry has been slow to take up this opportunity. There are limited pockets of collaboration between institutions, but in order to maximize the potential of the industry there need to be more serious engagements aimed at maximizing expertise and resources around a set of policy questions. If think tanks from different political sides could collaborate, this could also remedy the issue of "political tribalism" and ideological division—at least insofar as the recommendations being adopted goes. The goal should be to advance the best policy, regardless of politics.

For example, the Canada-India Track 1.5 Dialogue on Innovation, Growth and Prosperity is a three-year initiative between CIGI and Gateway House: Indian Council on Global Relations. Through the convening of experts, government officials, and business leaders, the dialogue seeks opportunities to work jointly on multilateral issues and identify areas where improved cooperation could benefit both countries. Sessions have examined issues related to cybersecurity, economic relations, geoengineering, and climate leadership, and have included a broader discussion on diplomatic relations between Canada and India.

Similarly, the Canada-EU Track 1.5 Dialogue is a joint effort with the EU Institute for Security Studies (EU ISS), Global Affairs Canada, the European External Action Service, and CIGI that works toward enhancing cooperation on issues related to international security and emerging technology such as artificial intelligence, quantum computing, IoT, and smart cities. Both initiatives are examples of how "transgovernmental networks" can serve as an avenue for sharing information, ideas, and resources, to facilitate a fluid and impactful response to emerging global governance challenges.

Finally, think tanks will need to show results, not simply write more papers or policy briefs. But real, tangible policy results. Democratic governments around the world have begun to search for a strategy for platform governance by initiating the International Grand Committee on Big Data, Privacy and Democracy (IGC). This coalition brings together a committee of politicians from around the world to comprehend and respond to the challenges posed by the surveillance capitalism practiced by global technology companies. Together, governments can build momentum and increase their capacity to address the power that global technology companies possess. To further support these efforts, CIGI has established a working group involving politicians, civil servants, and researchers who gather to discuss issues of platform governance and provide policy-focused research to government policymakers and the wider public on implementing components of the platform governance agenda. While this project is not wedded to the IGC, it engages with it as one venue for international collaboration and expands to a wider community beyond simply parliamentarians.

In addition, CIGI, with support from the Government of Canada, launched the World Refugee Council (WRC), an international group of global leaders and innovators aimed at advancing new solutions to the global refugee crisis. The work of the Council built on the New York Declaration, adopted by the United Nations General Assembly in September 2016, and the process to negotiate a Global Compact on refugees, led by the United Nations High Commissioner for Refugees (UNHCR). Not only did this initiative provide expert policy-focused research and recommendations by government, civil society representatives, and researchers, but its work was mirrored in a mandate letter from the Prime Minister to the Minister of Foreign Affairs (Office of the Prime Minister 2019). This demonstrates the capacity of think tanks to facilitate new solutions in response to global crises.

While think tanks are established to conduct research and policy evaluation, the underlying macro-level objective is to make people better off. In order to do that, the industry needs to advance positions that can create meaningful change in the lives of "ordinary people"—because if we cannot do that, then there is not much use for think tanks in general.

In fact, part of the problem is that think tanks have not been able to connect with or communicate with non-elites. This is partly driven by a false dichotomy; being well educated and having a privileged place within society where policymakers will listen to your views does not make you special, and it does not make you elite. Nor, does it make you better than anyone else. Rather, we are collectively wrestling with existential policy problems, so think tanks need to find ways to effectively communicate with policymakers, the academy, civil society, business, and the public.

The promise is there, and the opportunity is there, now it is our turn to seize it.

References

Centre for International Governance Innovation. 2019. CIGI-Ipsos Global Survey on Internet Security and Trust. https://www.cigionline.org/internet-survey-2019.

Office of the Prime Minister. 13 December 2019. Minister of Foreign Affairs Mandate Letter. https://pm.gc.ca/en/mandate-letters/2019/12/13/minister-foreign-affairs-mandate-letter.

Schultz, Jeff. 6 August 2019. How Much Data Is Created on the Internet Each Day? Microfocus Blog. https://blog.microfocus.com/how-much-data-is-created-on-the-internet-each-day/.

The Future of Think Tanks: Competing in the Digital Era

Luis Rubio and Verónica Ortiz

Abstract Luis Rubio and Verónica Ortiz , Mexican Council on Foreign Relations (COMEXI) in Mexico City, Mexico, explores the Future of Think Tanks and Policy Advice around the World.

Keywords Mexico · Policy advice · Think tanks

This is the time of immediacy. Two decades into the twenty-first century, the information revolution has benefited the work of think tanks by creating greater opportunities to communicate with wider audiences instantly, directly, and at a low cost. Mobile apps have made it easier for us to interact in a more immediate and simple way, making knowledge more accessible and interactive for the target audience as well as the larger public. However, as physical distances are cut shorter by technology, the barriers and deep differences between those at the top and those at the bottom become more evident. Even more relevant, social media has enabled debates that are not based on evidence but nonetheless compete for the public eye on equal grounds.

L. Rubio (✉) · V. Ortiz
Mexican Council on Foreign Relations (COMEXI), Mexico City, Mexico

© The Author(s) 2021
J. McGann, *The Future of Think Tanks and Policy Advice
Around the World*, https://doi.org/10.1007/978-3-030-60379-3_29

Undoubtedly, technology has been an ally for think tanks: from website builders, to open source software, to marketing automation platforms and direct access, and to consumers and users through social media. These resources have all greatly enhanced the work of these organizations. People around the world are now able to co-work in real time regardless of their physical location. Policy advice is benefiting from a hyper-connected world.

In times when data is becoming as valuable as gold, tech companies have looked for a new way to sell products through a bespoke segmentation of each user. Big data has enabled a myriad of opportunities. This tool, useful for marketing and widely used by private companies, is rapidly being adopted by think tanks, enabling them to directly target both their chosen audiences and their stakeholders. This is reducing the natural propensity of information to getting lost in the immensity of the internet.

The problem is that the tools think tanks have access to are equally available to everyone else and, in the vastness of the internet, every outlet has the same chance of influencing decision-makers and the public at large.

Hence, technology enables faster and more accurate communications, but it also empowers activists, politicians, and all sorts of special interests—entities with an ax to grind, usually with no analytical work behind them—to often overwhelm the debates through social media. These media outlets, which naturally privilege the extremes, have become a formidable source of competition for the people's attention and, thus, for the ability to influence decision-making.

Additionally, the immediacy of communication technologies is a double-edged sword. These platforms, including social media, challenge the relevance of intermediate institutions by bridging the gap between the political power and citizens.

Nevertheless, think tanks have a unique and privileged position at the crossroads of public and private sectors, as well as society. Their views and recommendations, independent of their political or ideological leanings, are multidisciplinary by nature. Yet, in the era of ubiquity of information, the true challenge is the oldest of the field: funding. Herein lies a key paradox: access to information and to target audiences has never been higher, but competition for funding has become unfathomable.

If raising funds is a challenge per se, competing in the digital era makes the task even more complicated in nations where philanthropy is not well established or is focused on immediate interests only. The question for funders often becomes the most primitive: if nonprofessional activists can do my bidding faster and cheaper, why fund serious, established institutions? The issue gets compounded by the very nature of think tanks, which must remain independent in order to fulfill their mission, but that very independence becomes an issue for funders. Furthermore, new sources of funding, particularly those from the tech sector, usually come with an agenda.

In this context, think tanks have no choice in so-called developing nations but to keep promoting the value of their work with every possible stakeholder. Gaining broader exposure becomes instrumental to getting greater traction. Reconciling independence and the interests of funders thus becomes a major challenge.

Social and political polarization poses a new threat to the existence of think tanks. The information revolution has greatly contributed to the development of humanity, while exposing, and even fueling, the current political and social fragmentation around the world. This "clash of civilizations" is now subnational and live-streamed.

But even if competition in social media is similar nowadays in every country, the nature of the problem is different. While the policy process in the United States heavily relies on the work of think tanks, which are considered not only legitimate, but also fundamental to the debate, the same cannot be said of many other societies. In the Mexican case, for example, the government itself, and the social forces it commands, actively attempt to delegitimize well established, professional, think tanks in order to advance agendas that do not fulfill even the most basic cost–benefit analysis. More worrisome, it also intimidates funders.

The real challenge thus becomes the interests and commitment of the average citizen. Paraphrasing Benjamin Franklin, if the people are not willing to defend their accomplishments and benefits, the work of think tanks in these nations becomes hopeless. At heart, the issue looking forward becomes how to get closer to every citizen, to understand his or her concerns in order to both attend to their far-reaching needs at a policy level as well as to develop more sustainable, long-term sources of funding. Funding can include crowdfunding—something alien to the Mexican tradition up to now. Funding for Mexican think tanks might evolve from big donors to fundraisers, not particularly common in the country, or might find its place in these platforms. Just as important, financial resources are instrumental for attracting the best talent available.

Nowadays, thanks to the information revolution, think tanks employ interdisciplinary and diverse teams that include social scientists working on policy questions, sound and video engineers for live-streaming their events, and researchers walking the streets conducting surveys and applying other opinion-measuring instruments. One of their most pressing challenges will remain the recruitment and maintenance of human capital, a true endeavor in the face of fake media and competition from other potential employers (like consultants) in terms of salaries and benefit packages. This has always been a fundamental challenge, but the digital revolution has enhanced it to the utmost.

Think tanks matter because they address topics and issues in an independent, nonpartisan way that would otherwise be ignored, forgotten, or left aside by both the public and private sectors. They also matter because their efforts help to find alternatives, policy proposals, and durable solutions, while governments deal with day-to-day questions of governance. The main challenge for think tanks in the years to come will be to keep them as safe havens for reflection and discussion shielded from political whims. In Mexico today, this becomes even more troublesome, for it is the government that is attempting to eliminate or neutralize each and every source of independence or counterweight.

This hostile environment should prompt us to reckon with an uncomfortable truth. Voters around the world are rebelling against political and intellectual elites disconnected from people's needs and aspirations. If think tanks are meant to prevail, they must reach out to the average citizen and build general support. They must do so in a twofold strategy. By translating such needs to the policymakers on one hand, while effectively communicating best practices and innovative policies to the general public on the other. For all the progress attained, societies in the twenty-first century are still facing no easy problems that convene every think tank's efforts to provide solutions. Improvising or oversimplifying answers is not an option.

But isolated efforts are often futile. It is in this ambiance that working with other think tanks becomes a natural response to the challenges posed by the political milieu. At the end of the day, think tanks need not be competitors among themselves: they were created to produce the best ideas and defend the highest ideals. Ultimately, that's the reason why think tanks matter.

Grab Your Sunglasses—The Future of Thinks Tanks is as Bright as Ever

Niels Veldhuis

Abstract Niels Veldhuis, President of the Fraser Institute in Vancouver, BC, Canada, explores the Future of Think Tanks and Policy Advice around the World.

Keywords Canada · China · Fundraising · Policy advice · Policy analysis · Think tanks · Western Europe think tanks

As leaders of think tanks consider the numerous challenges they face, I am reminded of Winston Churchill's famous quote, "a pessimist sees the difficulty in every opportunity; an optimist sees the opportunity in every difficulty." Having been in the think tank world for nearly twenty years, it is hard not to see opportunities all around us. Indeed, this is truly an exciting time to be involved with a think tank.

There is little question that we are experiencing dramatic changes that will impact think tanks, including innovations in technology, marketing, communications, artificial intelligence, and big data, to name but a few. But these changes should not be thought of as challenges. Rather, think

N. Veldhuis (✉)
Fraser Institute, Vancouver, BC, Canada

© The Author(s) 2021
J. McGann, *The Future of Think Tanks and Policy Advice Around the World*, https://doi.org/10.1007/978-3-030-60379-3_30

tanks that see them as opportunities, and innovate accordingly, will ultimately thrive and succeed in advancing their missions.

Indeed, there is nothing new about this phenomenon. One could imagine, for instance, think tank leaders worrying in the early 1980s as they marveled at the proliferation of cable and the introduction of 24-hour news stations like CNN. As Nobel Laureate F.A. Hayek observed, the only constant in society is change.

At the Fraser Institute, we have a very different view than many others regarding the process of creating change, which is shaped partly by our country's parliamentary political system. We believe that politicians in democracies—whose primary concern is invariably getting elected or reelected—generally follow, rather than lead the populace.

To us, the key to changing policy is to change the climate of opinion about what works and what does not work. The key to changing the climate of opinion is providing the widest possible audience well-researched, easily accessible, empirical information about how government policy impacts their lives. It's why for nearly 50 years the Fraser Institute has been headquartered in Vancouver, British Columbia, about as far away as one can get in Canada from the locus of national political power (i.e., Ottawa).

While many frets about increased polarization, particularly in politics, those of us involved in think tanks ought to remind ourselves that in a democracy, government policies must ultimately reflect the will of the people. Think tanks play a critical role in shaping how the public thinks about current policy, and changes that are needed, by providing analysis, measurement, constructive critiques, and most importantly, new innovative policy ideas. Indeed, the most important sources of policy change are not politicians or political parties, but rather the ideas generated from research in think tanks and other research organizations. That has, and will always be a large part of our value-add.

Empirical research and detailed policy ideas provide the unshakable foundations of successful think tanks. Being empirically driven, open and transparent with our data and methodologies, and encouraging replication and feedback have, and will continue to, stand the test of time. To this end, opportunities for innovative research are greater than ever because large data sets are more readily available, computing power is greater, and modeling is easier than ever before. Think tanks that are able to capitalize on these trends to produce timely, topical, and high-quality research will stand apart from the others.

But research isn't enough and never has been. Communicating research findings and policy recommendations are what have always set think thanks apart from universities. And today, the ability of think tanks to reach large, diverse audiences is probably the most exciting opportunity.

Innovations in technology have fundamentally changed the communications and marketing of think tank research and ideas. Twenty years ago, think tank scholars did research, made media appearances, did presentations, and met with policymakers. Communications departments were limited to, drafting press releases and handling media requests. Think tanks could connect directly with their supporters and friends through printed magazines and newsletters, and events, but the media retained the ability to heavily filter or even ignore the messages think tanks wished to bring to the attention of the public.

Today, our world is digital, traditional media is shrinking, and our ability to reach a much wider audience—directly, without the media's filtering of our message—is exponentially larger. While the media, particularly in the United States, has become more polarized, alternative platforms (including social media, email, SMS messaging, and video channels) allow us to potentially reach a much broader audience. This continuing revolution in communications and marketing is a major opportunity to present research and messages succinctly, supported by visual resources, in mobile-friendly ways, which can be easily shared through social media.

As the landscape continues to change, think tanks must continue to adapt. For example, with the ongoing consolidation and decline in traditional media, and a worrying recent development among major social media firms to censor speech and create algorithms that promote certain kinds of speech over others, the creation of direct distribution channels is becoming ever more important for think tanks aimed at educating the broader public.

Going forward, think tanks must engage with those that follow their work more directly and proactively—whether through email marketing and campaigns, mobile marketing (i.e., creating, targeting, sending, and tracking all mobile messaging) or connecting with followers in a much more personalized way. Those think tanks that innovate and embrace the challenge of a highly competitive, information-rich marketplace of ideas, will continue to succeed. Those who are unable to do so will increasingly become less effective, regardless of the quality of their research, and likely be the victims of creative destruction.

That applies equally to universities, which historically have been integral contributors to the marketplace of ideas. Unfortunately, many universities have increasingly become places of inflexible dogmatism and are less tied to solving real-world problems. As universities yield to growing activism on campuses that oppose differing opinions and ideas, think tanks will become ever more important.

In addition, with changing demographics and university professors wishing to remain active long after they officially retire, think tanks are able to provide that opportunity for leading scholars aimed at having real-world impact. Indeed, think tanks should cultivate relationships with professional scholars at all levels who are interested in contributing toward the think tank's mission—such scholars can provide great value in maintaining or improving research standards and in providing new ideas for think tanks to market.

Speaking of human resources, perhaps the biggest opportunities lie in creating the next generation of think tank scholars and leaders. Polls indicate that younger generations prefer employment with a wider purpose, and mission-driven think tanks provide just such opportunities. While we usually can't match the salaries provided by corporations or government, we can give young leaders opportunities to pursue their passion in ways these sectors cannot offer.

With respect to funding policy research, there is no doubt that the landscape here is also changing, with donors becoming less inclined to provide long term or general funding; instead favoring short-term projects aimed at specific results. But there is no shortage of potential funding, and here too think tanks must adapt by pursuing efficiency in their own operations, measuring their own performance more stringently so as to make their funding requests more persuasive, and by implementing new fundraising tools. In doing so, think tanks must defend their independence from funding sources.

The world is changing and perhaps more rapidly so. That makes it all the more exciting and allows for an even brighter future for think tanks that embrace change.

Asia Region

Asia, boasting the largest population and fastest growing economies of any region, is also a hotbed for development in the think tank sector. From 2011 to 2018, more than 500 think tanks emerged in Asia, double

Western Europe's growth, the next highest region, and comprising more than a third of new think tanks in the world. This growth is for good reason: Asia faces a number of new challenges and opportunities that require detailed policy analysis. Aging demographics in East Asian nations, security flashpoints between China and the United States, and climate threats in South Asia will have historic impacts on the region. Given these issues, it is imperative that the 1770 think tanks operating in the region step up to offer objective research and policy advice for these and other issues.

Asia Region

Asia, boasting the largest population and fastest growing economies of any region, is also a hotbed for development in the think tank sector. From 2011 to 2018, more than 500 think tanks emerged in Asia, double Western Europe's growth, the next highest region, and comprising more than a third of new think tanks in the world. This growth is for good reason: Asia faces a number of new challenges and opportunities that require detailed policy analysis. Aging demographics in East Asian nations, security flashpoints between China and the United States, and climate threats in South Asia will have historic impacts on the region. Given these issues, it is imperative that the 1770 think tanks operating in the region step up to offer objective research and policy advice for these and other issues.

The Future of Japanese Think Tanks: Policy Involvement and Regional Cooperation

Toshihiko Fukui

Abstract Toshihiko Fukui, President of The Canon Institute for Global Studies in Tokyo, Japan, explores the Future of Think Tanks and Policy Advice around the World.

Keywords China · Japan · Revolving door · Think tanks

Looking back on the history of think tanks in Japan, most of those which continue to operate were set up after 1960, although one of the first of its kind could date back to as early as the 1930s. Japan's sociopolitical environment surrounding think tanks, however, seems to have been quite different from their counterparts in other Western nations.

Japanese think tanks are characterized by the following three unique features:

The first is systemically low levels of independence.

Most of Japan's major think tanks are either government-affiliated research institutes or subsidiaries of megabanks, huge financial institutions, global trading firms, or other big private corporations. Many

T. Fukui (✉)
The Canon Institute for Global Studies, Tokyo, Japan

J. McGann, *The Future of Think Tanks and Policy Advice Around the World*, https://doi.org/10.1007/978-3-030-60379-3_31

213

executives in such think tanks are golden parachutes from their mother organs.

These think tanks tend to conduct research activities assigned by or in accordance with the Government of Japan or its affiliates for implementing government policies. Therefore, they seldom issue policy recommendations or action proposals that are truly independent of the government.

The second is the lack of "merit of scale."

There are many "independent" think tanks in Japan that consider their functions to be quite different from those of the Japanese government or big corporations. Having said that, their performances have not always been as good as they have hoped.

Unfortunately, many of those "independent" think tanks, mostly represented by a specific "star" individual or a small group of competent researchers, are not always financially affluent enough to be independent. Despite their competence in specific areas of expertise, their impact on the decision-making process is limited.

Finally, the third is the lack of "revolving doors" in Japan.

Whether we like it or not, the biggest and most effective think tanks in Japan have always been the government bureaucracies. This is mainly because the bureaucrats in each governmental ministry or agency monopolize relevant confidential information.

Without access to such confidential materials in Japan, the system of political appointment with revolving doors does not function in the way that we witness in the United States or European countries. Bureaucracies in Japan, therefore, tend to take less interest in, if not completely ignore, policy recommendations by private think tanks.

In addition, there are many other challenges think tanks in Japan face. For example, although many think tanks in Japan recognize that innovations in technology, communications, big data, or data visualization are rapidly changing their work, few seem to have been successful in fully utilizing them.

This is because the think tank sector in Japan has traditionally been highly compartmentalized. Most think tanks have their own areas of expertise, either economic, social, political, or scientific. Thus, they are not always capable of creating internal "synergy effects" by combining technological innovation with traditional research activities.

For smaller "one issue" think tanks, such innovations are becoming far less feasible due to their financial constraints. Even in larger think tanks, due to the shortage of AI/Big Data technologies and experts, it is not easy to internally coordinate varied expertise in economics, advanced mathematics, political science, or global issues.

Challenges could also come from new competitors such as law firms, advocacy groups, public relations firms, nontraditional media sources, or GAFA. Fortunately, such challenges are not yet tangible in Japan, but it is only a matter of time before such competition presents itself. To deal with this, think tanks in Japan must be equipped with technological knowledge and devices.

Another challenge facing Japanese think tanks is the need to change their strategy and structure. Traditional think tanks in Japan must be able to cope with interdisciplinary or cross-sectional intellectual issues instead of being solely focused on single issues in a compartmentalized manner.

All in all, it is undeniable that the roles which think tanks in Japan have played are quite limited. It is important for Japanese think tanks to encourage policymakers to change their interactions with think tanks and bureaucracy so that the think tanks can play more constructive roles in decision-making.

The Canon Institute for Global Studies, CIGS, a young Tokyo-based think tank, was established in 2009 to overcome the difficulties surrounding Japanese think tanks. Although solely financed by Canon, Inc., unlike other similar think tanks in Japan, CIGS has maintained its full creative and intellectual independence.

Over the past decade, CIGS has proposed various policy recommendations, mainly in the fields of its three pillars: macroeconomics, energy & the environment, and foreign policy/national security affairs. Particularly in the last few years, CIGS has reinforced its AI and Big Data workshop to collaborate internally with its fellow researchers.

CIGS's 50 researchers and its secretariat spare no efforts to spontaneously bring to bear "synergy effects" among those fifty with their various academic or professional backgrounds on new issues that Japan now faces such as the shrinking domestic population or the intensifying US-China hegemonic rivalry.

While Japan faces such domestic and foreign challenges, what is more ominous would be that "the best and the brightest" of new college graduates may not continue joining the Japanese bureaucracy. Sooner rather than later, a day may come when bureaucracy may no longer function as the largest think tank.

What is required from think tanks in Japan is not only full independence from the government. They should be able to spontaneously make proposals for policies the people of Japan need. They must be involved in the decision-making process by sending competent political appointees to the government.

CIGS, for example, has a program to recruit and train young candidates for future political appointments. These candidates are expected to not only plan and implement policies with the bureaucracy but also to take on political responsibility which the bureaucracy cannot. It is also important to remind politicians of the merits of such political appointees.

Think tanks in Japan should be able to share, through the revolving doors, the wisdom, expertise, and experience which those political appointees have acquired in the government. To diversify think tanks' financial resources, changes in tax systems for public contributions may be required.

Think tanks should also collaborate with like-minded think tanks in East Asia. The region has a great variety of think tanks with very competent scholars and researchers. Although their interests are not always identical, there are many common problems in East Asia which they can work together on. Such issues include joint research on countermeasures for the next pandemic in the region, post COVID-19 regional economic development, or maritime security in the South China Sea. Think tanks in Japan can and must further enhance contact with East Asian think tanks in addition to their counterparts in the United States and Europe.

Prospects and Possibilities for Think Tanks: A View from China's Non-Governmental Think Tank Sector

Wang Huiyao

Abstract Wang Huiyao, Founder and President of the Center for China and Globalization in Beijing, China, explores the Future of Think Tanks and Policy Advice around the World.

Keywords China · Multilateral cooperation · Policy advice · Research institutions · Think tanks

In recent years, China's rapid economic development and deepening global integration have increased the need for broad input into policy-making. Chinese think tanks have proliferated and play a growing role in this process. In addition to the government- or university-run institutions that make up the bulk of China's think tank sector, a new generation of non-governmental think tanks is also active in policy advice and international engagement.

Major shifts in economics, technology, and politics are reshaping the operating environment for think tanks. The world faces unprecedented transnational challenges, from climate change to pandemics, especially

W. Huiyao (✉)
Center for China and Globalization, Beijing, China

© The Author(s) 2021
J. McGann, *The Future of Think Tanks and Policy Advice Around the World*, https://doi.org/10.1007/978-3-030-60379-3_32

recently when the COVID-19 has unfolded into a global crisis that has impacted virtually every country on earth, but an upsurge of populism, nationalism, and protectionism has put considerable strain on international cooperation and multilateralism. The episode will also have far-reaching ramifications for institutions, the global economic and political structure, societies, and individual livelihoods and lifestyles, bringing forth profound questions about the future of humankind. With intergovernmental cooperation constrained and in need of reinvigoration, think tanks have a vital responsibility to fulfill.

Chinese think tanks are profoundly affected by these global changes, but also operate in a unique context given China's developmental path, political system, and evolving international role. This essay discusses prospects for China's non-governmental think tank sector, starting with a brief overview of the development of Chinese think tanks and then going on to outline the key challenges and opportunities that lie ahead and how best to adapt to them.

THE RISE OF "THINK TANKS WITH CHINESE CHARACTERISTICS"

Think tanks operate in a global context, but are also subject to local factors that shape their modes of operation and role in public policy. In industrialized Western nations such as the United States, think tanks have been around for over a century. They are part of a relatively mature policymaking ecosystem and exert influence on virtually all aspects of policy and decision-making.

In Asia and elsewhere, think tanks have a shorter history but are becoming more numerous, autonomous, and impactful as these economies rise. For example, in the BRICS countries, think tank development is strongly correlated with the pace of national development (Wang and Miao 2014: 10).

China has a long-standing tradition of intellectuals providing input to policy, but think tanks as an institutional form are relatively new. Since the launch of Reform and Opening-up in 1978, the demand for policy advice from the Chinese government has increased dramatically. China's political system also creates a unique role for think tanks. Given the lack of opposition political parties, they act as an institutional mechanism to broaden input into policy discussions and provide checks and balances.

In the early phases of development, the think tank sector was primarily made up of government-run institutions such as the Chinese Academy of Social Sciences and the Development Research Center of the State Council, as well as university-based research institutions.

In the twenty-first century, with China's rapid development and accession to the WTO, China's economy has become increasingly complex and intertwined with the global economy. Think tanks have come to play a more significant role in public policy and diversified in form, with the emergence of non-governmental and enterprise think tanks to provide fresh ideas and perspectives. The Center for China and Globalization (CCG), a non-governmental think tank established in 2008, is one such organization. Since it was founded, CCG has grown steadily in terms of size and impact, reflecting the growth of the sector at large as it becomes more internationalized and professionalized. As of 2019, the number of think tanks in China has grown to 507, with eight ranked in the world top 100 according to the 2019 Global Go To Think Tank Index.

THE WAY FORWARD: CHALLENGES FOR CHINESE THINK TANKS

Over the next decade, Chinese think tanks will continue to face rapid change in many spheres, from technology and media to economics and geopolitics. This creates challenges that Chinese think tanks must adapt to if they are to stay relevant and thrive. Four key features of this changing landscape are described below.

Fast-Paced, Competitive Communications Environment

The rise of mobile internet and interactive platforms such as Wechat has dramatically increased the availability of content and speed at which it is disseminated. At the same time, think tanks face a growing range of potential competitors in the policymaking space, such as business consulting firms, law firms, media, and big data platforms.

To adapt, think tanks must be creative with new media and business models to build communication platforms that can compete for social impact. While think tanks in North America and Europe have widely adopted effective use of social media, many Chinese think tanks lag in this area, particularly regarding English language content. This limits the reach of Chinese think tanks and their research findings.

The imperative to adapt and use new technologies has been under-scored by the COVID-19 outbreak, which has hampered the offline events that are a mainstay of regular think tank activities. Think tanks have been compelled to shift to webinars and other alternative formats, increasing the need to apply new media and business models. For example, during the outbreak, CCG held its first webinar series on "China and the world in times of coronavirus," convening experts both home and abroad.

Funding

Think tank funding from government, industry, foundations, and indi-viduals has been under pressure worldwide since the 2008 financial crisis, a trend that may be exacerbated by the coronavirus pandemic. Unlike government think tanks that have stable sources of internal funding, non-governmental think tanks such as CCG, which do not receive fixed funding from any government institution, must continuously seek new partnerships and ways to secure funding.

Changing Global Context

Recent years have seen a rise of great power rivalry and stifling of inter-national cooperation, particularly at the multilateral level. It is possible these trends will be exacerbated by the ongoing coronavirus pandemic. Economic relations, previously a catalyst for closer cooperation, are increasingly contentious, especially between China and the United States.

Chinese think tanks are exposed to such frictions and the politicization of international exchange. Bilateral think tank exchanges and conferences have been affected, in some cases hampering collaboration or restricting visits. Rising clamor about "Chinese influence" in Western capitals has also led to misreporting on the institutional affiliations and intentions of some non-governmental Chinese think tanks, threatening to chill bilateral think tank exchange when it is needed most.

CARVING OUT A NICHE: OPPORTUNITIES FOR CHINESE THINK TANKS

Despite the challenges laid out above, in many ways, prospects have never been better for Chinese think tanks to make a tangible impact, both in China and globally. Indeed, each of the major shifts laid out above—technological, financial, and geopolitical—create the imperative and opportunity for Chinese think tanks to grow and develop to the next level. This section outlines four promising areas for Chinese think tanks to focus on, namely domestic reform, innovative operational models, Track II diplomacy, and global governance reform.

Domestic Policy and Reform

China's reform process involves ongoing improvements to build governance, legal, and regulatory systems fit for an innovation-led, market-oriented economy. Think tanks are needed to help design and assess the feasibility of these new reform initiatives. Therefore, in comparison to industrialized nations with relatively more established legal and regulatory frameworks, there is a faster pace of reform and policymaking, and thus great scope for think tanks to impact key areas.

Promoting Administrative Reform

The creation of China's National Immigration Administration (NIA) is one example of how think tanks can contribute to administrative reform. In recent years, China, like other countries, is increasing efforts to attract global talent and manage migration effectively. Previously, relevant policy and implementation responsibilities were spread across multiple departments. Recognizing the need for a specialized immigration agency, CCG worked with partners for many years to produce reports and host events to promote the creation of a consolidated NIA, which was eventually formed in 2018 as part of a major bureaucratic overhaul. The creation of the NIA will facilitate better policy coordination and alignment with international mechanisms.

A Platform for Diverse Interests

The number of issues and sectors Chinese policymakers must grapple with is ever-broader and more complex. This includes fields, such as emerging industries, where relevant experience and expertise lie outside government. To bridge this gap, think tanks can function as third-party intermediaries to connect government agencies, industry, academia, and other sectors of society, allowing diverse views to feed into policymaking in an efficient, orderly manner. Non-governmental think tanks such as CCG can function as a platform for businesses to voice industry development needs or suggestions to the government, while also helping government agencies to understand and respond to reasonable requests from industry. This is done via regular submission of policy suggestions and memos to the government, roundtables, and major flagship conferences. For example, during the COVID-19 outbreak, CCG organized a number of online seminars featuring experts and business leaders, forwarding corresponding policy suggestions to the government and producing a report with recommendations on global responses to the pandemic.

DIVERSIFICATION AND INNOVATION IN OPERATIONAL MODELS

As mentioned above, non-governmental Chinese think tanks typically lack fixed funding from any single institution, so they must diversify sources of income to grow and fund research. This independence and entrepreneurial imperative allow non-governmental think tanks to explore new models of funding from commercial sources, private entrepreneurs, international institutions, and commercial sources, while also supporting an independent research agenda.

For example, as part of CCG's "platform role" outlined above, the think tank collaborates with industry and draws council members and advisors from companies in many sectors, from education and e-commerce to finance, tourism, and real estate. This diversity of industries and funding sources allows CCG to absorb and voice a variety of perspectives while ensuring it is not beholden to any particular government agency, industry, or company. This model, while more established in the West, is relatively new in China and there is potential for more think tank innovation in this area.

TRACK II DIPLOMACY

China's growing global role calls for think tanks to engage internationally and help tell China's story to the world. At the same time, international frictions, weakened intergovernmental dialogue, and the coronavirus outbreak have increased the need for trusted intermediaries to enhance mutual understanding and build trust.

Think tanks, in particular non-governmental think tanks, are ideally placed to bridge this gap as third-party "diplomatic messengers." Bilateral think tank exchange offers an informal channel to communicate candidly, reduce strategic mistrust, and float ideas and elicit reactions on ways to boost cooperation. Amidst US-China trade tensions, CCG carries out a series of Track II diplomacy missions to the United States, engaging think tanks and other government or business organizations, including the US General Chamber of Commerce, the US Department of Commerce (DOC), the US-China Business Council (USCBC), and the National Council for Foreign Trade (NFTC). Chinese think tanks can use this kind of outreach to supplement in-house research and propose concrete suggestions on how to improve China-US relations.

In addition to collaboration with United States and European institutions, which have previously been the focus, there is also growing scope for think tanks to share Chinese experience and engage with partners in developing countries, such as those participating in the Belt and Road Initiative.

Promoting Innovation in Global Governance

Lack of leadership and consensus has stalled multilateral reforms, as seen in the failure of the WTO Doha Round and failure of the 2019 United Nations Global Climate Change Conference. This has left gaps in global governance as institutions fail to keep up with shifts in the global economy and equip themselves to help fight global challenges such as pandemics.

Think tanks are well-placed to help break this deadlock and reinvigorate multilateralism by promoting reform and innovative solutions for global governance. This is especially true for Chinese think tanks, as China comes to play a more active role in global governance and promotes multilateral initiatives of its own.

Ways think tanks can fulfil this role include advocating that the government participate in global governance reform; shaping policy discussion agendas by organizing forums at the national, regional, and global level; and developing their own initiatives for global governance. CCG has proposed two such initiatives: an alliance of international talent organizations to foster policy coordination, and a global "D50" forum for e-commerce cooperation. To refine these proposals and secure international support, CCG held a series of events inside and outside of China and leveraged high-profile international platforms such as the Paris Peace Forum.

CCG also offers both domestic and international platforms for experts, Chinese officials, and scholars to exchange ideas, helping China engage in international affairs and global governance. This includes regularly hosting senior figures from international institutions such as the WTO and AIIB to discuss suggestions for multilateral cooperation. CCG also provides international channels for the voices of Chinese experts to be heard by organizing official gatherings at larger events such as the Munich Security Conference. This engagement generates ideas and momentum for innovation in global governance.

There is scope for global governance innovation in many other areas. CCG's experience shows how Chinese think tanks can use domestic and international platforms to refine and gain traction for their ideas and proposals.

Outlook: Adapting to a Changing Landscape

Chinese non-governmental think tanks have made great strides forward in the last decade. Like other organizations, they face challenges from rapid shifts reshaping the global landscape. Yet they are also uniquely placed to offer solutions to address these changes, serving as a bridge between policymakers, industry, and the general public, as well as between China and the rest of the world.

To succeed, Chinese think tanks must adapt to our changing circumstances, strategically positioning ourselves to build valuable networks and capabilities, while also retaining the flexibility to innovate and explore new ways of doing things. If we can do this, then the coming decade holds great promise for China's think tank sector.

Reference

Wang, Huiyao, and Lv. Miao. 2014. Global Think Tanks. People's Publishing House: 10.

China's Think Tanks in the New Era: Mission, Responsibility, and Direction of Development

Yuan Peng

Abstract Yuan Peng, President of the China Institutes of Contemporary International Relations (CICIR) in Beijing, China, explores the Future of Think Tanks and Policy Advice around the World.

Keywords China · Policy advice · Policy design · Research centers · Russia · Think tanks

Given its rise in the global community, China has taken a historic step to move closer to the center stage of international politics and economics, and with it, Chinese think tanks have also welcomed an unprecedented "era of opportunity and development." At the state level, China initiated the experimental work in establishing the first roster of top 25 national think tanks in 2015, which have now become the main explorers and propellers for the construction and direction of development for think tanks with Chinese characteristics. At the level of higher education, an assortment of think tanks with varied specialties have also sprung up like sprouts after rain in universities and colleges, with their born scholastic

Y. Peng (✉)
China Institutes of Contemporary International Relations (CICIR), Beijing, China

J. McGann, *The Future of Think Tanks and Policy Advice Around the World*, https://doi.org/10.1007/978-3-030-60379-3_33

attributes, forming a scene of diverse intellect. At the level of society at large, a number of media-type and local think tanks have also participated in this wave of development, whose diversified modalities are bound to add rich content and referable cases to China's think tank portfolio. The "think tank heat" is now displaying remarkable scenery in the new-era China.

At present, we are faced with "changes unprecedented in hundreds of years," in which China's security and prosperity is ever closely interconnected with global peace and development. China needs to understand the transforming world with greater depth; likewise, the world is increasingly focusing its sight on China, which itself is at the beginning of a new era of openness and reform. In line with this megatrend, China's think tanks have been progressively involved in the process of government policymaking, becoming an important "contributor" to China's approach to global governance as well as an intellectual source of "Chinese wisdom." Think tanks are thus playing an increasingly significant role in the modernization of China's system and capacity for governance. Meanwhile, as an indispensable "name card" for China's image as a major power, China's think tanks have become a "window," through which the international community looks to observe and inform of China's direction of development.

As demonstrated by international experiences, the evolution of think tanks has always been in synchrony with the stages of a country's overall development. The US think tanks flourished at the end of the nineteenth century and beginning of the twentieth century, which echoed the rise of America. Similarly, the current growth of think tanks in China is in line with the rise of China.

The mission of think tanks should conform to the grand strategy and serve the nation's needs. As unremittingly committed, China's grand strategy is to follow a path of peaceful development, foster a new type of international relations, and work to build a community with a shared future for mankind. In essence, the mission and responsibility of the Chinese think tanks in the new era is to serve this overarching goal.

However, compared with the mature think tank systems in Europe and America, the majority of Chinese think tanks are fresh and young, presenting a variety of problems. Some unreservedly simulate other countries' models, emphasize formality over substance, pursue massive media coverage but overlook research quality, or neglect the cultivation of professional crew, displaying a trending deficiency of "thinkers" in think tanks. A number of them still struggle with confusion on the direction of development, inadequacies of expertise, and restrictions by systems in place, and are still immersed in explorational processes. With a long way to go, the success of Chinese think tanks requires the collaborative efforts of experts and scholars of many generations to come, answering the call of the new era. In the current wave of think tank constructions, with more calmness and rationality, we should return to the intrinsic nature of the think tank, by means of which to pioneer the way ahead.

Firstly, the core competency of a think tank lies in its "expertise" and unique characteristics. The primary scenario to avoid is "homogenous" competition and repeated construction. There are significant differences in financing, advisory channels, and spheres of influence between governmental, educational, and societal think tanks. Different types of think tanks should position their distinct roles, exercise their respective expertise, and determine their individual paths of development. Some can conduct theoretical and foundational research, some strategic and policy-oriented, and others experimental and practitioner research. Think tanks should locate their varied potentials and cultivate diversified growth points while being able to come together to form a bigger picture. For example, the strategic studies and geographic area studies are the featured topics that the China Institutes of Contemporary International Relations (CICIR) focuses on. Among the fifteen institutes under the CICIR architecture, the ten of them cover geographic area studies of nearly all countries and regions worldwide. Most researchers associated with the country/area institutes are interdisciplinary experts that are familiar with both the native languages and relevant issues of their designated regions. In addition to the institutes, CICIR has also set up thirteen research centers to address the functioning topics of varied themes. In this sense, the human powers in the institutes and centers are largely overlapping, as the researchers not only cover their respective countries or regions of expertise but also look into those specific topics that function in the designated areas. Through meticulous studies and accumulated works along two or even multiple tracks of expertise, the CICIR researchers benefit from this unique model of integrative growth and suffice to accomplish interdisciplinary works. This is the reason why when problems arise in whatever countries or spheres, be them major countries like the USA, Russia, Europe, and Japan, or rather the smaller states, it is most probable to find authoritative CICIR researchers of corresponding expertise to contribute valuable analyses.

Secondly, the nature of think tanks is to provide decision-making service, not publicity for policies. The main function is to get involved in the process of decision-making, provide intellectual support to policy-makers, help solve developmental dilemmas, dissolve potential crises, and outline future strategies, particularly in crucial times of a country's needs. Research products of the think tanks should be objective, professional, and policy-oriented, as opposed to common media coverage, and should especially be independent of opinionated public pressures. Thus, although the media can be employed as a tool for publicizing findings, think tanks should keep a reasonable distance from them in order to avoid becoming media-like.

Think tanks need to cultivate distinct cultures in accordance with respective functions and attributes, thus forming unique brands of their own. For instance, the unique culture that CICIR pursues is emphasizing collective research work over individual achievement; favoring solid analysis over media coverage; convening closed-door sessions with selective panelists rather than international forums of big-name and fame; not asking what your country can do for you, but asking what you can do for your country; avoiding impetuous manners while upholding the principled mottos; and seeking self-fulfillment by providing strategic, forward-looking and policy-oriented research products to decision-makers.

Thirdly, exchanges and communications between think tanks should have a greater effect on international relations. International exchanges of extensive ranges and in-depth contents provide inexhaustible energy and worthy vitality for research works. Again as an example, CICIR maintains regular contacts/partnerships with more than eighty think tanks of forty-odd countries, sending over a hundred delegations annually for academic exchanges abroad. With such an extensive exchange network in place, CICIR practically keeps round-the-clock contacts with the top think tanks around the world. By way of such exchanges, CICIR and its counterparts learn from one another and add valuable assets onto the existing institutions. For instance, to better facilitate research work, CICIR has applied its understanding on the modes and operations of international think tanks to its own day-to-day administration by creating tools to host principal experts, task forces of varied topics and administrative assistants.

In the present context of international politics, with increasing signs of a return to realism and the complications of country to country relations, strategic dialogues and exchanges between think tanks play an essentially important role. As of today, China has initiated a number of influential platforms for global conversations, among which are the Xiangshan Forum and Boao Forum. Along this line, the annual CICIR forums have also evolved into weighty platforms for track II dialogues between CICIR and its foreign counterparts. Think tanks should take on the task of functioning as the "bridges and bonds" as well as "lightning rods" between countries, and yet communications among themselves should not be interfered with by their respective political agendas. For instance, in the context of increasing tension over US-China trade, Chinese and American think tanks should seek to defuse crises by enhancing dialogues, instead of "decoupling" to intensify conflicts. Track II diplomacy between think tanks should have more roles to play, which is also a core mission of China's think tanks in the new era.

Looking into the future, Chinese think tanks should draw on the advanced experiences of global counterparts to further enhance the overall strength and international influence by making more explorations in the following areas.

The first is to strengthen institutional innovation. For many Chinese think tanks in traditional forms, there are more or less institutional constraints like inflexibility in personnel recruitment and use of funds, lack of integrated coordination in deploying resources, unitary forms in the circulation channels of the research products as well as the way they present, and the restraints of track II dialogues & field trips overseas by a few binding rules and regulations within the institution. In the years ahead, Chinese think tanks should learn from the managerial mechanisms of the international counterparts, increase innovative efforts combined with their own actual conditions, and take unique approaches to hatch institutional innovations.

The second is to augment the use of science and technology in research endeavors. A good example is the application of video conferencing systems, which may transcend the traditional conferences in terms of organization and formality, and provide conveniences for inviting global participation in the themed discussions and research projects here, thus boosting the joint research between think tanks in China and overseas. Other technology tools are digital libraries, modern databases, big data systems, new statistics systems for public surveys, strategy simulation systems, and systems for risk analyses and early warning, which may help visualize the research products and add on the perceptual intuitions.

The third is to enhance international communications. The core of communication power lies in good analyses, which demands persistent refinement of research works. While inviting international colleagues to "come in" and engage, Chinese think tanks should also make strides at promoting their research products and facilitating the Chinese scholars to "go out" for exchanges. This requires the cultivation of personages who are familiar with international communications. Ideally, such researchers should have thorough understandings of the policies and conditions of the home country as well as the situations in countries or areas of their expertise, amid excellent foreign language skills as well as high proficiency in using modern tools for mass communication, such as the internet and new media.

The fourth is to strengthen strategic studies. China today has approached closer to the center of the world stage like never before, concurrently entering a critical period of economic transformation and upgrading. In response to the series of practical problems and realistic challenges, answering the urgent calls for novel strategic planning and top-level policy design, the think tankers should further enhance the strategic studies on "grand, deep and long-term" issues, while setting base on "micromesh, in-depth and substantive" studies. With such unremitting efforts, the conundrum of development can be expected to decode, the potential risks be resolved, and the future-oriented strategies be worked out. In a word, continuously broadening the international horizon and industriously deepening strategic studies are the missions of Chinese think tanks in the new era as well as the shared responsibilities of Chinese scholars as of today.

Reorganize, Renew, Reformat: The Future Think Tanks

Manjeet Kripalani, Neelam Deo, and Satish Kamat

Abstract Manjeet Kripalani, Executive Director; Neelam Deo, Director; and Satish Kamat, Executive Board Member of Gateway House: Indian Council on Global Relations in Mumbai, India, explore the Future of Think Tanks and Policy Advice around the World.

Keywords India · Ivory tower · NGOs · Policy advice · Think tanks

It's been a century since think tanks came to be established and earned a place for themselves in the global intellectual firmament. Now, the world wars that propelled their founding and thinking are long over, a new technological era has arrived, and the authoritative voice is no longer as compelling or widely heard. What, then, is the future of think tanks?

The future of think tanks is one of reorganization, renewed relevance, and reformatting output. The think tank of the future will be part old think tank, with its intellectual and research depth; part journalist; part technocrat; less ivory tower; less Western; and more Asian.

M. Kripalani (✉) · N. Deo · S. Kamat
Gateway House: Indian Council on Global Relations, Mumbai, India

J. McGann, *The Future of Think Tanks and Policy Advice Around the World*, https://doi.org/10.1007/978-3-030-60379-3_34

This is a good evolution, reflective of ongoing global shifts. Three dimensions of think tanks are in transition and looking for a refresh: the model, the money, and the medium.

The **model** for global think tanks was the institutions of the West, particularly in the United States, which started out as *sotto voce* advisors to their governments, producing policy papers that reflected their society's needs. They were never part of the establishment, although over the years, they were often staffed by numerous former governments and political experts. The Council on Foreign Relations, headquartered in New York and still one of the world's premier think tanks, was founded and first funded in 1919 by financiers who wanted a pragmatic and participative policy environment and outcome.

There was also military involvement in framing foreign policy, exemplified by institutions like RAND in the USA, RUSI in the UK, and the United Services Institute and Centre for Air Power Studies in India. These think tanks were either excessively militaristic in the United States, supportive of colonial pretensions in the United Kingdom, too close to the military-industrial complex in Europe, or ignored in India.

Still, these elite and powerful purveyors of policy attracted substantial funding, especially from individuals who believed in developing bright minds for future strategic and policy planning. Companies, too, found evidence-based research to be a more respectable and admirable form of lobbying with government and the public, as they tried to shape the global environment for their operations in what has come to be termed 'globalization.'

Since then, a global industry of think tanks has developed, largely based on the Western model of having a bank of deep scholarship on specific issues, with former government officials moving through the institutions, keeping them familiar with government policy and vice versa. They operate with a mix of both government and private funding.

The Western financial crisis of 2008 precipitated a change in both the model and the **money**. With easy Wall Street money drying up, think tanks, which had become almost corporate, with global centres outside their countries and scholars flying business class around the world to swanky conferences, found themselves adrift. Several, especially in the West, have turned to using their well-regarded brands to lobby with their own governments for private interests and for governments of other countries. In Asia and Latin America, where government funding dominates, the think tanks are now more dependent on the state than ever before, and continue to reflect its voice in their research. European think tanks still have some independence, but even there, the political party foundations now pick up some funding functions. Counter-intuitively, however, the number of think tanks in the world grew in the decade of 2008–18, from 5465 to 8348, according to the TTCSP Index.

Simultaneously, other actors have stepped into the policy space, which is often conflated with lobbying. These include consulting firms like McKinsey, international NGOs like the Gates Foundation, global media giants like Bloomberg and the Economist, multinational corporations with vast policy and lobbying teams across the world, mega conference managers like the World Economic Forum, and industry associations like the Confederation of Indian Industry. Even the international accountants like PWC and E&Y are now in the game, with their rapidly expanding government practices enhancing their profits and access to officialdom.

Consequently, interest in and funding for the interdisciplinary research that think tanks do is ceding space everywhere. Governments are seduced by the consultants and lobbyists, and private players invest more in their own targeted lobbying. Apart from governments themselves, few of these new actors keep society and the state as their lodestar for research.

Exacerbating these changes is the new **medium** of communication. Technology and the tyranny of urgency have enabled policy to be boiled down to 280 pithy characters, making the books and long-form research papers that scholars at think tanks toiled over for months before publication virtually irrelevant.

It's a good time, at the cusp of a new era, for think tanks to re-envision their model, money, and medium. From the old model, think tanks will keep their unique expertise of deep institutionalized research and memory of leading intellectual and policy thought. This will be more relevant if it is bottom-up research, rather than top-down, ivory-tower translation to society. Conveying it effectively to society and the state necessitates a more journalistic wordsmithing, and of course, an unambiguous social media message. With journalists now moving into think tanks, the communication of policy will get better, thanks to their research skills and lucid, accessible writing.

That's the easy part. Funding will be the hardest transition for think tanks to make. Older and more established institutions with uninterrupted funding from foundations or governments and large infrastructure costs to carry will take time to find a new way. Younger think tanks, who are more recently dependent on fickle annual funding from individuals, corporations, and the government are reorganizing their study to reflect current national concerns over the broad, blue-sky thinking and ideas for the future that the think tank world has long represented.

This may be easier to do in Asia, where rising prosperity and aspirations have made states amenable to policy ideas and advice from outside of government—not from foreign think tanks, but new domestic players, whose national interests remain rooted at home. Western think tanks which have expanded into other countries are finding fewer doors open to them, and will do well to instead collaborate both bilaterally and multilaterally with in-country players on research.

Countries like India, with few legacy think tanks, can be nimble players in the new think tank era. Many existing think tanks are largely imitative of the US-UK models, which have worked well until now. In New Delhi, the establishment institutions have gained fame by serving as event organizers, able to draw in politicians and bureaucrats to enhance their convening power and stature. But new think tanks are breaking out, some based on ideology, others on civic issues, and others still on bilateral engagements, especially with China. These are increasingly being seen as a career option by young Indians, whose refreshing outlook to old questions produces new answers.

With India undergoing several simultaneous transitions—social, political, economic, technological, geopolitical, generational—there is a greater need for think tanks to study and illuminate these trends. Since businesses are hesitant to invest in think tanks, as they don't see direct benefits which will help drive immediate solutions, it is necessary to enable easier funding for policy think tanks—for instance, through the Corporate Social Responsibility route. They will find that, in fact, think tank research can solve big governance problems.

After all, think tanks are multi-abled and therefore ever-relevant. As Dr. Hyun Oh-Seok, the former Deputy Prime Minister of Korea and Chairman of Korea's National Diplomatic Academy, said last June in Mumbai, think tanks are able to:

> "Think like government/policy-makers;
> Analyse like professors;
> Write like journalists;
> Communicate like diplomats;
> Manage like businessmen."

New Trends of University-Affiliated Think Tanks in China: A Brief Overview

Dong Wang

Abstract Dong Wang, Executive Director of the Institute for Global Cooperation and Understanding, IGCUPeking University in Beijing, China, explores the Future of Think Tanks and Policy Advice around the World.

Keywords Policy advice · Policy formulation · Public engagement · Policy making · Research institutions · Revolving door · Think tanks · University-affiliated

Overview of Think Tank Development in China

Think tanks serve to develop new concepts, influence policymaking, guide public opinion, promote public education, store and provide talents, and conduct Track II dialogues. They are called the "fourth force" as an addition to a country's legislative, administrative, and judicial systems, and are highly valued by governments and societies all across the world in the twenty-first century.

D. Wang (✉)
Institute for Global Cooperation and Understanding,
Peking University, Beijing, China

© The Author(s) 2021
J. McGann, *The Future of Think Tanks and Policy Advice Around the World*, https://doi.org/10.1007/978-3-030-60379-3_35

Over the past 40 years, China's think tanks have risen and made headway alongside reform and opening-up. This history of reform and opening-up also records the development of China's think tanks. Coming into the 2020s, China's think tanks are entering a new phase of institutional development. The Chinese government has realized that the high-quality development of think tanks is indispensable in the modernization of the country's governance systems and capacity, and considers developing "new-types of think tanks with Chinese characteristics" (juyou zhongguo tese de xinxing zhiku) as a strategic move to comprehensively deepen reform and realize the Chinese dream of the great rejuvenation of the Chinese nation. For this reason, the Chinese government has released a series of important documents, including the "Plan to Promote the Development of New-Types of Think Tanks with Chinese Characteristics" and the "Opinions on Strengthening the Development of New-Types of Think Tanks with Chinese Characteristics." Chinese President Xi Jinping emphasized "strengthening the development of new types of think tanks with distinctive Chinese characteristics" in his report at the 19th Communist Party of China (CPC) National Congress, elevating it to a national strategy. In this context, "national high-end think tanks" (guojia gaoduan zhiku) have played an exemplary role in the development of China's think tanks. Government-affiliated think tanks are continuously enhancing their innovation capacity, university-affiliated think tanks are springing up rapidly, and corporate, media, and social think tanks are thriving.

As a major type of think tank, university-affiliated think tanks play an increasingly pivotal role in the building of a system of new-types of think tanks with Chinese characteristics. The development of such think tanks is characterized by three features.

First, the size of university-affiliated think tanks in China is large and growing rapidly, covering a wide range of varieties. They are vital to China's efforts to build new-types of think tanks with Chinese characteristics. According to the Chinese Think Tank Index (CTTI), there are a total of 341 university-affiliated think tanks in China, accounting for 57.41% of the 594 think tanks surveyed. University-affiliated think tanks far outnumber government-affiliated think tanks, and their proportion is larger than that of any other type of think tanks. With regard to the increase in number, nearly 30 new think tanks have emerged since 2015, six of which are university-affiliated. Moreover, university-affiliated think tanks cover almost every aspect of public policy, including economic, political, legislative, social, cultural, educational, science and technology, ecological, and international issues.

Second, university-affiliated think tanks are steadily exerting growing influence on policy formulation, academic development, and society, all at an international level, as universities have been investing generously in their think tanks over the past few years. According to the Chinese Think Tank Report released by the Shanghai Academy of Social Sciences (SASS) from 2013 to 2018, think tanks affiliated with top universities such as Peking University, Tsinghua University, Renmin University of China, and Fudan University have always remained in the top ten list of best think tanks in China, along with government-affiliated think tanks, as measured by the criteria of comprehensive influence.

Third, some top universities have become trailblazers of China's efforts to build high-end think tanks by conducting pilot programs with their disciplinary advantages. In 2015, a total of six university-affiliated think tanks, including the National School of Development (NSD) at Peking University, were incorporated into the list of 25 National High-end Pilot Think Tanks, which means that university-affiliated think tanks became the second largest source of think tanks apart from their official counterparts.

DEVELOPMENT OF CHINA'S UNIVERSITY-AFFILIATED THINK TANKS: OPPORTUNITIES AND CHALLENGES

Globalization and Information: Response and Innovation

Think tanks primarily serve to provide professional and forward-looking policy advice to governments, which indicates that the development of think tanks should constantly advance institutional reform in response to changes over time, in line with their respective characteristics. University-affiliated think tanks boast the unique advantages of a complete set of disciplines, abundant talent, favorable scientific research environments, and widespread international exchange. Given that globalization and informatization are two major trends of the contemporary world, the pivotal mission of building think tanks lies in identifying ways to leverage the advantages of university-affiliated think tanks in the new era.

To begin with, university-affiliated think tanks in the era of globalization are trending toward internationalization (guojihua).

Generally speaking, globalization has brought about global challenges, such as global warming, the proliferation of weapons of mass destruction (WMDs), epidemics, and terrorism. No country can hope to resolve these challenges single-handedly. On this account, every think tank must engage in research on international issues with a global outlook. Many international think tanks, such as the US-based Brookings Institution and Carnegie Endowment for International Peace (CEIP), the Sweden-based Stockholm International Peace Research Institute (SIPRI), the International Institute for Strategic Studies (IISS) in the UK, and the Nomura Research Institute (NRI) in Japan, consider internationalization an important development strategy, actively employ international researchers, develop branches worldwide, and conduct international exchanges and collaboration.

More importantly, China has become a driving force of globalization, and its emergence has set off a process of what has been called "re-globalization." As a reformer in this new round of globalization, China takes as its core values joint contribution, shared benefits, and shared governance for a community of shared future for humankind. The international development of China's university-affiliated think tanks will be reflected in Chinese wisdom, plans, and roadmaps toward globalization.

Furthermore, the era of big data is further defining the basic format of university-affiliated think tanks.

Big data is not only expanding the vision and ideas of university-affiliated think tanks in research, but also raising higher requirements for the timelines and scientific grounding of research outcomes. Prior to the era of big data, traditional research at universities often had problems such as long research cycles and narrow visions, so cutting-edge issues were hardly examined in a timely manner. The acquisition of massive data and application of new computer technology allows these issues to be examined beyond the capacity of traditional technical approaches. The development of big data helps increase the size of samples for analysis, and facilitates researchers in the analysis of unstructured data resources. Readily available validation of this kind often results in unexpected achievements. All in all, think tanks can discover new variables emerging from the dynamics of social development and dig out more factors via big data.

Moreover, big data improves the readability of think tanks' presentation of research results and prioritizes the use of new technology to publicize research so as to "deliver results to the most appropriate people in the most appropriate fashion at the best time." Chinese university-affiliated think tanks are aimed at providing policy consultation, influencing the media, and educating the public. Policy makers with tight schedules can only spend a limited amount of time reading reports prepared by think tanks every day, while the public is now accustomed to fragmented reading due to increased dependency on social media. Therefore, traditional lengthy research reports or white papers with hundreds of pages can no longer garner the interest of their targets. Cutting-edge think tanks in China, including university-affiliated ones, now seek to visualize the stories behind data via diagrams and graphs enabled by big data technology while publishing and transforming their research results. The visualization of research outcomes enabled by technology at think tanks helps decision-makers identify effective information promptly and understand principal views of relevant think tanks, thus raising the efficiency of decision-making. Meanwhile, it helps the media more effectively report and spread information and establish interactive mechanisms with think tanks. It also simplifies and communicates complex ideas to the public and increases public engagement in, and recognition for, the policymaking process and research outcomes.

Translating Affiliation with University into Competitiveness

In particular, affiliation with universities presents these think tanks with some unique challenges. First, typically, university-affiliated think tanks in China boast a comprehensive discipline system and strong interdisciplinary collaborative and innovation abilities, which is not only the main advantage of university-affiliated think tanks but also the future direction of think tank development. For major research universities in China, development of think tanks is increasingly viewed as a key instrument for galvanizing talents, pushing forward cutting-edge, interdisciplinary research, and promoting infusion of basic research and applied research. For these think tanks, however, affiliation with a university does not automatically translate into capabilities. They have to innovate rigorously, strategize development models, create mechanisms and incentive structures to pool talents together, and adapt agilely in the age of rapid technological change and information flow. Moreover, the university itself should not become a boundary constraining the reach of a university-affiliated think tank. While universities sometimes might fall to the pitfall of "peer competition" that precludes deep collaboration between competing peers, a university-affiliated think tank should reach out to various universities and think tanks and actively forge collaboration with actors from different fields. It is not unusual for a major Chinese university to boast hundreds of university-affiliated think tanks—all research institutions and centers affiliated with a university can be broadly defined as university affiliated think tanks. However, given resource scarcity and the fact that the distribution of resources among these think tanks is uneven, university-affiliated think tanks inevitably face a (sometimes fierce) competition for resources and support.

Second, talents are among the core competitiveness of a think tank, and high concentration of scientific research talents is another unique competitiveness of university-affiliated think tanks in China. At present, however, there are some obstacles to giving full play to the advantages of talents. Just to name a few: the emphasis on academic publication in the evaluation system of university faculty's professional title and research, the lack of a scientific evaluation mechanism for policy-oriented research, the lack of incentives for university faculty who usually value teaching and pure academic research to policy-oriented researches, and lack of nuanced understanding of the complexity in policy making. In this regard, most Chinese universities can optimize and innovate on think tank systems in the following three directions.

1. Chinese universities should incorporate policy-oriented researchers into faculty's professional title appraisal and academic evaluation system, thereby forming a positive incentive cycle.
2. Seek systematic breakthrough and design on the use and training of talents, so as to improve the talent team structure of think tanks. Many Chinese university-affiliated think tanks learn and borrow from the "revolving door" mechanism in Western countries, try to attract talents by competence, recommend think tank experts to take a temporary post in government, and attract some retired officials to enter university-affiliated think tanks to exert their abilities. These measures can help effectively strengthen the "transmission belt" between university-affiliated think tanks and the government.

For example, headed by former Chinese Vice Foreign Minister Fu Ying, the Centre for International Security and Strategy of Tsinghua

University is a successful attempt for former government officials to opti-mize the talent structure of university-affiliated think tanks utilizing the "revolving door" mechanism. In addition, there are many university-affiliated think tanks dedicated to building a high-quality "revolving door" platform. For instance, sitting on the Advisory Board of Insti-tute of Global Cooperation and Understanding at Peking University are about 30 former and incumbent state and ministerial level leaders such as Chee-hwa Tung, Vice Chairman of Chinese People's Political Consulta-tive Conference and former Chief of Hong Kong Special Administrative Region, Academician Han Qide, former Vice Chairman of the National People's Congress, Li Zhaoxing, former Minister of Foreign Affairs, Xu Guanhua, former Minister of Science and Technology, Qiu Yuanping, former Minister of the State Council's Overseas Chinese Affairs Office, and Cui Tiankai, Chinese Ambassador to the United States, accompa-nied by over 100 leading scholars and experts from a wide range of disciplines. Take Institute of International and Strategic Studies, Peking University, for another example. With former State Councilor Dai Binguo as Honorary Dean and prominent international relations scholar Wang Jisi as Dean, the Institute of International and Strategic Studies at Peking University has developed into a premier university-affiliated think tank since its establishment in 2007.

Third, encourage researchers of university-affiliated think tanks to carry out long-term, comprehensive and forward-looking studies. Unlike government-affiliated or corporate think tanks that are quick to respond to hot-button issues, university-affiliated think tanks should give full play to the advantages of the universities' strong basic scientific research ability and produce studies with a long-term perspective in a wide range of fields covering humanities, social sciences, and science and technology.

CONCLUSION

All things considered, despite challenges, the development of university-affiliated think tanks in China faces many opportunities. First of all, it will continuously capitalize on its advantage of superior capacity for fundamental research vital to long-term national development and render substantiated theoretical support for well-informed decision-making. It will leverage the advantage of a complete set of disciplines to carry out integrated multidisciplinary research on major policy issues and put forward targeted and feasible policy suggestions. It will tap into the advantage of cultivating talent to set up a reliable talent pool in support of building new types of think tanks with Chinese characteristics. It will employ the academic advantage of universities to solve problems and guide public opinion. It will utilize the advantage of widespread international exchange to actively develop academic communication and advance public diplomacy.

KIEP's Strategic Response to Challenges in Policy Research

Chul Chung

Abstract Chul Chung, Senior Vice President of the Korea Institute for International Economic Policy (KIEP) in Seoul, Republic of Korea, explores the Future of Think Tanks and Policy Advice around the World.

Keywords Inclusive growth · Republic of Korea · Policy advice · Research institutions · Think tanks

SURMOUNTING CHALLENGES AND KIEP

The Korea Institute for International Economic Policy (KIEP) was founded as a national research institute to guide the government's international economic policies. KIEP conducts forward-looking studies which provide in-depth analysis of changes in the international economic environment and forecasts of future developments. KIEP began its operation in 1990, with the Cold War coming to an end and the Korean government engaging its neighbors to the north in a policy of Nordpolitik. In order to effectively prepare and deal with all the unfamiliar issues of the Uruguay Round negotiations, which were opening markets around

C. Chung (✉)
Korea Institute for International Economic Policy, Seoul, Republic of Korea

© The Author(s) 2021
J. McGann, *The Future of Think Tanks and Policy Advice Around the World*, https://doi.org/10.1007/978-3-030-60379-3_36

243

the world and bringing new international rules, the Korean government established KIEP as a think tank particularly specializing in international economic policy research.

In the midst of economic turmoil caused by the 1997 Asian financial crisis, KIEP devoted itself to developing policies that could guide the Korean economy out of crisis, such as promoting trade and foreign investment. Another major area of research was how to prevent such a financial crisis from recurring, prompting the institute to expand its capacity in the area of international macroeconomics and finance. When free trade agreements (FTAs) began to proliferate across the globe in the 2000s, KIEP helped the Korean government pursue a multi-track simultaneous approach to FTAs with rigorous research on this new policy area. As a result, Korea emerged as a hub of FTAs, which in turn facilitated trade and contributed to economic growth.

Back in 2008, when the global financial crisis pushed the world economy into deep recession, KIEP supplied the Korean government with various direct and indirect policy measures to position Korea as an important player in the new global economic order. Korea hosted a G20 summit in 2010 and made significant contributions to the global agenda at the time of the crisis. More recently, KIEP has expanded research into new trade and investment issues combined with development cooperation and an environment agenda, as well as policy research oriented at strategic regional cooperation with northern countries including Russia and Central Asia, and southern countries such as India and Southeast Asia (namely, the New Northern Policy and New Southern Policy, terms coined from the perspective of Korea).

KIEP is now embarking on its thirtieth year of operation. The past 30 years were a dynamic and exciting period for KIEP, marked by navigating the turbulent waters of globalization. During the past 30 years, the Korean economy has grown drastically, not only in measures of size, but also in the virtue of quality. With the Korean economy, KIEP has also grown out of a fledgling institute in the peripheries of the world into a core think tank with significant intellectual contribution to the global economy.

UNCERTAINTY AND UNPRECEDENTED CHALLENGES IN POLICY RESEARCH

One of the biggest challenges KIEP is facing is increased uncertainty. The "anti-globalization sentiment" together with the rise in protectionism and nationalism we have witnessed coming into the 2010s as well as the ongoing COVID-19 pandemic are posing immense challenges to the global economy and KIEP's policy research. In addition to the dampening effect on global trade caused by the US-China trade war, Korea has navigated unexpected trade interruptions caused by Japan's export restrictions. Now COVID-19 is causing a great deal of uncertainty. All of these changes and increased uncertainty bring about new challenges and opportunities to think tanks like KIEP. After all, KIEP has grown through grave challenges over the years by showing the way forward for the Korean economy.

In order to respond to the uncertainties and challenges caused by US-China trade war and to manage risks of too much reliance on the G2 countries, Korea is gearing up for policies to build sustainable and mutually beneficial relationships with emerging economies such as the New Northern and New Southern regions in the area of trade and economic cooperation. At the same time, Korea is responding to increasing demands from the international society to shoulder a larger role and set of responsibilities in accordance with its now higher economic status and size. Therefore, as it proceeds with its New Northern and New Southern policies, Korea needs to implement effective ODA policies that measure up to the expectations of developing economies while improving efficiency in its current system.

On the internal side, the uncertainties troubling the Korean economy are the fall in its growth potential and increasing economic inequality. The Korean economy is struggling to develop new growth engines, as labor productivity falls and birth rates continue to drop while the Korean population is rapidly aging, leading again to a fall in its potential growth rate. Meanwhile, the inequality in income and employment opportunities is one of the core factors of social conflict that should be addressed sooner rather than later.

Another important change for KIEP in its policy research is the rapid development of new technologies. As the Fourth Industrial Revolution continues to accelerate the convergence of different industries and technologies, our tasks involve how to realize certain benefits associated with new value creation, economic growth, and improvements in the quality of life in our research design and policy recommendations. As data accumulated by societies grows in value, there is a rising demand for measures to effectively utilize them. ICT developments are also bringing about a transition from closed and separated research to open and platform-based research that promotes joint research projects and collaboration with outside experts. These developments naturally increase demand to share research outcomes with the outside world through a wider range of dissemination channels.

KIEP's Strategic Response

KIEP is striving in various directions to respond to these changes in the environment for policy research. First, KIEP's research focuses on developing international economic policies, including trade policy, that can support inclusive growth, contributing to the growing body of arguments against new protectionist measures and preparing the nation for structural changes in the existing world trading system. Researchers at KIEP are working to formulate a framework for policies that can promote social integration and cohesion. Furthermore, KIEP's research emphasizes trade policies that are mutually beneficial with emerging economies; hence, these policy measures can enhance inclusive trade by promoting the internationalization of small and middle-sized enterprises (SMEs).

Korea's potential economic growth rate is on the decline while its population is aging rapidly. There is an increased demand for a new and innovative paradigm for growth in Korea. Therefore, another research focus of KIEP is to analyze innovation strategies of major economies to keep pace with the Fourth Industrial Revolution as well as topics such as digital trade and financial innovation. In response to multi-dimensional changes in the economic environment, KIEP is also conducting research that can combine various trade and economic cooperation issues with local economies and soft power.

KIEP has been expanding the channels of dissemination for its research findings and implementing new media to communicate its research to a broader audience by turning text-based research papers into video clips that can be shared online. In order to improve the utilization of our research results, English subtitles are provided so that global researchers can have access to the content and implications of KIEP's research. KIEP is also widening the scope of video contents to include live broadcasts of seminars, video summaries of our major policy analyses, and interviews with prominent scholars and leaders who participated in international conferences organized by KIEP.

The best way to respond to changes in the research environment and unanticipated challenges, such as the COVID-19 pandemic, is to prepare for an uncertain future with rigorous research and policy recommendations that contain worst-case scenarios and creative policy measures. It is crucial for a think tank like KIEP to embrace uncertainty and tackle issues that may be complicated and challenging. Given a world with rising inequality, deglobalization, and the Fourth Industrial Revolution, research institutions are facing a tall order, since they have to come up with policy recommendations that can incorporate new technology and contribute to inclusive growth with innovation. All things considered, international cooperation and facilitation of communication between KIEP and global think tanks is more imperative than ever in order to shed light on the future.

Think Tanks in an Emerging India: A Struggle for Relevance?

Samir Saran

Abstract Samir Saran, President of the Observer Research Foundation (ORF) in New Delhi, India, explores the Future of Think Tanks and Policy Advice around the World.

Keywords Digital platforms/Digitization · India · Policy advice · Privately funded · Research institutions · Think tanks · Transparency

Multilateralism and global governance today can best be described as being in a state of gridlock. Pandering to the shrill cries of parochial constituencies at home and to those agitated by the unmet promises of globalization, countries have become more inward-looking. Digital technologies and platforms have only amplified this tide against collective action. Gains made globally over the past few decades are being undermined; rising protectionism, zero-sum approaches across sectors, widening inequality, the spread of disinformation, and the undermining of democratic processes and institutions are all manifestations of this turbulence. Think tanks are not immune to these changes either and

S. Saran (✉)
Observer Research Foundation, New Delhi, India

are struggling for space, relevance, and credibility in this unsparing environment.

How did we get here? Modern think tanks were devised in the early twentieth century by transatlantic diplomats and academics to consolidate the gains of the First World War and to promote new "internationalist values." Their establishment was very much a political project. These institutions and the ideas they represented were an intellectual support structure for the social contract and economic consensus that modernized the West. Their counterparts in Asia and other parts of the developing world meanwhile were incubated during the heady days of globalization in an effort to consolidate this process and create new favorably disposed geographies. Nevertheless, contemporary headwinds have caught most think tanks around the world off guard, with governments and peoples questioning their relevance and ability to be honest interlocutors in these evolving times.

Those working at and with think tanks closely aligned themselves with their global brethren—and, in the process, created echo chambers that became increasingly detached from those on the "outside." While fixated on the global picture, think tanks overlooked globalization's impact on, and the agency of, individuals and communities at home. Ironically, it is the individual that is at the heart of the Lockean contract—globalization and its soldiers claimed to improve her lot but ultimately lost sight of this nucleus of global governance. This neglect has manifested in contemporary political choices across the world that ostensibly seek to reverse the trend of globalization, and "re-assert" popular will.

And the individual has found an ally in new technologies which allow them to script discourses outside of formal institutional arrangements. Indeed, the shifts in our material reality have also coincided with changes in our information environment. The rapid diffusion of digital technologies and the democratization (and subsequent polarization) of speech have made it harder for think tanks to maintain legitimacy and/or relevance outside of narrow political constituencies. Why has this been the case? Have think tanks struggled for relevance because of the velocity of change brought about by the medium (technology), or is it because there is something fundamentally wrong about their message (globalization)? Is it possible at all for think tankers to keep individuals and communities at the center of their policy prescriptions and simultaneously evangelize greater connectivity and exchange among states and societies globally? These questions when and if answered will perhaps rejuvenate this once important segment of the public sphere.

PLATFORM NATIONS

Indeed, think tanks are in dire need of a structural and institutional re-imagination. These organizations are tied to the societies in which they operate and should adapt to societal dynamics. Digital technologies are radically restructuring social relations, forcing dislocations from traditional sources of identity: family, gender, and even the factory floor. A monolith organization with formal hierarchies, partisan ideologies, and uniform demographics is unlikely to be able to comprehend, or even operate in, such societies.

Instead, just as our nations have become increasingly "platforma-tised"—relying extensively on flexible social, political, and economic arrangements that technology enables—think tanks need to morph into far more agile institutions. After all, we relentlessly remind governments and businesses that nimble organizations will succeed in the Fourth Industrial Revolution. It is time for our community to internalize these recommendations. Technology undoubtedly offers a new and viable business model for think tanks. We live in the age of Uber, where shared assets are increasingly becoming the model driving value generation.

This "uberization" is arguably more useful to think tanks in India and the developing world at large. The "platformization" of public policy engagement allows them to overcome the constraints of finance, infrastructure, and human capital. The Indian Software Product Industry Roundtable (ISPIRT) is one organization that has adopted this model from inception. They rely primarily on a core group of "volunteers" from the technology industry and a loose coalition of experts from business and academia to shape the technology policy environment in India.

"Platformisation" will certainly be a tall order for larger think tanks like ORF, which were originally organized around the traditional bricks and mortar model. Nevertheless, it is increasingly a crucial part of our global strategy. Unlike philanthropically funded think tanks like Carnegie or Brookings, ORF's engagement with new geographies and communities will not be dependent on a permanent physical presence. Instead, we have invested in platforms and convenings in emerging geographies like Africa and Southeast Asia and in older ones like the United States and Europe. This allows us to engage with the policy debates in these regions and draw their expertise into Indian conversations without large institutional burdens.

This may indeed be the future of many think tanks in India. The brightest individuals will wear multiple hats, often straddling the world of think tanks, business, and academia. Think tanks from the emerging world, unconstrained by the organizational structures of their established counterparts, may well be run by a core group of "curators" that manage this larger universe of talent. Flexible organograms and their capacity to source and pool talent for individual projects will survive and thrive.

A New Information Environment

Flexible organizational structure alone will not stem the rising mistrust in the credibility and "expertise" of think tanks. In a world shaped by falsehoods that proliferate through viral media, think tanks, as repositories of facts and knowledge, often find themselves disconnected from the debates that matter the most to the societies they serve. Part of the challenge certainly relates to the new media environment within which think tanks operate. Social media and digital technologies have changed the grammar and vocabulary of communications. In an age of hashtags and memes, long-form research rarely finds an audience. Giving fresh legs to traditional long-form research is a central poser for all.

For too long, think tanks have been occupied by a needless debate about whether they should operate as media organizations or not. Think tanks must leverage this new media moment to repackage their expertise and scholarly output and operate as all information platforms do—after all, the age of hashtags lends ammunition not just to advocacy groups, but also to think tanks. Think tanks must invest in bite sized and tweet length morsels of information that can cut through today's cluttered media environment to deliver knowledge to communities that seek it and are likely to propagate it more efficiently. New Media influencers must be made allies, and their reach can help think tank research travel faster and further.

This new information environment also gives us an opportunity to reconsider the time sensitivity of our research. Traditionally, our output tends to focus on long-term trends that are driving change, while ignoring immediate policy concerns and issues. Peer reviewed journals and annual long forms may well incubate excellent scholarship, but what is their utility in an era where news cycles are rapid and public attention on any one topic is diffused and temporal? We must rethink how our products find space in the minds of those continuously saturated with new information. Again, we should not make binary choices. Journal articles and nifty blogs are equally important, and researchers must now be able to produce both.

Think tanks in the emerging world should also welcome this new era for its potential to democratize access to and the dissemination of information. While these organizations are equally susceptible to the menace of polarization and misinformation, digital technologies have allowed them to script narratives that are not anchored to the intellectual idiosyncrasies of the developed world. Where the production of knowledge was once jealously guarded by "reputable" journals, social media and digital technologies have created a level playing field for think tanks in countries like India to find an audience for their research.

The digitization of the public sphere also offers Indian think tanks the ability to engage with policy debates in vernacular—shedding the old elitism and monopoly of English language experts. The Centre for Internet and Society in Bangalore, for instance, has long invested in an Access to Knowledge project that scales vernacular open source research and output from universities and research organizations. ORF is also investing heavily in providing a voice and platform to local language research scholars—with our pages now supporting research in Hindi and Marathi. Indeed, not only must Indian think tanks find new audiences for their research, they must amplify the voices of those who may not be able to otherwise engage in global debates.

REIMAGINING FINANCE

Credibility is also a factor of how institutions are financed. Inequality has exploded in many parts of the world, leading to a backlash against "the Davos man" and those that are a part of "the establishment." Think tanks cannot and should not escape the scrutiny that will follow. There are, after all, no sacrosanct sources of funding that are somehow free of any expectations. At the same time, think tanks must certainly access global pools of finance if they are to scale and inform larger audiences.

Think tanks, especially those from India, have traditionally been poor at this. Research organizations that are funded by large businesses are seen as outliers or as biased by advocacy groups. At the same time, businesses and industry organizations are uncertain about the value of think tanks and are hesitant to invest in them. Even today, these communities remain more interested in marquee events and platforms that generate attention but hold little in policy value or in the production of pure knowledge and novel policy ideas.

Philanthropies and businesses must invest in human capital, in technical capacities, and in the skill sets of institutions that are likely to champion good governance and informed policy positions. And complete transparency about the source and utilization of funds must underlie this relationship, enabling consumers of information to benchmark a think tank's knowledge products against the interest of its funders. Disclosures are important and allow consumers to choose wisely and as per their own value systems. Diversity is another key word. Diversification of funding sources enhances credibility and this must be a mantra for all.

Of course, the Fourth Industrial Revolution also offers think tanks new options. Why should young think tanks from India and the emerging world remain wedded to extant cultures of wealth management? Can they find new and innovative means of raising finance? The Takshashila Foundation in Bangalore, for instance, relies in part on its short-term educational offerings to individuals for funding. But can other think tanks scale such models? Can the agency provided by digital platforms, for example, also be used to spur investments by individuals in research? Alongside a few "tentpole" funders, newer think tanks may well be able to tap into the wallets of thousands of individuals who are able to contribute to their growth. The Internet Freedom Foundation, a new Indian digital rights advocacy organization, already relies entirely on crowdsourcing funding from interested individuals. This may sound like a tall order, but crowdfunding is going to increasingly dominate the treasury operations of research institutions.

Communities and Collaboration

Finally, think tanks must also reimagine how they relate to and inform diverse sets of communities. It is evident that politicized communities have been able to mobilize and propagate ideas better, faster, and fiercer than think tanks ever can. But the messages and means of their mobilization are easily perverted by identities, ideologies, and the internet. Indeed, this has created new fault lines that were earlier brushed under the carpet or erased from intellectual discourse.

Think tanks must learn to communicate to and across these identities, including those in their teens—the Greta Thunbergs of this and future generations. After all, many entering the workforce today see policy and research as a first career choice—a generational shift in attitude with respect to organizations that were once dependent on those already pursuing established careers in government, business, or media. We must encourage and support this ambition, especially in emerging economies that will host the largest pool of human capital and talent. ORF has partnered with several organizations, most notably "Youth Ki Awaaz," to co-opt the voice of the young in policy debates. Just last year, we jointly released a "Youth Manifesto," outlining the concerns and policy recommendation of India's student communities.

Beyond the next generation, think tanks in the developing world must also invest in a new relationship with the state. In emerging economies like India, the state and its machinery have previously seen think tanks as intrusive or hostile and perhaps even irrelevant. Even today, many retired bureaucrats and defense personnel tend to join government funded think tanks like the Indian Council on World Affairs or the Institute for Defense Studies and Analysis. A culture that values more extensive engagement with privately funded organizations will certainly go a long way in allowing human capital to be utilized more effectively in India. While it is incumbent on the state to revise this posture, it is equally essential for think tanks to strike a balance that preserves autonomy and independence while continuing to engage with institutions and leaders that are receptive to ideas and research. These institutions must offer a value proposition that is appealing to policymakers.

A healthier relationship with the state will allow Indian think tanks to escape the limitations of responding only to local policy debates. This is antithetical to the interests of nations and societies that are fast shouldering regional and global responsibilities. Future regimes around trade, investment, technology, and security will be scripted in capitals around the world from Washington to Beijing—and Indian think tanks and their emerging economy brethren must engage with and inform these communities. Indeed, one of the earliest Indian think tanks to have recognized this was the Centre for Science and Environment, whose advocacy in the United Nations in the 1980s and 1990s was instrumental in highlighting the hypocrisy of the so-called Global North in climate change negotiations.

There is an important lesson here for Indian think tanks: we cannot serve local interests unless we shape global opinion and choices.

Of course, no think tank is likely ever to have enough talent, or for that matter, the institutional resources to address and respond to local, regional, and global debates. This is why think tanks must stop competing with each other and collaborate. To some extent, this is already happening. The Think Tanks and Civil Societies Program at the University of Pennsylvania, for instance, is a valuable effort. Such initiatives amplify ideas being produced by scholars attached to a cluster of institutions. Collaborations that transcend geographical and ideological barriers will allow the think tank community to more accurately study and represent the full extent of churn underway around the world.

CONCLUSION: IN DEFENSE OF EXPERTISE

Going forward, it is inevitable that think tanks must evolve to meet the needs of the twenty-first century, some of which have been discussed here. For think tanks in countries like India, the challenge is especially acute. Just as these countries have begun to develop a culture of think tanks, creating platforms, and producing knowledge to serve communities from business, government, and academia, their expertise and value is suspect to many. They will bear the burden of producing knowledge and curating communities at a time when the academic and organizational foundations that think tanks carefully crafted over the past century are becoming less relevant.

Even today, unfortunately, many in the think tank world find refuge in their intellectual fortresses, looking on with worry as the "nativists" attempt to reverse the gains of the past century. This cannot be further from the truth. The nativist is not contesting the values of globalization, merely the means to exercise influence over the distribution of its benefits. There is a growing belief that, far from being the propositional and ideational organizations of the twentieth century, think tanks are vehicles to consolidate the status quo. In other words, it is not expertise itself that is under scrutiny, but the purpose to which it is put.

These times must compel us to interrogate ourselves just as we have others in the past and ask if our policy prescriptions correspond in any meaningful way to the realities and expectations of those we seek to inform. It may well be that think tanks from the developing world will shoulder this responsibility. After all, they are not constrained by decades of institutional habits and rituals. Indeed, the successes of the past and the disruptions of the present must not blind us to the demands of the future. The coming decade will test the ability of think tanks, especially those from the emerging world, to adapt to new circumstances. These disruptive times must be seen as an opportunity for think tanks to reclaim their social value—produce research, offer innovative solutions, and create talent and human capital in the context of this truly digital century.

The Future of Think Tanks and Policy Advice: Lessons from South Korea's Combating COVID-19

Haksoon Paik

Abstract Haksoon Paik, President of the Sejong Institute in Seongnam, Republic of Korea, explores the Future of Think Tanks and Policy Advice around the World.

Keywords Policy advice · Policy community · South Korea · Think tanks · Transparency

I will examine the key strategic and operational challenges facing think tanks, including the Sejong Institute in the Republic of Korea (South Korea), and discuss the lessons and implications for the think tanks to learn from South Korea's remarkable role model and approach in combating the novel coronavirus disease of 2019 (COVID-19). I will also share my thoughts on the impact of COVID-19 on international cooperation, democracy, and political leadership, as well as the role of the think tanks. To conclude, I will identify the special status of think tanks in the policy community, despite various difficulties they experience, and the contribution of the Think Tanks and Civil Societies Program

---

H. Paik (✉)
Sejong Institute, Seongnam, Republic of Korea

© The Author(s) 2021
J. McGann, *The Future of Think Tanks and Policy Advice Around the World*, https://doi.org/10.1007/978-3-030-60379-3_38

(TTCSP) of the University of Pennsylvania in playing a brokerage role as an international knowledge hub.

Allow me to begin with the task to identify, locate, and deal with the key strategic and operational challenges facing think tanks such as technological innovation, rivalry with old and new competitors, increased polarization of politics, growing funding difficulties, etc. Prudent attention and creative response to these challenges will strengthen our capacity to prepare individual think tanks for solving institution-specific problems and also the think tank community for jointly dealing with the local and global issues of our time.

Above all, think tanks operate in a dramatically changing environment brought about by unprecedented technological developments such as IT, CT, and ICT in the Fourth Industrial Revolution. In this environment, think tanks have to deal with the unprecedented nontraditional, transboundary, and transnational man-made disasters including the COVID-19 pandemic, climate change, global warming, air pollution, nuclear safety, marine plastic waste, aging societies, etc.

Most recently, a brilliant role model to emulate in combating COVID-19 pandemic was created by South Korea, which combined creative, problem-solving knowledge and ideas with highly innovative technological support. South Korea's "trace, test, and treat" approach, which was systematically organized and time-saving for treatment, proved to be a huge success in combating the pandemic. This approach is exactly what we think tanks should learn from when dealing with new challenges and in finding solutions to them. Therefore, we ought to study South Korea's approach to fighting COVID-19.

The first thing that was required was creative, problem-solving ideas and knowledge combined with time-saving but reliable technology. South Korea "managed to design and create a test, set up a network of labs across the country, and get it all to work in 17 days." A biotech company in South Korea developed a test kit for the coronavirus using AI technology. South Korea could test nearly 20,000 people every day and as many as over 260,000 cases in less than a month, which was incomparably fast. The mortality rate of COVID-19 in South Korea was as low as 0.9% as of March 16, 2020, the global average being 3.4% according to the WHO.

Another innovative idea in the South Korean case is the "drive-through" testing of suspected cases of COVID-19. The process could be done in a matter of minutes. The United States, the inventor of the drive-through system at fast food restaurants, has now decided to copy South Korea's system in fighting COVID-19.

Here, in a larger perspective, allow me to share with you three thoughts related to the impact of COVID-19 on international cooperation, democracy, and leadership, and the role of the think tanks.

One is the impact of COVID-19 on the international community in terms of how to cooperate and prepare for such unpredictable, devastating pandemics in the future and also on think tanks in terms of what role they must play to establish a more effective system of governance in fighting disasters at both local and global levels. Notably, South Korean President Moon Jae-in has already taken the initiative to help develop such a global system of governance by proposing a special video conference summit of the G20 for international solidarity and cooperation in fighting COVID-19 and promoting economic recovery. The Sejong Institute intends to play whatever role it must to help establish such a system of governance in cooperation with the government.

Another thought relates to how and to what extent COVID-19 has impacted the relationship between the state and society in terms of the sustainability of democracy at the time of emergencies—i.e., whether democratic systems can continue to function during disasters of such magnitude as COVID-19. Emergencies like the COVID-19 outbreak require strong intervention by the state in the society, tipping the balance of power toward the state. It is a red light, though, for democracy which basically balances the state and the society in such a way that the society has the power to check and balance the power of the state. Think tanks are obliged to produce public discourse and policy ideas to make democracy sustainable even during emergencies and disasters.

Still, another thought concerns what type of political leadership is more suitable and effective in dealing with emergencies like COVID-19. South Korea, unlike China, Italy, Iran, Japan, and North Korea, dealt with the pandemic by emphasizing the importance of openness, transparency, and democracy and by seeking public cooperation instead of taking measures like municipal or regional lockdowns. This carries a significant political implication in helping us discern what type of leadership—e.g., strong man vs. democratic leader—could deal with such disasters in a more accountable and responsive way. We think tanks could open a serious debate over this subject.

Now let us turn our focus to other important challenges—increased rivalry with old and new competitors, ever-growing polarization of politics, and constant funding difficulties, among others—as well as the steps needed for effective responses to them. To clarify, I would like to first share my experience at the Sejong Institute, which is South Korea's leading non-governmental, non-partisan, independent think tank in the areas of foreign affairs, security, and Korean unification.

The Sejong Institute, like other institutions, operates in competition with two kinds of rivals: existing think tanks and the newcomers in the field equipped with AI, big data, SNS, global connectivity, etc. The question is how to excel in competition by expeditiously adopting new technologies, strategies, and restructuring our institutions so as to not be left behind. We are doing what we have to in that regard, but it is just a matter of time before other think tanks catch up with us.

The best way to overcome such hardship is to form knowledge partnerships with competitors, particularly with the newcomers in the field, and cooperate in packaging and disseminating our products. In addition to recruiting well-qualified researchers and staff, we can also reeducate and retrain our researchers and staff.

Another challenge for us is the increased political polarization of our society, reducing the space of non-partisan, middle-ground, public discourse, and policy advice. South Korean society is divided along two lines: how to deal with North Korea and how to ensure fairness and socioeconomic justice. My institute, as an independent think tank, enjoys more freedom and creativity when engaging with public discourse and policy proposals than other government-affiliated institutions in Korea. While appreciating these advantages of independent think tanks, we should also create more space for autonomous and independent think tanks around the world.

Funding is undoubtedly one of the most serious problems for think tanks at the time of global economic hardship and shrinking trade. The Sejong Institute depends on three sources of funding: dividends from investment funds, government and public foundation funded projects' benefits awarded through open competition, and benefits from education and training programs of domestic and foreign government officials and diplomats. As was proved by my institute, adding education and training programs to the research and policy programs can be a reliable way of securing material resources with which to maintain the quality and independence of research and also to enable basic operations of think tanks.

Despite the aforementioned problems facing us, we think thanks are enjoying a special place and status in the policy community thanks to "bridging the gap between knowledge and policy." For example, whenever presidential elections are held in democratic societies, the expertise of think tanks and their experts—their knowledge and policy—are eagerly sought out by candidates and their teams. Besides individual think tanks and their experts, the Think Tanks and Civil Societies Program (TTCSP) of the University of Pennsylvania has greatly helped think tanks and their experts by playing a brokerage role as an international knowledge hub. The TTCSP annually holds AI think tank summits as well as regional and global think tank summits to provide a venue for think tanks to make the policy community an epistemic community based on knowledge partnerships. TTCSP, whose motto is "helping to bridge the gap between knowledge and policy," should be credited for their critical role and contribution.

Navigating the Future: Roles for Think Tanks and Policy Advice in Southeast Asia

Simon Tay and Lee Chen Chen

Abstract Simon Tay, Chairman and Lee Chen Chen of the Singapore Institute for International Affairs in Singapore explore the Future of Think Tanks and Policy Advice around the World.

Keywords China · Government-funded · Indonesia · Policy advice · Policy analysis · Policy community · Singapore · Think tanks

Introduction: Context and Changes

Changes in the past decade have reshaped the context for the future of think tanks globally and also in Southeast Asia. Since the global financial crisis, questions about globalization, unfair competition, and inequality have risen to prominence. The responses, right or wrong, include more populist, nationalist, and protectionist tendencies. These pressure the international system and global order. Another source of pressure is the increasing recognition of the climate crisis with urgent calls for action from some countries and sectors of society and the economy in the face of inertia and refusal from others.

S. Tay (✉) · L. C. Chen
Singapore Institute for International Affairs, Singapore, Singapore

J. McGann, *The Future of Think Tanks and Policy Advice Around the World*, https://doi.org/10.1007/978-3-030-60379-3_39

In these questions, national, regional, and global reactions and policies are implicated. Technology is also a factor that has grown markedly in the last decade. It is an enabler and a disruptor, and while it can be used for our common public good, it can also be divisive. The world and each of our societies have evolved into a highly competitive, information-rich, global marketplace of ideas and policy advice, but it is also one that is more divided, partisan, and exclusionary.

Think tanks are responding in different ways to these changes. In considerable part, this is inevitable. The current conditions give rise to a war of ideas and convictions among governments, corporations, and peoples—in their roles as citizens and also as consumers. Today's think tanks must take a position and attempt to advocate and influence in a world that is more fragmented, polarized, and partisan.

It is in this milieu that think tanks in Singapore and the region must respond and adjust. When there are compliments about the role of think tanks in the country and within the regional group of the Association of Southeast Asian Nations (ASEAN), we have to recognize a number of factors that have favored the role of think tanks. First, the efforts of policymakers to prefer rational policymaking, and to try to improve policies and implementation. Second, within Singapore, a limited political spectrum of differences and partisan contestation, create a relatively coherent policy community with many consistent, long-term participants. Third, among ASEAN, continuing efforts to improve the regional Community with better policies and implementation, and also an emphasis on both the cohesion and responsiveness that necessitates processes to find consensus and acceptable compromises among the ten ASEAN member states and its key interlocutors, as well as to align priorities and agendas.

This positive context can change, however, and not for the better. Indeed, there are already signs and evidence of shifts. These are driven by global and national forces. Witness the increasing competition and conflict between the United States and China. This is not a contest between two different systems and ideologies but rather one that is taking place largely within a set of rules that were once largely agreed and embedded within a number of international institutions. The Sino-American conflict is, in this regard, not only about whether one or the other prevails but also whether the international rules-based order and regional arrangements can survive.

So what can and should think tanks in ASEAN do?

Rising Above the Sino-American Conflict and Partisan Populist Politics

Think tanks in ASEAN have always had to negotiate their spaces and purposes within the assertive states of the region. This continues; the independence that many Western-based think tanks assume cannot be taken for granted. Where the state is more neutral or open to differing views, this provides a positive to benign milieu for the think tank. However, politics today is far removed from that.

The Sino-American tensions create spillovers that affect the smaller states of the region. For more than a decade, the overhanging question has been of choosing sides in the conflict. This continues but has grown more complex in two dimensions. The first is that the conflict not only relates to politics and security, but also a much broader range of issues including climate, trade, technology, social values, and cultural allegiances. The second is that it is no longer only governments that will provide answers to that question of choice. Different constituencies in society and the economy can and will differ in their perspectives. At the regional level for ASEAN, the conflict is driven by fundamental differences in outlook between one member state and another.

In this multi-issue, multi-actor context, think tanks face a number of challenges. An effort to uphold the international rules-based order can seem retrograde, without regard for changing circumstances of economic inequalities and influence. So might the status quo belief in the United States as the guarantor of the region's security, given the unpredictable perambulations of the Trump administration. An effort to relook at how a country or ASEAN as a group should reconsider its engagements with China or the USA can be colored (fairly or otherwise) as partisan or even procured and paid for by financing and agents of influence.

To some extent, think tanks in ASEAN are inured to this as most of them have strong links to the state, as they were established and funded by their governments to contribute toward salient policy tasks. For example, within the ASEAN Institute of Strategic and International Studies (ISIS) network of think tanks, more than half of the members are affiliated with the Ministry of Foreign Affairs and serve as analytic bodies within these agencies including the Diplomatic Academy of Vietnam, Lao Institute of Foreign Affairs, and ISIS Malaysia. Government-funded think tanks are not, however, fully immune against external interference in foreign policy, as a recent incident involving a China-born American academic who was expelled from Singapore illustrated. The academic, Professor Huang Jing, was accused of acting as an agent of a foreign country, presumably China, to influence Singapore's foreign policy and public opinion through his role as the Director of the Centre for Asia and Globalisation at the Lee Kuan Yew School of Public Policy. Debates about the rise of China and its growing influence, including within the intelligentsia community, are not limited to just ASEAN; countries such as Australia and New Zealand are also struggling to come up with a coherent strategy to respond to it.

Similar pressures can also arise when societies become more participative but also more partisan and populist. Social movements and non-governmental organizations are increasingly assertive and their voices can often be louder than those of think tanks. They compete and, where the politics shifts toward populism, can prevail, for better or worse. In the case of Indonesia, it held one of its most divisive presidential elections in 2019 where Islam was used as a tool to create divisions within the country's population of 260 million. In the face of rising radical Islam and identity politics, Jakarta-based think tanks such as CSIS Indonesia and the Centre for Policy Indonesia Studies face the challenge of remaining non-partisan and providing fact-based, objective policy analysis to the general public.

When the government of the day is beholden to only one segment of the polity, it can turn the apparatus of the state to that partisan cause. In such circumstances, the effectiveness of an independent think tank will be extenuated. Its continuity may also be pressured. If the think tank disagrees with the partisan populist state, it may be summarily labeled as disloyal or against the people and considered a surrogate of political opponents.

Innovating Against Increased Competition for "Noise" and Funding

Think tanks in ASEAN have long provided a platform for debate and a sounding board for policy discussion and opinion-making. Since its establishment in 1988, the ASEAN-ISIS network of think tanks has facilitated numerous Track 2 diplomacy dialogue on various issues and submitted policy recommendations to ASEAN governments through its formal affiliation with the regional grouping. Similarly, the Council for Security and Cooperation in the Asia Pacific (CSCAP), which is comprised of strategic studies centers from ten countries in the Asia-Pacific region, has been engaging ASEAN governments actively on geopolitical and security issues.

What used to be the exclusive domain of think tanks, i.e., creating "noise" in a society, is now gone.

The private sector—including public relations companies, consulting groups, law firms, and advocacy organizations—has strengthened its capacity to analyze and influence policy. To that end, many of the new technology giants such as Amazon, Google, Facebook, and Grab have set up multiple policy and regulatory units within the company. Media organizations—facing their own pressures—have gone beyond their traditional roles of informing the public and now seek to demonstrate thought leadership and influence outcomes.

At the same time, the proliferation of social media and misinformation has created a growing trend of echo chamber dialogue which poses new challenges for think tanks in ASEAN. Fake news, in particular, had a strong influence on several political events within Southeast Asia in 2017, i.e., elections in Indonesia, Myanmar's Rohingya crisis, and the Philippine drug war. In these instances, the spread of misinformation was used to bolster hate speech, stereotypes, and propaganda.

Confronted with rising digital and political disruptions, think tanks in ASEAN and the rest of the world must pursue rigor, innovation, accessibility, and accountability with greater fervor than ever before in order to remain relevant and impactful. Increased competition for thought leadership and funding also challenges think tanks to respond in various ways: by defining and sticking to its own unique identity; by engaging and partnering with one or more of these actors; and by hybridizing its own work and programs.

As an independent think tank, the Singapore Institute of International Affairs navigates some of these challenges through strategic partnerships with international organizations such as the United Nations Environment Program on the issue of green finance. In other instances, we have worked with multinational corporations such as Google on the digital economy, and with HSBC Bank on sustainable infrastructure. In such cases, we have consciously strived to identify the topics and approaches of our programs ourselves, prior to seeking out partners; this helps limit the risk that these or other institutions that are larger and better funded than we are would potentially dominate the work, and ensures that there is true collaboration.

Using Media and Technology, or Being Used

There are ongoing innovations in technology, communications, big data, and data visualizations that have impacted the work of think tanks and can potentially disrupt them. How policy research and advice are packaged and disseminated is changing rapidly. Many policymakers today are uninterested in the outputs of think tanks unless they have resonance beyond expert circles, among widely defined groups of stakeholders and even the public. Established think tank techniques of using task forces and study groups will continue, but think tanks must focus on mobilizing wider interest and support for their ideas and engage with broader segments of society in order to influence policy.

ISIS Malaysia, for example, has started to develop an active online platform on YouTube, whereby researchers and analysts provide commentary on current affairs. The aim is to encourage a healthy public debate among policy makers, scholars, and citizens. A few years ago, CSIS Indonesia partnered with the Economic Research Institute for ASEAN (ERIA) to launch a website for economic discussions to assist the Indonesian government in policymaking. The SIIA ourselves has also consistently produced online content and continued to adjust our format to be more appealing to new and wider audiences.

At present, the situation is still in flux. No single actor or sector has monopolized the best way of deploying these new resources and new packaging to influence opinion and policy. The think tank—with its traditional emphasis on qualitative assessment, words, and paper—can be overwhelmed. But there is time to adapt. Much will depend not only on resources and capabilities but mindset; perceiving the need to adapt is a precondition and cannot be taken for granted for established think tanks. Successful think tanks must be able to message policymakers and a community of stakeholders and thus must also adapt or risk being sidelined. Outreach must become a central function of think tanks to find audience and resonance in the new milieu.

What Changes and What Remains?

The need for policy that is clearly understood, well communicated, and effectively implemented has never been greater, given the complexity of the issues the world faces and the turbulent situations in our politics, economies, and societies. There has never been more need for effective and legitimate think tanks.

Perhaps, there is no single model of think tank that is extant today. When we look forward, with all these factors of change and new actors, this is even more unlikely in the future. The variety of think tanks will likely expand, with many hybrids and experiments—by think tanks individually, or in consortium, or by working with one or more of the different actors and institutions that have entered into the same or proximate spaces in the policymaking arena. Adaptation is necessary. Experimentation must be expected.

In adapting, however, there can be concerns about whether think tanks can stay true to their mandate or, to use media world jargon, retain its USP (unique selling point). While there are many fast-moving changes, leading think tanks share established values. Among the most critical of these are independence and the effort to provide a well-grounded and rational assessment of situations and policy responses.

Building from that foundation must be the outreach effort by think tanks to deliver those insights in a timely manner to policymaking communities and also a wider spectrum of actors in the society and economy. In this, there must be efforts to go beyond the idea of these actors as "audience" and instead see them as vital actors, collaborators, and stakeholders. Increasingly, these efforts will involve the use of new media as well as traditional and often confidential dialogues. These efforts—both experimental and more established—can gain from exchange among think tanks. Those of us who face similar challenges and hold similar values can and should find more avenues for exchange and collaboration.

How Think Tanks Need to Change

Somkiat Tangkitvanich

Abstract Somkiat Tangkitvanich, President of the Thailand Development Research Institute in Bangkok, Thailand, explores the Future of Think Tanks and Policy Advice around the World.

Keywords Civil society · Civil society organizations · Think tanks · Thailand · Transparency · Policy advice

When TDRI was established over 35 years ago, the Thai policy landscape was not as complicated. Under a "semi-democratic" regime, technocrats had a leading role and were capable of implementing policies. Conducting policy research in those days was relatively simple: just applying economic theory and technical knowledge to solve problems and forwarding the policy recommendations to the government, who would then order the bureaucrats to implement and bring to fruition those policies.

After the country became fully democratized in the 1990s, think tanks were required to communicate their ideas to the public. The primary channels were through conducting seminars, giving interviews to TV reporters or publishing op-ed articles in major newspaper outlets. During

S. Tangkitvanich (✉)
Thailand Development Research Institute, Bangkok, Thailand

© The Author(s) 2021
J. McGann, *The Future of Think Tanks and Policy Advice
Around the World*, https://doi.org/10.1007/978-3-030-60379-3_40

that period, TDRI had gradually learned to work with the media to connect with the public. We now have a weekly television program on Thai PBS, the country's public broadcaster, a weekly radio program, and two bi-weekly op-ed columns in local English and Thai newspapers.

However, it has become increasingly challenging to connect with the public. During the past ten years, the media has become fragmented with the proliferation of the internet, making it almost impossible to reach all segments of society. Numerous magazines and newspapers have closed down and many television stations have gone bankrupt. Radio is primarily tuned in only when urban drivers are commuting to work or stuck in traffic. With the rise of many new forms of online media, the general public now primarily consumes news through countless social media outlets.

As a result, we can no longer maintain our communication with the public through traditional outlets which would only limit our audience to the middle-aged and the elderly. These changes require us to rethink how we can disseminate our research and communicate with the public.

We have created a small but efficient knowledge management (KM) unit to connect with the public through such social media such as Facebook and Twitter, while maintaining traditional media channels. By presenting content with friendly infographics and easy-to-understand messages, we have been successful in increasing our audience base. As of 2019, we have more than 60,000 Facebook friends, 5500 Twitter followers, and 10,000 Youtube subscribers. Despite our efforts, a lot of work still needs to be done for us to truly reach all significant segments of Thai society.

Economic and social problems have also become much more complex. At the same time, the capacity of the bureaucratic system to implement the proposed policy solutions has declined due to noncompetitive wages in the public sector and political meddling in the implementation. As a result, the government can no longer solve problems alone and needs sustained engagement from society. Meanwhile, business sectors and civil societies have grown to share increasing roles in solving problems facing the country.

Under this environment, we have engaged more deeply with the business sectors and civil societies in designing, advocating, and implementing policies. For example, our anti-corruption research team works closely with civil society organizations, such as the Anti-corruption Organization of Thailand (ACT), in promoting and implementing the "regulatory guillotine" project to get rid of outdated regulations, and in improving transparency in public procurement of construction projects. Our education reform team works closely with over 25 public agencies, big corporations, startups, social enterprises, and civil society organizations to design and implement an "education sandbox" under the concept of "Innovative Education Zones," which cover over 100 schools in three provinces. Our transport policy research team engages with consumer groups in designing new bus routes for the Bangkok Mass Transit Authority (BMTA). The list goes on and on.

A constant flow of funding is always important to maintain a think tanks' ability to produce quality research and the source can often determine their independence. TDRI, a non-government nonprofit institution, has diversified its funding sources from a few major donors to more than 80 public agencies and corporations to maintain our independence from any dominant sources that may detract us from evidence-based research.

Above all, managing human resources is perhaps the most important challenge. We need to heavily invest in people, from offering competitive salaries based on the market rates, providing "self-development fringe benefits" to our researchers that allow them to acquire new skills according to their specific needs, to the rewarding of Ph.D. scholarships to promising young researchers.

We also conduct active talent scouting and recruitment by organizing policy talks at local and overseas universities, opening our house for student visits and internships, conducting "policy competition" events, and creating referral networks.

The ability to evolve and adjust strategies will allow think tanks to remain relevant in a fast-changing environment and allow us to continue to create impact at the policy level.

Managing Opportunities in Joining the Global Think Tank Community

Yerlan Abil and Aigul Kosherbayeva

Abstract Yerlan Abil, Rector and Aigul Kosherbayeva, Vice-Rector for Strategic Development at the Centre for Applied Research and International Partnerships in Astana, Kazakhstan, explore the Future of Think Tanks and Policy Advice around the World.

Keywords Analytical centers · Kazakhstan · Think tanks · Policy advice · Research centers · Transparency

ANALYTICAL CENTERS AS SUBJECTS OF THE POLITICAL PROCESS

The study of think tanks as policy subjects is relevant for the following reasons:

Firstly, analytical centers perform an important function in ensuring the quality of decisions made in the modern political system. The constant complication of political processes today leads to the inevitable increase in the role of think tanks.

Y. Abil (✉) · A. Kosherbayeva
Centre for Applied Research and International Partnerships, Astana, Kazakhstan

Secondly, analytical centers in developed countries take on the mission of educating citizens and articulating the interests of various social groups and segments of the population; that is, they serve the society. Thus, analytical centers can contribute to solving urgent issues of general importance and protect and promote public interests, thereby contributing to the development and strengthening of democracy.

Politicians and government agencies are faced with the problem of attracting the knowledge and experience of specialists to develop solutions to problems. Power needs reliable, accessible, and valuable information to make smart decisions. They need knowledge about the effectiveness of public policy, alternative ways of implementing decisions, expected costs, and consequences. These needs of government agencies contribute to the emergence of organizations engaged in specific research, forming a community of think tanks.

In modern conditions, we are experiencing increasing problems not from lack of information, but from its excess, which increases the demand for systematic and prepared knowledge. The presence of a developed structure of think tanks as basic elements of the national expert community has become a critical indicator of the effectiveness of management decisions and the state as a whole.

Thus, increasing requirements for efficiency and rationality in making political decisions and their implementation leads to the fact that analytic various types of think tanks.

ACADEMY ON THE WAY TO BE A THINK TANK

Many think tanks in Kazakhstan work closely with government leadership. They provide some innovative policy solutions for the strategic development of the country. After gaining independence in 1991, the need for policy think tanks in Kazakhstan has increased.

The Academy of the Public Administration under the President of the Republic of Kazakhstan is the only institution of higher education in Kazakhstan with a focus on training and retraining for its civil servants. It's affiliated with the Agency of the Republic of Kazakhstan for Civil Service Affairs, Anti-corruption Agency of the Republic of Kazakhstan, and the Executive Office of the President of the Republic of Kazakhstan. The strategy of the Academy is aimed at modernizing the national occupational training system, which is able to respond quickly to the changing needs of the professional state apparatus and thereby create, preserve, and disseminate knowledge for the benefit of the country and the world. Furthermore, to expand educational programs in the foreign and domestic markets of Kazakhstan, foreign students are attracted, and consulting services are organized for certain CIS countries.

The Academy now has three research centers: Center for Applied Research and International Partnership, Center for Interethnic and Interconfessional Studies in Central Asia, and Research Center of Studies on the Anti-corruption Issues.[1]

The Center for Applied Research and International Partnership is responsible for conducting, supporting, and promoting research as well as for the liaison affairs.

The Research Center of Studies on the Anti-corruption Issues is in charge of developing analytical and educational support in the implementation of the state policy on anti-corruption.

The Center for Interethnic and Interconfessional Studies in Central Asia, which is affiliated with the Assembly of People of Kazakhstan, is responsible for educational training, conducting empirical research, and international networking.

The Centers contain a considerable selection of manuscripts published in the Scopus database and Web of Science. The publications contribute to the general development of public administration and good governance in Kazakhstan. The research staff is often invited to contribute to international research consortiums. Notably, 19 scholars have been involved in expert activities and four of them have been working with international organizations such as the Scientific and Advisory Council of the Commonwealth of Independent States Anti-terrorism Center, the United Nations Office on Drugs and Crime, and the International Organization for Migration.

The scholars of the Centers are always encouraged and supported to participate in international research conferences. The research conferences are also organized by the Centers themselves.

---

[1] The research products of the Center for Applied Research and International Partnership are available at https://www.apa.kz/en/center-for-applied-research-and-international-partnership/public-administration-research/; The research products of the Center for Interethnic and Interconfessional Studies in Central Asia are available at: https://www.apa.kz/en/brief-information-about-the-center-for-interethnic-and-interconfessional-studies-in-central-asian-region/research-projects/; The products of the Research Center of Studies on the Anti-corruption Issues are available at https://www.apa.kz/en/research-center-for-the-study-of-anti-corruption-issues/current-research/.

Within the framework of the Astana Economic Forum, the Global Conference "Practice and Challenges of Public Administration in the Digital Era" was held in 2018 and another conference "Managing opportunities: Global Challenges to Leadership" was held in 2017 for world leaders, international experts, scientists, politicians, representatives of financial institutions, and entrepreneurs. In 2019, the Centers participated in the organization of the Global Conference "Transformational Leadership in a Changing World," offering its proposals and recommendations for the formation of a new leadership culture capable of managing challenges of the modern world.

On October 2, 2019, the Academy, with the support of the International Anti-Corruption Academy, organized a regional seminar "Anticorruption cooperation in Central Asia and Afghanistan." The seminar was a part of the VIII session of the Assembly of Participants of IACA.

This year, 20 staff members of the Academy have become ISO 37001 certified professionals after completing a training course on the anti-bribery management system arranged through the PECB, a Canadian certification body, and the Research Center of Studies on the Anti-corruption Issues.

The Academy is a state-owned enterprise, and internal reports, policy briefs, and recommendations are an integral part of its work. The academic and research staff are often invited on various occasions by state organs to submit reports, policy briefs, and recommendations on certain issues of public administration and civil service. Proper dissemination and utilization of research products are necessary through the organization of regular workshops and seminars where scholars present their research and the websites where they can publish their findings.

State and Prospects of Analytics Development in Kazakhstan

Kazakhstan is open to social, economic, legal, political, and other innovations and is flexible to consider the latest trends in a particular sphere. The scope of research has a wide range of issues, and Kazakhstan aims to strengthen its economic, social, legal, and political affairs. However, the lack of visibility of research products makes it difficult to provide enough data on the work of think tanks in Kazakhstan. Some of them conduct research for certain stakeholders and do not effectively transmit or utilize their reports, summaries, policy recommendations, and other products.

Thus, it is likely that the research conducted by domestic think tanks sometimes does not reach key audiences.

Consequently, the presence of Kazakhstan research centers in the ranking is a very important indicator of the positive changes taking place in the country. Firstly, the demand for analytical products from state bodies indicates their horizontal orientation toward cooperation. Secondly, scientists want to, can, and should be influential in society, and the "Brain Trusts" provide this opportunity to enter the "Corridors of Power" and directly participate in the design of public policy. Thirdly, the international rating of brain trusts allows combining the efforts of research centers around the world, creating conditions for cooperation in analytical projects, and providing a more accurate and adequate picture of their world in proposals for national governments.

In the Think Tanks and Civil Societies Program's 2019 Global Go To Think Tank Index rankings of Central Asian think tanks, one can witness the existence of some Kazakhstan-based institutions such as Kazakhstan Institute for Strategic Studies, Economic Research Institute, Center for Strategic and Military Research, and others. As an alert to domestic and international think tanks not represented in the rankings, more effort needs to be invested in the publication and proper dissemination of research products in English. The research products might need to be planned in a language practical to use in the international community.

The "think tanks" of Central Asia are very poorly represented in the world ranking of think tanks, with some exceptions, which indicates their insufficient recognition in the global expert community.

To obtain international recognition, the analytical centers of Central Asia need to:

- ensure the transparency of their work, the availability of research, analytical products, and services for citizens, politicians, scientists, business and financial circles, not only in their countries and the region but also abroad.
- establish active international cooperation with leading foreign "thought factories."

Since most of the "think tanks" in Central Asian countries are created and operated under state bodies and are financed primarily by the state, in crisis conditions of economic development, it is necessary to not reduce funding for research and analysis, but rather to increase it, since it is essential to search for effective solutions to the problems of the state, society, and the economy.

In the era of increased social and economic turbulence, think tanks can provide a range of strategies and best practices for transforming public policy and government institutions. The Academy think tank represents the state-affiliated model, targeted to support public core operations and programs. We strive to become a knowledge institution to serve the country through knowledge generation and management for promoting international cooperation among the regional members bringing mutual gains to them all. Our scope of work includes forecasting emerging regional challenges and common sector issues, as well as exchanging experiences and building research capacity.

As the coronavirus pandemic continues to influence how our society functions, we are learning how to adapt to this new reality. One of the most important things we must protect during this time is the brand of our organization: the value-added of the Academy think tank. In the prospect to come, we are going to prioritize effective communication and information-rich expertise that would be required in a post-pandemic global marketplace of ideas.

Conclusions

Are Think Tanks Fit for an Uncertain Future?

James McGann

Abstract James McGann, Director of the Think Tanks and Civil Societies Program, Lauder Institute for Management and International Studies, University of Pennsylvania in Philadelphia, PA, explores the Future of Think Tanks and Policy Advice around the World.

Keywords Brazil · Civil society · Fundraising · Hungary · Think tanks · Philippines · Policy advice

Throughout the last six to eight years, the world witnessed a rise in populism, nationalism, and protectionism; all signaling a challenge to the post-WWII order and multilateralism. At the same time, transnational challenges—such as: growing trade tensions, economic turbulence, increasing economic inequality, climate change, mass migration, and

---

Electronic supplementary material The online version of this chapter (https://doi.org/10.1007/978-3-030-60379-3_42) contains supplementary material, which is available to authorized users.

J. McGann (✉)
Think Tanks and Civil Societies Program, Lauder Institute for Management and International Studies, University of Pennsylvania, Philadelphia, PA, USA

refugee crises, as well as traditional and nontraditional security threats—demand that countries and institutions cooperate more frequently and effectively. In the past five months, we have been forced to deal with a pandemic that not only threatens our lives and livelihoods, but also demands that think tanks around the world respond.

We are entering a period of significant change, uncertainty, and instability, where the previously established order—as well as the international organizations that work to sustain relative peace and prosperity—are under assault. Meanwhile, enduring and emerging existential and transnational threats are growing. The post-WWII economic, political, and security order is being challenged and redefined by national and regional tectonic shifts in domestic and international politics. Presently, we are living through a dynamic moment in world history. As such, it is important to take stock of the technological, political, economic, and organizational trends and disruptions that are taking place in real time. The COVID-19 crisis and the economic, political challenges that follow will test think tanks like they have never been tested before. These unprecedented times provide us with an opportunity to assess the cross-sectional issues and trends in order to develop effective responses. These are daunting challenges, and so it is essential that we marshal our intellectual and institutional resources to prepare for the turbulence and turmoil that we are likely to face in the upcoming decade.

There are four key trends that flow from the Fourth Industrial Revolution that will ultimately transform all of our jobs and lives over the next ten years. These four forces drive the digital and political disruptions that are sweeping across the globe. They are:

- The disruptive power of social media, artificial intelligence, and big data;
- The dramatic increase in the rate of technological change;
- The increased velocity of information and policy flows; and
- The promise and the peril of the Information Age and the Fourth Industrial Revolution.

Human and digital networks, such as the internet, are constantly enhanced by new technologies that increase both the volume and velocity of information flows around the world. In this world of rapid moving information, it is possible to manage and manipulate massive amounts of data, to the effect of disrupting business, politics, and public policy.

Henry Kissinger famously said that being a policymaker is like being at the end of a fire hose. Today, we are all at the end of a high pressure stream of information.

These trends in information and technology serve as a catalyst that fuels the political discontent and disruptions which are on the rise in the USA, France, Britain, Italy, the Philippines, Hungary, Brazil, and other countries around the world. Policymakers have erroneously attributed the source of this discontent as the backlash against globalization. In reality, it is much more complex and it involves a number of issues and problems that—thanks to the internet, social media, and social networks—have become omnipresent and inescapable. The increasing uncertainty of our time has created a sea of insecurity, making people concerned and confused about the future of their work and well-being. This sea of insecurity consists of seven factors that have intensified over the last seven to 10 years. The failure of government or elected officials to address these issues, due to political polarization and policy paralysis, has left citizens around the world disillusioned and discontent. These factors help explain why people are gravitating to nontraditional politicians who promise security and quick fixes to complex problems. The sea of insecurity is composed of the following factors:

1. **Economic Insecurity**: Jobs, entire careers, and professions are being re-engineered—or simply vanishing. The income gap is growing and the opportunities for the current generation may not be as promising or secure as it was for us or our parents.
2. **Physical Insecurity**: We are reminded on a daily—even hourly—basis of terrorist attacks, the impact of climate change and other catastrophic events, such as the prospects of a nuclear conflict. This increases the collective sense of insecurity.
3. **Loss of National and Personal Identity**: Changing demographic patterns—namely, regular and irregular migration—are raising questions about national identity. In twenty years, Asians, Hispanics, and those of European descent will be of equal numbers in the United States. Similar changes are taking place in Europe. This change is disconcerting to many and is compounded by other economic and social factors.
4. **The New World Disorder**: The balance of power that was characteristic of the Cold War and bipolarity provided a degree of order and security that is currently missing. History tells that the most

unstable and dangerous periods are the ones in which there are multiple power poles or those in which powers are rising and falling. We are in precisely such a period: everyone is in charge—and no one is.

5. **Information Insecurity**: The Information Age has given us unprecedented access and convenience, but this comes at the cost of privacy, security, loss of identity, and—to a certain extent—humanity. The flood of information, which includes disinformation, misinformation, and attempts to manipulate portions of the population, makes us feel uncertain and insecure. Advancements in technology will also change the way we live and fight, but also the way our world is organized.

6. **Constant and Disruptive, Change**: We live in an age of unprecedented change and disruption, where technology has accelerated the rate of change and, essentially, made change the only constant in people's lives. In addition, the rise of new powers and a shift in the center of gravity of economic, military, legal, social, and political influence, from the global North and the West further fuels insecurity. In brief, we are currently undergoing a fundamental reassessment of how power and influence is expressed through the world. These changes permeate every aspect of our lives and are profoundly unsettling, leaving many feeling adrift and insecure.

7. **The Insecurity of No Answers and No Escape**: The most unsettling aspect of all is the inadequacy of our leaders and institutions, neither of which are not focused on these key issues. They are not addressing these concerns; it is therefore no mystery why there has been a loss of trust and confidence in governments and elected officials. This is where think tanks can play a critical role, by helping to create policy answers and action that is needed in many societies today. Think tanks play a critical role in analyzing, developing, and promoting policy solutions, particularly in times of extreme disruption and change. However, these organizations now operate in information-rich societies where facts, evidence, and credible research are often ignored—and where disinformation is gaining influence.

Let me be clear: the future is not bleak, and I am convinced that emerging technologies will help solve many of the world's problems, whether they be pandemics, water and food shortages, or climate change.

Think tanks need to be on the front lines, not the side lines, by helping to analyze these issues and prepare society for the transformative changes we face now and in the future. To remain relevant and impactful, think tanks and policy institutes must simultaneously pursue rigor, innovation, accessibility, and accountability more than ever before. In short, think tanks must adapt and innovate by transforming their organizations to be smarter, better, faster, and more mobile. We should always keep in mind that for each disruption, a window of opportunity opens to create new products, a larger audience, and new ways of implementing policy. Think Tanks should approach every challenge by asking: "What can we learn from this? What can I do differently? How can we turn adversity into an opportunity for growth and change?" Think tanks can provide a range of strategies and best practices for transforming public policy and institutions, even in an era of digital and political disruptions, as well as increasing social and economic turbulence. While these challenging times, there is also an opportunity for those institutions that can develop new and innovative solutions to the complex problems we face.

New Business Models for Think Tanks

Think tanks today face increasingly intense political and technological changes in the world, all of which pose serious challenges and even existential crises. In 2015, a Washington Post columnist, Amanda Bennett, asked "are Think Tanks obsolete?" (Bennett 2015). To answer this question: think tanks are not obsolete, but some of their strategies are. In order to overcome the numerous predicaments imposed by the current era, think tanks must innovate their business models. The goal of this study is to highlight some of the critical threats and opportunities that think tanks face globally, by those who are grappling with them on a daily basis: the senior executives of some of the leading think tanks around the world. These threats are best expressed by the so-called four mores': more issues, more actors, more competition, and more conflict. These indicate the challenges that all think tanks will face: competitive challenges, resource challenges, technological challenges, and policy challenges. Ultimately, effective responses to these threats and opportunities should focus on the "Five M's": mission, market, manpower, mobility, and money. In the global marketplace of ideas, think tanks need to develop national, regional, and global partnerships while also creating new and innovative platforms to deliver their products and services to an ever-expanding audience of citizens, policymakers, and businesses around the world. The think tanks that are innovative and agile will be the ones best positioned to seize the opportunities that this new and dynamic policy environment presents to think tanks across the globe.

A New Operational Context

Today, think tanks face the "NGO pushback" in which external forces are using legal and extralegal means to limit the number, role, and influence of civil society. This "pushback," coined in the 2015 Global Go To Think Tank Report, resulted, in part, from the rise of partisan politics and political polarization. These forces eroded effective decision-making and blurred the lines between policy advice and advocacy for think tanks (McGann 2015: 11). The general public, influenced by this partisanship and the rise of populism, has expressed a distrust in higher-power institutions, including research institutes such as think tanks. The funding landscape for think tanks has also changed drastically. The so-called golden age of think tanks in the seventies and eighties is gone. Today, with the recent rise of global philanthropy, donors focus more on projects that are short term, specific, and high impact (McGann 2015: 11). Furthermore, in the face of rapid technological advancements, think tanks now find themselves no longer the only actor in the knowledge-brokerage industry, but as the sole of its competitors in the "global marketplace of ideas," vying with other actors such as media organizations, advocacy groups, consulting and law firms (McGann 2015: 11). Given this context, adapting new business models seems inevitable and, therefore, worth studying. Frankly, the traditional academic-centric model has come to an end. The business models for think tanks are transitioning from "the manner by which the think tank delivers value to stakeholders, entices funders to pay for value, and converts those payments to research with the potential to influence policy" to a condign that incorporates innovative strategies in management, communication, financing, and technologies, all without undermining the quality and rigorousness of research and publication (Ralphs 2016).

Management

The leadership of think tanks is being called to change. The desire for a scholarly head of a think tank, like the motto previously maintained, "research it, write it, and they will find it," no longer holds true. Today, think tanks not only need scholars, but also managers. In a world of research, where the competition for ideas and influence is intense, think tanks need to demonstrate the value they add to public discourse and public policy. The competition that think tanks face today has led some funders to decide that they are only willing to fund the products and services of think tanks that have the "highest impact." In today's environment, everyone can be a think tank—at least virtually. Think tanks face competition from advocacy organizations, for-profit consulting groups, and law firms, in addition to every means of electronic competition—an increasingly efficient competitor (Ralphs 2016). As noted in the 2015 Global Index Report, "Big data, which involves the collection and analysis of massive amounts of information to pinpoint critical data and trends, may render think tanks and their staffs superfluous. This new analytic capability enabled by supercomputers, maybe the think tanks of the future" (McGann 2016: 15). However, big data, and any other competitors cannot replace the potential insight that only an organization devoted solely to policy research can generate. Accordingly, think tanks must figure out how to market their product most effectively.

Think tank executives hold vast influence over the direction their institution takes. In the wake of these global shifts, all of which directly impact think tanks, executives need to wield their influence with these challenges in mind.

STRATEGIC COMMUNICATION

There are at least three audiences with which think tanks must communicate—donors, policymakers, and the general public. In order to catch the attention of these key audiences, a think tank must be able to deliver the analytical information it promises in a timely and effective manner.

In an age of near-instant information dissemination via social media, think tanks must keep pace. Active blogging, social media use, online interactive forums, and infographics are examples of methods to achieve this. Once a think tank has garnered attention on social media platforms and more generally online, they simultaneously raise their donor profile. As funding becomes an issue, the burden falls heavily on the public image of the institution. Thus, strategic communication of the goods and services that a think tank can offer is an important way of maintaining necessary funding. These communication strategies are the vehicles in delivering research results, and as such, are crucial in generating an impact on the policymaking community (Kuntz 2013: 23).

Innovative Funding Strategies

While Benjamin Franklin wrote: "...nothing can be said to be certain, except death and taxes," think tank leaders today may say "...nothing can be said to be certain, except death and short-term project funding"—if any funding is to be certain at all (Avins 2013). Increasingly, think tanks are moving toward endowment-based funding in order to increase long-term stability. Other executives have suggested the establishment of funds, such as a shared reserves fund or an emergency bridging fund, to help think tanks build capacity and avoid financial risks. In short, an effective and successful fundraising strategy should build the organizational strategy and related processes into researchers' everyday work: for example, having a Monitoring and Learning (M&L) system in place that communicates real impact while generating useful information and more importantly, be explicit about the connection between the strategy and funding needs.

Big Data Analytics

Accompanying technological advancements is the increasing amount of data and the use of big data analytics. Some estimations suggest a 4300% increase in annual data generation by 2020—44 times greater in 2020 than it was in 2009 (Numanović 2017). According to studies conducted by the European Parliament Research Service in 2016, big data analytics could identify efficiencies that can be made in a wide range of sectors, leading to innovative new products, greater competitiveness, and economic growth (Numanović 2017: 3). The McKinsey Global Institute (MGI) stressed that "there are no industries in which the ability to continuously integrate new sources of data of any format and quality would not generate improvements" (Henke et al. 2016: 73). Think tanks are no exception.

While there are certainly complex regulatory concerns and technical loopholes with the appearance of new technologies, big data analytics could help think tanks better measure their influence in a quantitative way. In 2016, Tsinghua University in China released the 2016 Big Data Report on Chinese Think Tanks, which measured the influence of Chinese think tanks by assembling 110 thousand websites, 18 million active WeChat—a Chinese social media app—official accounts, 150 million active Weibo—the so-called Chinese Facebook—accounts, 6155 online forums, and

930 thousand news Apps for smartphones (Zhu 2017, 24). This effort suggests that the seemingly immeasurable "influence" of think tanks could be measured into a quantifiable number of citations, articles, and mentions on various platforms—a technique that, while limited, could be adopted and used to gain more insights regarding the communication strategies and level of social and political impact of think tanks.

CONCLUSION

In order to survive these ever-escalating changes, think tanks recognize the need for constant innovation more and more. With the understanding that the global context is constantly changing, think tanks should push to innovate management tactics, strategic communication plans, fundraising strategies, and big data analyses. On the other hand, this new business model should not go against think tanks' original mission to produce quality and influential research, intended to help policymaking. Think tanks need to find a delicate balance between innovating their business models and committing to the quality and rigorousness of their research and products. None of this should come at the expense of the other. It is only with an innovative business model and unwavering commitment to the excellence of research that think tanks will be able to survive and excel in today's world.

REFERENCES

SUBMISSIONS

Bennett, Amanda. 5 October 2015. Are Think Tanks Obsolete? Washington Post: In Theory. https://www.washingtonpost.com/news/in-theory/wp/2015/10/05/are-think-tanks-obsolete/. Accessed 7 February 2020.

McGann, James G. 2015. 2015 Global Think Tank Innovations Summit Report: The Think Tank of the Future Is Here Today. TTCSP Global and Regional Think Tanks Summit Reports. http://repository.upenn.edu/ttcsp_summitreports/15.

McGann, James G. 2016. *The Fifth Estate: Think Tanks, Public Policy, and Governance*. Washington, DC: Brookings Institution Press.

Conclusion

Avins, Jeremy. 25 November 2013. Strategy Is a Fundraising Necessity, Not a Luxury. *On Think Tanks*. https://onthinktanks.org/articles/strategy-is-afundraising-necessity-not-a-luxury/. Accessed 7 November 2018.

Bennett, Amanda. 5 October 2015. Are Think Tanks Obsolete? *The Washington Post*. https://www.washingtonpost.com/news/in-theory/wp/2015/10/05/are-think-tanksobsolete/?noredirect=on&utm_ter&utm_term=.20802394eb95. Accessed 7 November 2018.

Henke, Nicolaus, Jacques Bughin, Michael Chui, James Manyika, Tamim Saleh, Bill Wiseman, and Guru Sethupathy. December 2016. The Age of Analytics: Competing in a Data-driven World. McKinsey Global Institute. https://www.mckinsey.com/business-functions/mckinsey-analytics/our-insights/the-age-of-analytics-competing-in-a-data-driven-world. Accessed 6 November 2018.

Kuntz, Fred. 11 July 2013. Communications and Impact Metrics for Think Tanks. Centre for International Governance Innovation. http://www.cigionline.org/articles/communications-and-impact-metrics-think-tanks. Accessed 7 November 2018.

McGann, James G. 9 February 2016. 2015 Global Go to Think Tank Index Report. Scholarly Commons, University of Pennsylvania. https://repository.upenn.edu/think_tanks/10/. Accessed 7 November 2018.

Numanović, Amar. 11 July 2017. Data Science: The Next Frontier for Data-Driven Policy Making? Medium. https://medium.com/@numanovicamar/https-medium-com-numanovicamar-datascience-the-next-frontier-for-data-driven-policy-making-8abe98159748. Accessed 7 November 2018.

Ralphs, Gerard. 14 June 2016. Think Tank Business Models: The Business of Academia and Politics. *On Think Tanks*. https://onthinktanks.org/articles/think-tank-business-models-the-business-ofacademia-and-politics/. Accessed 7 November 2018.

Zhu, Xufeng. 23 June 2017. A New Ranking: The 2016 Big Data Report on Chinese Think Tanks. *On Think Tanks*. https://onthinktanks.org/resources/a-new-ranking-the-2016-big-data-report-onchinese-think-tanks/. Accessed 7 November 2018

Correction to: Connecting Politics and Society: A Way Forward for Think Tanks

Pol Morillas

Correction to:
Connecting Politics and Society: A Way Forward for Think Tanks
in: J. McGann, ***The Future of Think Tanks and Policy Advice Around the World*****, https://doi.org/10.1007/978-3-030-60379-3_8**

The original version of this chapter was inadvertently published with an incorrect chapter author name "Pol Morrillas" instead of "Pol Morillas", which have now been corrected. The correction to the book have been updated with the changes.

The updated version of this chapter can be found at
https://doi.org/10.1007/978-3-030-60379-3_8

© The Author(s) 2021, corrected publication 2021
J. McGann, *The Future of Think Tanks and Policy Advice
Around the World*, https://doi.org/10.1007/978-3-030-60379-3_43

C1

APPENDIX

Author Biographies

ABDEL-LATIF Abla Dr. Abla Abdel-Latif received her Ph.D. in Economics from the University of Southern California. She is Chairman of the Presidential Advisory Council for Economic Development, Executive Director and Director of Research of the Egyptian Center for Economic Studies, an Expert Member in the Coordinating Council of the Central Bank of Egypt, Professor of Economics at the American University in Cairo, and a Board member of the National Bank of Egypt. Dr. Abdel-Latif was appointed by presidential decree to represent the Federation of Egyptian Industries in the writing of the New Egyptian Constitution in 2013. Dr. Abdel-Latif's positions continue to make her one of the most influential academics in Egypt.

ABDELMOULA Ezzeddine Since 2007, Dr. Ezzeddine Abdelmoula has been a part of the Al Jazeera Center for Studies, where he now leads as the Director of Research. He received Masters degrees in international politics and political philosophy from SOAS University and La Sorbonne, respectively. He earned a Ph.D. in Politics from Exeter University in 2008. The author of "Al Jazeera and Democratization: the Rise of Arab Public Sphere" and "Arabs and Democracy in the age of Multiple Screens," Dr. Ezzeddine is a preeminent scholar on democratization in the Arab world.

© The Editor(s) (if applicable) and The Author(s), under exclusive license to Springer Nature Switzerland AG 2021
J. McGann, *The Future of Think Tanks and Policy Advice Around the World*, https://doi.org/10.1007/978-3-030-60379-3

ABDULLA Shaikh Dr. Shaikh Abdulla bin Ahmed Al Khalifa is the Chairman of the Board of Trustees at the Bahrain Center for Strategic, International and Energy Studies, in addition to serving as Undersecretary for International Affairs at the Ministry of Foreign Affairs of the Kingdom of Bahrain, a post he has held since August 2015. Previously Shaikh Abdulla held the post of Director-General for External Communications (2014) at the Information Affairs Authority, during which he played a pivotal role in drawing up and implementing a strategy for strengthening the country's national communications and public engagement. Shaikh Abdulla was awarded a Ph.D. in International Relations and Diplomacy from the École des Hautes Études Internationales, France. In 2008, he earned a Master of Law (LLM) from Queen Mary College, University of London, UK, focusing on negotiation and mediation. He also holds a Diploma in Political Development (Honors) from the Bahrain Institute for Political Development, and a Bachelor of Law (LLB) (Honors) from the Applied Science University, Jordan.

ACQUAH Emmanunel Emmanuel Acquah founded the Africa Center for Entrepreneurship and Youth Education (ACEYE) with the goal of providing entrepreneurial opportunities for Africa's youth in mind. Before ACEYE, however, he developed his leadership skills as a Business Head under the Africa Business Bureau and as President of the Cajole Foundation: another nonprofit dedicated to human development.

ASAVISANU Torpong Dr. Torpong Asavisanu joined the Thailand Development Research Institute (TDRI) as an advisor to Public Health Policy Research and Human Resources Management in 2013. In 2018 he was appointed Executive Vice President. His area of expertise includes healthcare management and public health policy. He held previous positions as hospital director responsible for the management of healthcare service to the general public under the Social Security and Universal Healthcare Coverage schemes.

He graduated with a B.Sc. from the University of California, Irvine (UCI) in Biological Sciences and Healthcare Management and a Doctor of Medicine from Chulalongkorn University.

BAUQUET Nicolas Nicolas joined the Institute in September 2018 after eight years serving the French cultural diplomacy. As Head of the Culture and Cooperation Section of the French Office in Taipei from 2014 to 2018, he worked on the development of French soft power in Asia. From 2010 to 2014, he was Cultural Counselor at the French Embassy to the Holy See and Director of the Center Saint-Louis, the French cultural center in Rome. As a historian, he devoted his doctoral thesis to the question of the relationship between religion and politics in communist Hungary. A graduate of Ecole normale supérieure and holder of an agrégation of history, he has taught at Sciences Po and Harvard.

BAUSCH Camilla Dr. Camilla Bausch is Scientific & Executive Director of Ecologic Institute in Europe.

Her main fields of research are environmental, climate and energy policy. Dr. Bausch was a long-standing contributor to the German Delegation to the UN climate negotiations. She has been active in the introduction and reform of the emissions trading system in Germany as well as ongoing developments of energy law. The implementation and effects of the German energy transition on neighboring European countries is an important aspect of her work as well as the ongoing development of European climate and energy policy.

Dr. Bausch is Spokesperson for the Ecological Research Network (Ecornet). She is Associate Editor of the journal Carbon & Climate Law Review (CCLR) and is invited regularly to speak at conferences and events. Dr. Bausch is Co-Founder of the Climate Talk event series and was personally responsible for the initiative for a decade. She is also the initiator and head of the EnergyTransitionArt project. She is member in several boards/advisory groups/juries.

Camilla Bausch is a trained lawyer with a focus on European and environmental law. She received a Ph.D. in law from Humboldt-Universität zu Berlin (Germany). Dr. Bausch has received research fellowships and scholarships from numerous institutions, including the German Research Foundation (DFG), the German Academic Scholarship Foundation, the German Marshall Fund, and the Twenty-first Century Trust Oxford. She has lived abroad for extended periods in the USA, Belgium, and Russia.

BIGORGNE   Laurent Laurent   Bigorgne   has   directed   Institut Montaigne, a French independent public policy think tank, since 2011. He is a French expert on education and higher education issues.

Before joining Institut Montaigne, Bigorgne served as first Dean of Studies and later Vice President of Sciences Po (2000–2008). He also spent a year in London on secondment at the London School of Economics (2009). He started his career as a History teacher.

Passionate about education, Bigorgne also chairs two nonprofit organizations, Agir pour l'école and Le choix de l'école, and he is a member of the Board of Directors of the Lycée International de Londres Winston Churchill in London. He graduated from Sciences Po and holds an "Agrégation" in History.

BONIFACE Pascal   Dr. Pascal BONIFACE is the founding Director of the French Institute for International and Strategic Affairs—IRIS, based in Paris.

He is professor of international relations in the "Institut d'Etudes européennes" (Institute for European Studies) in the University of Paris-8. He is the Director of the quarterly journal "La Revue internationale et stratégique" (International and strategic review) since 1991, and the Editor of "L'Année stratégique" (Strategic Yearbook) since 1985.

Dr. Pascal BONIFACE has published more than sixty books dealing with International Relations, Nuclear Deterrence and Disarmament, European Security, French International Policy, Sport in the International Relations (he developed the concept of *Geopolitics of Sport*) and also the conflict in the Middle East and its impact in France. Several have become classics, reissued on a regular basis and translated in several languages.

Dr. Pascal BONIFACE publishes several articles in international and strategic reviews, is regularly present in the media national or international, written or audiovisual, and gives many conferences in France and abroad. He's one of the most followed geopolitical analysts on social networks (Facebook and Twitter). He also analyzes international issues on his own YouTube channel and weekly podcasts "Comprendre le monde" (Understand the world), as well as on his blog (IRIS & Mediapart).

Pascal Boniface is a member of the National Ethical Commission at the Fédération française du football (FFF—French Football Federation). He has been made a Chevalier of the French Award for distinguished services in public and private capacity and Officier of the Legion of honor. He has received the "Prix Vauban" in 2011.

CHUNG Chul   Chul Chung is currently acting president and senior vice president of the Korea Institute for International Economic Policy (KIEP), and vice-chair of the Korea National Committee for Pacific Economic Cooperation (KOPEC). Dr. Chung is serving as a member of the Presidential Commission on Policy Planning (PCPP) of the Republic of Korea. In the Korean government, he has served as trade advisor to the Minister of Trade, Industry, and Energy as well as a member of the

Long Term Strategy Committee chaired by Deputy Prime Minister, and Policy Advisory Committee member of the Ministry of Foreign Affairs.

Dr. Chung is serving as the editor-in-chief of the East Asian Economic Review. He is Vice President of the Korean Association of Trade and Industry Studies. Prior to joining KIEP, he taught international economics as a professor in the School of Economics at Georgia Tech in the United States. He also held an adjunct professorship in the Graduate School of International Studies at Seoul National University.

While on leave from KIEP (2009–2012), Dr. Chung worked on the ratification of the Korea–United States FTA as chief economist of the Korea International Trade Association (KITA) in Washington, DC. He has published numerous academic articles and policy research papers on international trade, economic geography, and regional integration issues including APEC. He received Ph.D. in Economics from the University of Michigan, Ann Arbor.

DE CONING Cedric Cedric de Coning is a Senior Advisor on Peace-keeping and Peacebuilding for ACCORD. He is also a Senior Research Fellow in the Peace Operations and Peacebuilding Research Group at the Norwegian Institute of International Affairs (NUPI) and he is also a Special Advisor to the Head of the Peace Support Operations Division of the African Union Commission. He serves on the editorial boards of the journals Global Governance and Peacebuilding. Cedric has a Ph.D. from the Department of Philosophy at the University of Stellenbosch. Cedric's main research focus is on AU, EU, and UN peacekeeping and peace-building policies and practices. He has a special interest in the implications of complexity theory for the planning, management and evaluation of peace missions. Recent publications include: Rising Powers and the Future of Peacekeeping and Peacebuilding (2013), Understanding Peace-building as Essentially Local (2013), and The BRICS and Coexistence: An Alternative Vision of World Order (2014).

DEO Neelam Neelam Deo has served as the Indian Ambassador to Denmark and Ivory Coast with concurrent accreditation to Niger, Guinea, and Sierra Leone. She has also served in the Indian embassies in Rome, Bangkok and Washington, DC, where she liaised with the US Congress, the State Department, and the National Security Council on strategic issues. Her last assignment was as Consul General in New York from 2005 to 2008. During the course of her assignments in the Ministry of External Affairs, she held the position of Joint Secretary for the divisions dealing with Bangladesh, Sri Lanka, Myanmar, and the Maldives. At different times over the course of her career, she has dealt with Bhutan, South East Asia, and the Pacific, as well as countries in West Asia and North Africa. She is an invited speaker on strategic issues and India–United States relations at numerous think tanks and universities, in India, Europe, and the USA. Apart from her articles and commentaries written exclusively for Gateway House, Neelam occasionally writes for mainstream publications, and is a frequent commentator for television news channels. She has a Master's degree from the Delhi School of Economics and serves on the Editorial Advisory Board of the Indian Foreign Affairs Journal. She has served on the board of Oxfam India and as trustee of Breakthrough, a human rights organization. She has also served as an Independent Director on the Boards of Mumbai-based corporations.

DONG Wang Wang Dong is Executive Director of the Institute for Global Cooperation and Understanding (IGCU), Peking University. He also holds appointments as Deputy Director of the Office for Humanities and Social Sciences, Peking University; Associate Professor at School of International Studies at Peking University. He sits on the advisory committees of several prestigious academic institutions and think tank including Member of the Steering Committee of the East Asian Security Forum, Western Returned Scholars Association; Member of the International Advisory Council of the Shanghai Academy of Global Governance and Area Studies; Member of the Advisory Committee of the "China-U.S. Young Scholars Forum," the Global Times-the Carter Center; Member of the Academic Committee, the Institute for Asia Pacific Studies, Peking University; General Secretary, the Academic Committee of the Pangoal Institution, a leading China-based public policy think tank.

Wang Dong received his bachelor in law from Peking University and Ph.D. in political science from UCLA. Dr. Wang has previously taught with a tenure-track appointment at the Department of History and Political Science, York College of Pennsylvania, and served as Research Associate at East Asian Peace Program, University of Uppsala. Dr. Wang has written extensively on international relations and China's foreign policy. His articles appear in *Diplomatic History*, *The Pacific Review*, *The New York Times* as well as other top academic and news outlets. Author of a new book *Re-globalization: When China Meets the World Again* (in Chinese, 2018) (in English, with Routledge, forthcoming).

He has served as Chinese speaker/delegate for preeminent international fora such as World Economic Forum, Munich Security Conference, and Shangri-La Dialogue. Dr. Wang has received many awards and was named a "Munich Young Leader" in 2016. He was selected by the inaugural program of "Preeminent Young Scientists" of Beijing in 2018 (ranked No. 1 in humanities and social sciences).

DYKIN Alexander President, Primakov National Research Institute of World Economy and International Relations (IMEMO), Russian Academy of Sciences (RAS), Academician, Dr. of Science (Economics). In 1998–1999 A. Dynkin was the Economic Advisor to the Chairman of the Government of the Russian Federation. In 1994, 1996 he was invited as a visiting professor and lecturer to Georgetown University (USA, Washington, DC).

His research areas comprise the issues of economic growth, forecasting, energy, international comparisons, the patterns of innovation development, global issues, international relations, and international security.

FISCHER-BOLIN Peter Peter Fischer-Bollin has been Head of the Konrad-Adenauer-Stiftung Division Analysis and *Consulting* in Berlin since January 2020. Born in 1966 in Westphalia he did his military service in 1986/1987. He holds a Master's degree and a Ph.D. in Political Science, History, and Constitutional Law from the University of Mainz, Germany. He has taught Democratic Transitions and Political Systems at the Landivar-University in Guatemala, the University of Bonn and the Humboldt-University in Berlin. After working for some years in the Bundestag and the private sector he joined Konrad-Adenauer-Stiftung in 1996. Since then he has worked for the foundation abroad and at its headquarters: as Representative in several Latin American countries (El Salvador, Guatemala, and Brazil) and back in Germany as Head of the Department for Europe/North America from 2004 to 2007 and Head of the Human Resources Department within KAS from 2012 to 2017. In 2011/12 he worked for the CDU state-organization in North Rhine-Westphalia. 2017–2019 he was a Deputy Head of KAS's Department for European and International Cooperation.

In his position as head of the division he coordinates six departments responsible for tackling current and future political challenges. The departments provide analyzes of the political landscape and consult (political actors) on German, European, and Global policies.

FORD Elaine Elaine Ford is the director and founder of Democracy & Development International (D&D International) based in Lima, Peru. She is the director and creator of the Digital Democracy Program promoted by D&D International. President of the Internet Society (ISOC) Peru Chapter and Member of the Steering Committee of ISOC Chapters Advisory Council. Member of the Committee of Women Leaders of the Americas. Professor of the Communications Faculty of the Peruvian University of Applied Sciences (UPC). She is Master in International Studies of the University of Chile, approved with Maximum Distinction. Postgraduate Studies in International Human Rights Law of the University of Nottingham, England. Journalist of the Peruvian University of Applied Sciences (UPC). She has a Specialization in Collaborative Solutions and Innovation in Government at Harvard Kennedy School, Harvard University, United States.

She obtained the "Woman Leader and International Entrepreneur Award" (ODM Peru, 2019), the "Iberoamerican Leading Woman 2018 Award" (Peru, 2018), "Young Leader Award" from the International Young Leaders Foundation (Argentina, 2010) and was designated "Distinguished Visitor" by the Urban Morgan Institute for Human Rights, of the University of Cincinnati School of Law in Ohio (United States). She was invited by the German government to the Digitalization Program in the cities Berlin and Hannover (2018). She has won the Chevening Scholarships of the British Council and Fulbright. He has participated in the programs: International Visitors Program and Youth Leaders of the United States Department of State.

Author of the book: "The challenge of digital democracy. Towards an interconnected citizenship" (2019), presented in the cities of Lima, Berlin, Santo Domingo, and Panama City.

FUKUI Toshihiko Mr. Fukui joined the Bank of Japan in 1958 after graduation from the University of Tokyo. Having served for three decades in several positions, he took up the position of Executive Director in 1989–1994, and Deputy Governor in 1994–1998. He left the Bank of Japan once in 1998. In 1998–2003 he worked as Chairman at Fujitsu Research Institute. Then he was appointed the Governor of the Bank of Japan and served for the period between 2003 and 2008. Since December 2008, he has been at the current position of the President of the Canon Institute for Global Studies.

GARRIDO Diego Lopez DIEGO LÓPEZ GARRIDO is an economist, and has a Chair in Constitutional Law. Elected as MP for six terms, he was member of the Convention for drafting the European Constitution, representing the Spanish Parliament (2002–2003). He has been representative in various legislatures and Secretary of State for the European Union. He has produced numerous works on legal, economic, and political issues, and regularly works with major news organizations. Currently he is a parliamentary counsel to the Spanish parliament and Executive Vice President of Alternativas Foundation.

Specialist in human rights, and author of many books on politics and European Community Law. His last books published are: Lecciones de Derecho Constitucional de España y de la Union Europea (Vols. I and II).

Paraisos Fiscales, libros de la Catarata y Fundacion Alternativas., Madrid 2016, and: The Ice Age. Bailing Out the Welfare State in the Era of Austerity, London Publishing Partnership, 2015.

Along 2016, he will publish, as Editor and co-author, the book: Derecho Constitucional Comparado (Tirant lo Blanc).

He speaks four languages: Spanish, English, French, and Italian. Married with four children.

GIAVARINI Adalberto Rodriguez Adalberto Rodríguez Giavarini is president of the Argentine Council for International Relations and former Minister of Foreign Affairs of the Argentine Republic. He previously served as a member of the National Congress, as Minister of Economy (Buenos Aires City) and as Undersecretary of the Treasury and Secretary of Defense at the beginning of the current democratic period. Rodríguez Giavarini is a member of the advisory council and grand jury at Konex Foundation, and runs the foreign affairs chapter of the Political Action Network Foundation. Rodríguez Giavarini also chairs the executive board of his consulting group specializing in national, regional, and international political economy as well as many private universities. He is Vice President of the National Academy of Education in Argentina, and is the treasurer of the board of directors at the National Academy of Moral and Political Sciences. Rodríguez Giavarini has participated as a main speaker in several seminars and conferences in Argentina and abroad. He has published numerous essays and articles in national and international newspapers and magazines. He is a professor honoris causa at Soka University, Japan, and has been decorated by sixteen countries. Rodríguez Giavarini received his degree in economics from the University of Buenos Aires, where he later returned as professor of macroeconomics.

GOUNDEN Vasu Dr. Vasu Gounden established the African Center for the Constructive Resolution of Disputes (ACCORD) in 1992. It is today a globally recognized conflict management institute and the largest in Africa. In 2018 Vasu established Global Peace (www.globalpeace.me) to mobilize a global constituency to strengthen multilateralism and to build a better world.

Over the last 28 years Vasu has worked in some of the most protracted and violent conflicts in Africa, including Burundi, the Democratic Republic of the Congo (DRC), Liberia, Sierra Leone, Somalia, and Sudan. He has prepared conflicting parties in negotiations and has supported the mediation efforts of former Presidents Obasanjo of Nigeria, Masire of Botswana, Chissano of Mozambique, and former South African Presidents Mandela, Mbeki and Zuma. He has also been involved in assisting parties in Madagascar with their negotiation strategy development.

Vasu serves on the Boards of several Institutions across the world involved in conflict management. He has addressed the UN Security Council on three separate occasions. He was recognized in 2000 by the World Economic Forum as one of its Global Leaders of Tomorrow for his work in peace and security, and was awarded with an honorary doctorate in social sciences by the University of KwaZulu-Natal in 2016 for his contribution to the field of peace and security.

HASSAN Idayat Idayat Hassan holds an LL.M. in Legal Theory from the European Academy of Legal Theory in Brussels. She is interested in democracy, accountability, peace and security, and transitional justice in West Africa. She has served as the Deputy Regional Coordinator with the Movement Against Corruption and has held Fellowships in several universities across Europe and America including SOAS and Yale. As Director of the Center for Democracy and Development she is the key figure in advancing the institution's mission of advancing West African democracy and development.

KAMAT Satish Satish Kamat is a Chartered Accountant with over thirty-eight years of corporate experience in finance and general management functions. His significant employments have been with Glaxo India as its Corporate Treasurer, with Cargill Inc. as a member of its founding and leadership team in India, and as a Director of Cargill India. He has held senior positions in various businesses of the Mahindra Group. He is an independent Director on the board of LIC Mutual Fund Asset Management Limited. He has been associated with Indian Council on Global Relations—Gateway House, from its inception and is a member of its Executive Board. He is currently associated with various non-for-profits institutions.

KOSHERBAYEVA Aigel B. Vice-Rector for Strategic Development, Research and International Partnership Doctor of Economics, Associate Professor. In 1990 Aigul Kosherbayeva graduated from the Faculty of Philosophy and Economics of Kirov Kazakh State University (now Al-Farabi Kazakh National University) majoring in political economy. Aigul Kosherbayeva began her career in 1991 as a research assistant at the Department of Economic Theory at Al-Farabi Kazakh National University. From 1995 to 2001 she worked as the lecturer at the Department of International Economic Relations, from 2001 to 2002 as the Director of the Center for the World Market Studies at the RSBSE "Economic Research Institute," from 2005 to 2012 as the Director of the project analysis and evaluation group of "Kazmunaygas Consulting," Senior Manager of LLP "United Chemical Company" of JSC "Samruk-Kazyna," Director of the Center for the development of manufacturing industries at JSC "Kazakhstan Institute of Industry Development."

Since 2014 she has been working at the Academy of Public Administration under the President of the Republic of Kazakhstan as an Associate Professor (part-time), a full-time Professor at the Institute of Management. From December 2016 to February 2018 Aigul Kosherbayeva worked as the Vice-Rector for Strategic Development, Research and International Partnership. From February to September 2018 she worked as the Director of the Institute for Applied Research at the Academy of Public Administration under the President of the Republic of Kazakhstan. In September 2018 she was appointed as the Vice-Rector for Strategic Development, Research, and International Partnership of the Academy of Public Administration under the President of the Republic of Kazakhstan.

KRAMER Andreas R. Andreas Kraemer, Founder & Director Emeritus of Ecologic Institute in Berlin, Germany, and Chairman (pro bono) of Ecologic Institute US in Washington, DC, is currently Senior Fellow of the Center for International Governance Innovation (CIGI) in Waterloo (Ontario), non-executive Director of the Fundação Oceano Azul in

Lisboa (Portugal), and Visiting Assistant Professor of Political Science and Adjunct Professor of German Studies at Duke University. He is also Initiator and Convenor of the Arctic Summer College and Advisory Board Member of The Arctic Institute. His research focuses on the role and functions of science-based policy institutes or "think tanks" in theory and the practice in different political systems, the interactions among policy domains and international relations, and global governance on environment, resources, climate, and energy.

R. Andreas Kraemer is also Manager (pro bono) of the Konrad von Moltke Fund and active as Co-Chairman of the Advisory Board of OekoWorld, which sets global investment criteria for ethical and "green" investment funds or mutual trusts, and Member of the Practice Board for the Master Course on "Strategic Sustainability Management" at the University of Applied Sciences in Eberswalde (HNE Eberswalde). Since 1993, R. Andreas Kraemer has lectured an annual full-term course on European integration and environmental policy for the Duke in Berlin Program of Duke University. From 1995 to 2015, R. Andreas Kraemer served as Scientific Director and Chief Executive Officer of Ecologic Institute, Berlin, Germany and concurrently from 2008 to 2013 in the same function at Ecologic Institute, Vienna, Austria. In 2015, he was Visiting Scholar at the Massachusetts Institute of Technology (MIT), Center for Energy and Environmental Policy Research (CEEPR). From 2011 to 2014, R. Andreas Kraemer was Speaker of Ecornet, the Ecological Research Network of independent, trans-disciplinary environmental research institutes in Germany. From 2015 to 2018, he was Senior Fellow at the Institute for Advanced Sustainability Studies (IASS), Potsdam, Germany, and in 2018 and 2019 Mercator Senior Fellow of the Mercator Foundation, Essen, Germany.

KRIPALANI Manjeet Manjeet Kripalani is the co-founder of Gateway House: Indian Council on Global Relations, and acts as the executive director of the institution. Prior to the founding of Gateway House, Kripalani was India Bureau chief of Businessweek magazine from 1996 to 2009. During her extensive career in journalism (Businessweek, Worth and Forbes magazines, New York), she has won several awards, including the Gerald Loeb Award, the George Polk Award, Overseas Press Club and Daniel Pearl Awards. Kripalani was the 2006–2007 Edward R. Murrow Press Fellow at the Council on Foreign Relations, New York, which inspired her to found Gateway House. Her political career spans being the deputy press secretary to Steve Forbes during his first run in 1995–1996 as Republican candidate for US President in New Jersey, to being press secretary for the Lok Sabha campaign for independent candidate Meera Sanyal in 2008 and 2014 in Mumbai. Kripalani holds two bachelor's degrees from Bombay University (Bachelor of Law, Bachelor of Arts in English and History) and a master's degree in International Affairs from Columbia University, New York. She sits on the executive board of Gateway House and is a member of the Rotary Club of Bombay.

LAZAREVIC Milena Milena Lazarevic is one of the founders and Program Director at the European Policy Center (CEP), independent, nonprofit think tank based in Belgrade, Serbia. As the Program Director, she is in charge of the overall programmatic strategy of CEP as well as developing and managing the quality assurance system and processes within the organization. She also takes the lead on numerous good governance-related projects implemented by CEP.

Milena is a proven expert in the field of public administration reform, in Serbia and the Western Balkan region. Between May 2014 and March 2015, in addition to her work in CEP, she also acted as the Special Adviser to the Serbian Deputy Prime Minister in charge of public administration reform. As a consultant, she has worked for SIGMA/OECD, Regional School for Public Administration (ReSPA), the World Bank and several major international consultancy companies. Before co-founding CEP, she worked for almost six years as a civil servant in the Serbian administration, dealing with public administration reform and administrative capacities for EU accession, first in the EU Integration Office of the Serbian Government (SEIO) and later in the Ministry of Public Administration.

As a Soros scholar, Milena obtained her BA degree in European Studies and International Relations *magna cum laude* at the American University in Bulgaria (AUBG), after which she completed with honors an advanced MA program in European studies at the College of Europe, on a King Baudouin Foundation scholarship. She later also graduated from the Diplomatic Academy of the Ministry of Foreign Affairs of Serbia and obtained an MA in European Administrative Law at the Law Faculty of the Belgrade University.

LEACH Melissa Melissa Leach is the Director of the Institute of Development Studies (IDS). She co-founded and co-directed the ESRC STEPS

(Social, Technological, and Environmental Pathways to Sustainability) Center from 2006 to 2014, with its pioneering pathways approach to innovation, sustainability, and development issues. She is a Fellow of the British Academy and was awarded a CBE in 2017 for services to social science.

A social anthropologist and geographer, her interdisciplinary, policy-engaged research in Africa and beyond links environment, agriculture, health, technology and gender, with particular interests in knowledge, power, and the politics of science and policy processes. Among external roles, she was vice-chair of the Science Committee of Future Earth 2012–2017, lead author of the 2016 World Social Science Report 2016 on Challenging Inequalities and the UN Women's World Survey on the Role of Women in economic Development 2014. She is a member of the International Panel of Experts on Sustainable Food Systems (IPES-Food) and the Strategic Coherence of ODA Research (SCOR) Board.

LIMA Marlos Marlos Lima is the Executive Director for Latin America and Deputy Director for International Affairs at FGV. He is also a professor on postgraduate courses in Strategic Planning, Public Policies, Prospective Scenarios, Future Studies, and Decision Making under Uncertainty. Marlos has been involved in many projects in private and public initiatives abroad and in Brazil. He is an economist at Brazilian School of Economics, holds a master's degree in Public Administration and a Ph.D. at FGV. Marlos Lima is also visiting professor at many universities in Latin America, and founding member of Latin American Group for Public Administration (GLAP/IIAS), and American Academy of Management.

MAGRI Paolo Paolo Magri is Executive Vice President and Director of the Italian Institute for International Political Studies (ISPI) and Professor of International Relations at Bocconi University. He is also Member of the Strategic Committee of the Italian Minister of Foreign Affairs and Member of the Europe Policy Group of the World Economic Forum (Davos); member of the Strategic Committee of the Italian Minister of Foreign Affairs; Member of the Board of Directors of the Italy-China Foundation and of the Advisory Board of the Italian Entrepreneurial Association of the Lombardy region (Assolombarda). He is a regular speaker, writer and commentator to diverse media outlet on global issues, US foreign policy, Iran, and Middle East.

Previously, he served as Program Director to the UN Secretariat in New York and, up to 2005, as Director of International Affairs at Bocconi

University in Milan. He has also been consultant for several International Organizations and companies such as Italian Ministry of Foreign Affairs (Albania), European Union (Poland), Italcementi (Egypt).

He is author, among others, of: Big powers are back. What about Europe? (*ISPI, 2018*); Post-Vote Iran: Giving Engagement a Chance (*ISPI, 2017*); The Age of Uncertainty (*ISPI, 2017*); The Trump Era (*Mondadori, 2017*); Il mondo di Obama. (*Mondadori, 2016*); Twitter and Jihad. The Communication Strategy of ISIS (*Mondadori, 2016*); Le nuove crepe della governance mondiale. (*ISPI, 2016*); Iran After the Deal: The Road Ahead (*ISPI, 2015*); I BRICs e noi. (*ISPI, 2011*).

McGANN James James McGann is a Senior Lecturer of International Studies at the Lauder Institute, Director of the Think Tanks and Civil Societies Program and a Senior Fellow at the Fels Institute of Government at the University of Pennsylvania. Dr. McGann has served as a consultant and advisor to the World Bank; the United Nations; the Asian Development Bank; the United States Agency for International Development; the Soros, Rockefeller, MacArthur, Hewlett and Gates foundations; the Carnegie Corporation; and foreign governments on the role of nongovernmental, public policy and public engagement organizations in civil society. He has served as the Senior Vice President for the Executive Council on Foreign Diplomats, the Public Policy Program Officer for the Pew Charitable Trusts, the Assistant Director of the Institute of Politics, John F. Kennedy School of Government at Harvard University. He also served as a Senior Advisor to the Citizens' Network for Foreign Affairs and the Society for International Development. Dr. McGann earned his M.A. and Ph.D. from the University of Pennsylvania. He has authored over 15 books on think tanks and is the creator and editor of the annual Global Go To Think Tank Index.

MORILLAS Pol Pol Morillas is general director and Senior Research Fellow at CIDOB (Barcelona Center for International Affairs). He is a political scientist, holds a Ph.D. in Politics, Policies, and International Relations from the Universidad Autónoma de Barcelona (UAB) and a master's in International Relations from the London School of Economics. He is also an Associate Professor at the UAB, where he teaches European Foreign Policy and the Theory of International Relations, and a member of the Observatori de Política Exterior Europea. Previously, he has been Head of the Euro-Mediterranean Policies field at the European Institute of the Mediterranean (IEMed), Coordinator of the Political and Security Committee of the Council of the EU, and Advisor on External Action at the European Parliament. His numerous published research papers for academic journals and think tanks, like his opinion articles, cover the dynamics of European integration, the institutional developments of EU external action, the Common Foreign and Security Policy, the EU's security strategies and Euro-Mediterranean relations, among other subjects. His latest book is Strategy-Making in the EU. From Foreign and Security Policy to External Action published by Palgrave Macmillan.

MWONGERA Nahashon Nahashon M. Mwongera is a Senior Policy Analyst at the Kenya Institute for Public Policy Research and Analysis (KIPPRA). Over the last 15 years he has worked with both public and private sector institutions in conducting public policy research and analysis; reviewing and developing new products and services for financial service providers; writing strategic plans, development blueprints, and technical reports. His research interests include role of think tanks in supporting the evidence-to-policy linkage; environment and natural resource management; tourism sector inclusive growth and development; mainstreaming inclusive green growth strategies and policies in development planning; micro, small, and medium enterprise sector development; macroeconomic and financial sector analysis. Prior to joining KIPPRA, Mr. Mwongera worked in the private sector for five years as a research manager and consultant focusing on project management, capacity building, design and development of financial products and services for commercial Banks, Microfinance Institutions, Savings and Credit Cooperatives to enhance uptake of financial services by the poor in Eastern and Central Africa.

Mr. Mwongera holds a Bachelor of Arts (Economics and Mathematics) degree from Egerton University in Kenya, a Master of Arts (Economics) degree from the University of Botswana and is currently a Ph.D. (Economics) student at Kenyatta University in Kenya. While at KIPPRA, over the last 10 years, he has written technical reports and published several public policy research papers, participated in research dissemination forums, workshops, policy round tables, policy taskforces and technical working groups. In 2019, he was part of the team that organized *The 6th Africa Think Tank Summit* convened at Nairobi on 24–26 April 2019 and commissioned by the African Capacity Building Foundation (ACBF) in partnership with the Government of Kenya and KIPPRA[1].

In addition, he was part of the KIPPRA team that organized *The 2nd Kenya Think Tanks Forum* in 2019; and the *Launch of the 14th Global Go-To Think Tank Index report* on 30th January 2020 at Nairobi in Kenya[2], produced by the Think Tank and Civil Societies Program (TTSCP) of the Lauder Institute at the University of Pennsylvania.

Some of his recent publications include the following: a chapter on *"Enhancing policy uptake in Africa: Role of think tanks,"* published in 2019 in the ACBF compendium on Lessons Notes on Capacity Development in Africa[3]; A discussion paper and policy brief on *"Coastal Tourism and Economic Inclusion in Indian Ocean Rim Association States"* published in 2018 with The South African Institute of International Affairs[4]; A journal article on *Assessment of Kenya's Tourism Source Markets*, published in 2015 in the Journal of Travel & Tourism Marketing[5]; Report on the Kenya Green Economy Strategy and Implementation Plan 2016–2030, produced in 2016 by the Government of Kenya with support from development partners (UNEP, WWF, AfDB and GiZ)[6]; and a working paper on *"Fiscal Policy Scoping Study for Kenya"* published in 2015 by the United Nations Environment Program (UNEP) under the "Fiscal Policy Reforms for Green Economy" project[7].

NGUGI Rose Dr. Rose Ngugi is the Executive Director of the Kenya Institute for Public Policy Research and Analysis (KIPPRA). She is involved in providing technical guidance and capacity building on policy and strategy formulation to the Government of Kenya and other stakeholders, with the overall aim of contributing to the achievement of national development goals. Before then, she was a Senior Advisor in the Office of Executive Director, Africa Group 1, International Monetary Fund, and Washington, DC. Dr. Ngugi has been a member of Central Bank of Kenya, Monetary Policy Committee and has vast teaching experience in the University of Nairobi, School of Economics. Dr. Ngugi has published widely. Her research interests are in public policy, financial sector, investments, reforms, and institutional issues. She holds a Ph.D. from Business School Birmingham University, UK specializing in Financial Markets, a Masters and Bachelors degree in Economics from the University of Nairobi, Kenya.

OKEKE-UZODIKE Ufo Dr. Okeke-Uzodike pursued his early education in Nigeria and continued his studies at Wake Forest University, the University of South Carolina, and the University of North Carolina, Chapel Hill. He earned his Ph.D. in Political Science with subfields in international political economy, international relations, US Foreign Policy, Conflict Transformation, and Peace Studies in Comparative Politics. His areas of interest are peace, justice, security, and development in Africa. His publications have addressed foreign policy, regional integration, democratization, economic development, women's rights, religion, and conflict transformation.

Dr. Okeke-Uzodike has acted as the Dean of the School of Social Sciences at the University of KwaZulu-Natal South Africa. He is also the editor of Afrikka: Journal of Politics, Economics, and Society as well as Ubuntu: Journal of Conflict Transformation. As Executive Director of the African Heritage Institution, one of Africa's most well-respected think tanks, Dr. Okeke-Uzodike leads the institution towards its goal of contributing to African democracy and prosperity.

ORTIZ Veronica Ms. Ortiz graduated from Law School at the Universidad Panamericana in Mexico City and pursued graduate courses on Law and Society at Oxford University.

She started her legal practice in the international firm Baker & McKenzie and then joined public service in the Legal Office of the President, the Ministry of Commerce and the Mexican Banking and Securities Commission.

From 2008 to 2012 she was a consulting partner with GEA, Grupo de Economistas y Asociados. Since 2013 she was an independent political analyst for domestic and international corporations and audiences.

She was appointed Executive Director of the Mexican Council on Foreign Relations (COMEXI) on October 2019.

She is also a member of the National Consulting Committees for the Mexican Institute of Finance Executives (IMEF) and of the Private Sector Economic Studies Center (CEESP/CCE).

She writes a biweekly editorial for El Heraldo de México newspaper. As TV anchor she co-hosts along with journalist Leonardo Curzio the series "Incursionando" for the Mexican Congress public network.

PAIK Haksoon Dr. Haksoon Paik is President of the Sejong Institute, the leading independent think tank in the Republic of Korea (South Korea). He is a member of Board of Directors of the Kim Dae-jung Peace Center—the memorial center for the late South Korean President Kim Dae-jung, the Nobel Peace Prize laureate in 2000. He was formerly an advisor in various capacities to South Korea's Ministry of Unification,

Ministry of Foreign Affairs, and National Assembly. He was the Executive Director of the Seoul-Washington Forum, the Chairman of the Policy Committee of the Korea Council for Reconciliation and Cooperation, a news commentator for the Korean Broadcasting System (KBS), and a columnist for major Korean national newspapers. He was a Vice President of Korean Political Science Association and also a Vice President of the Korean Association of North Korean Studies.

Dr. Haksoon Paik earned his Ph.D. in political science from the University of Pennsylvania and was a post-doctoral fellow at Korea Center, Harvard University. He has written extensively on North Korean politics, inter-Korean relations, North Korea–United States relations, and North Korean nuclear and missile issues. He is author of numerous books and monographs written in Korean, including: *Park Geun-hye Administration's Policy on North Korea and Unification: Comparison with Previous Administrations (2018), North Korean Politics in the Kim Jong Un Era, 2012–2014: Ideas, Identities, and Structures* (2015), *The U.S.–North Korea Relations During President Obama's Second Term, 2013 2014: Threat of the Use of Nuclear Weapons and the Collapse of Relations* (2014), *The U.S.-North Korea Relations during President Obama's First Term, 2009–2012* (2012), and *The History of Power in North Korea: Ideas, Identities, and Structures* (2010). His most recent published articles and book chapters include: "Inside Kim Jong Un's Assertive Mind" (2017) and "Kim Jong Un's Leadership in Diplomacy, Security Affairs, and Unification" (2017).

PENG Yuan Dr. Yuan Peng, Research Professor and Doctoral Advisor, is the President of China Institutes of Contemporary International Relations (CICIR). He earned his Ph.D. in World History in 1997 from Northeast Normal University. He was once a visiting scholar at the Atlantic Council (1999–2000) and Brookings Institution (2003–2004). Previously, he served as CICIR's Vice President and Director of CICIR's Institute of American Studies. He has been engaged in American studies for decades, particularly focusing on US foreign policy, Sino–United States relations and Asia Pacific security. He is the author or editor of several books such as American Think Tanks and Their Attitudes toward China (Current Affairs Press, 2003), China and the US Accommodating in the Asia Pacific: China, America, and the Third Parties (Current Affairs Press, 2013), From Westphalia to a New World Order (China CITIC Press, 2016). He was elected to be Vice-Chairman of Chinese Society of

International Relations, Executive Director of Chinese Society of American Studies and Executive Director of All China Association for Taiwan Studies. He is fluent in English.

RANCHOK Anatoliy Anatoliy Rachok is the Director General of the Razumkov Centre, one of the oldest and most renowned nongovernmental think tank in Ukraine. He has been in this role since 1999. The Razumkov Centre was founded in 1994 as the interdisciplinary analytical institute with the objective of research on various aspects of national security.

After his appointment Anatoliy Rachok focused efforts on creating the environment for steady Center's performance irrespective of political and socioeconomic changes in the country, establishing balanced project activities of different Center's programs, choosing staff with high-level expertise and practical experience of public sector employment and ensuring regular publication of the Razumkov Center's "National Security and Defence" journal. Different elements specific to the top think tanks of the United States and Germany set an example for the development of the Centre. His long-standing commitment has led the Razumkov Center to leading positions in Ukraine and Central and Eastern Europe, and to the list of TOP-50 best think tanks in the world.

Mr. Rachok graduated from Romano-Germanic Department of the National Taras Shevchenko University of Kyiv. After studies he started public service in the information and publishing sphere, at the end of 80s he governed the Kyiv Agency of the International Association of Detective and Political novels and during 1994–1999 he served as the Deputy Director of Konrad Adenauer Foundation Office in Ukraine, assisting civil society formation in Ukraine, e.g., formation of political parties, youth organizations, nongovernmental think tanks.

SARAN Samir Dr. Saran earned his Bachelors in Electrical and Electronics Engineering from Manipal Institute of Technology before going on to receive his Masters in Media Studies from the London Institute of Economics and Political Science. He completed his Doctoral Studies at the Global Sustainability Institute.

As a notable author on Indian issues, Dr. Saran has written four books. In 2011 his first book, *Re-imagining the Indus: Mapping Media Reporting in India and Pakistan* studied water management coverage in Indian and Pakistani media. Then in 2016 he published both *Prospects for EU-India Security Cooperation* and *India's Climate Change Identity: Between Reality and Perception*. His most recent work, *The Road to Universal Health Coverage* was released in 2018.

As President of the Observer Research Foundation, one of Asia's most influential think tanks, Dr. Saran sets high-level strategies for all the organization's work. He is the co-founder and curator of the *Raisina Dialogue*, the most respected platform for Indian geopolitics and geoeconomics. As Chair of CyFy, he leads India's premier cybersecurity and internet governance conference. Dr. Saran engages with the global community through his roles on the Global Commission for the Stability of Cyberspace both the World Economic Forum's Global Future Council on Geopolitics and its South Asia Advisory Board.

SCHMIDT Roland Dr. Roland Schmidt holds the position of the Friedrich-Ebert-Foundation's Secretary-General.

FES is an independent, private and nonprofit foundation under German law. As a political foundation it is affiliated to the Social Democracy. Its mission is the contribution to political information and debate in Germany and abroad in order to foster the progress of society and democracy and Germany's good relations with foreign countries. The FES-network comprises branch offices in more than 100 countries worldwide. As a political think tank the foundation provides scientific policy advice and supplies research at the interface between science and politics.

After having passed the second bar examination Dr. Schmidt worked initially as Assistant Lecturer at the University of Kiel. He started his professional career in the Federal Ministry of Finances which he ended as Under Secretary. In the context of the German reunification he was posted to the EU Commission in Brussels. Subsequently he served as Administrative Director and Legal Adviser to the Social Democratic Party in the German Bundestag.

Dr. Schmidt majored in law and social sciences and was awarded a doctorate in law by the Christian- Albrechts-Universität of Kiel. He published essays on European Law.

SHULL Aaron As CIGI's managing director and general counsel, Aaron Shull acts as a strategic liaison between CIGI's research programs and other departments while managing CIGI's legal affairs and advising senior management on a range of legal, operational, and policy matters.

A member of CIGI's executive team, Aaron provides guidance and advice on matters of strategic and operational importance, while working closely with partners and other institutions to further CIGI's mission. He also serves as corporate secretary.

Prior to joining CIGI, Aaron practiced law for a number of organizations, focusing on international, regulatory, and environmental law. He has taught courses at the University of Ottawa, Faculty of Law, and the Norman Paterson School of International Affairs and was previously a staff editor for the Columbia Journal of Transnational Law.

Aaron graduated from the University of Waterloo, placing first in his class as a departmental scholar, with a B.A. (honors) in history and political science. His keen interest in international affairs and political history led him to pursue an M.A. in international affairs at Carleton University's Norman Paterson School of International Affairs, where he graduated with distinction. He concurrently pursued his LL.B. from the University of Ottawa, where he graduated cum laude with first-class honors. Aaron received his LL.M. from Columbia Law School, where he graduated as a Harlan Fiske Stone scholar.

Aaron lives in the Waterloo Region, where he spends time with his family.

TANGKITVANICH Somkiat Dr. Somkiat Tangkitvanich is the President of the Thailand Development Research Institute (TDRI) since 2012. His areas of expertise include Media and Telecommunications Policy, Economic Analysis of Laws, International Trade and Investment Policy, and Research and Development Policy. An Eisenhower fellow, he has received numerous awards in research. He was the main architect of the establishment of Thai PBS, the first public television broadcaster in Southeast Asia and many media laws in Thailand. Under his leadership, TDRI was nominated "Person of the Year" in 2012 by the Bangkok Post.

Dr. Somkiat, upon completion of his B.E. (summa cum laude) in Computer Engineering from Chulalongkorn University, was awarded the Monbusho scholarship from the government of Japan. He earned his M.S. and Ph.D. in Computer Science from the Tokyo Institute of Technology.

TAY Simon SC Associate Professor Simon Tay is Chairman of the Singapore Institute of International Affairs. He is concurrently a tenured Associate Professor, teaching international law at the National University of Singapore Faculty of Law. He is also Senior Consultant at WongPartnership.

His book, Asia Alone: the Dangerous Post Crisis Divide from America (Wiley 2010) was well-reviewed in the Economist, Financial Times and regional media. His commentaries feature regularly in regional newspapers. Professor Tay is also a prize-winning author with five books of stories and poems. In 2010, his novel City of Small Blessings was awarded the Singapore Literature Prize. He recently published a collection of short stories titled "Middle and First".

From 1992 to 2008, he served in a number of public appointments for Singapore. These included serving as Chairman of Singapore's National Environment Agency; and as an independent Nominated Member of Parliament (1997–2001). In 2006, Professor Tay received a National Day Award.

VELDHUIS Niels Niels Veldhuis is President of the Fraser Institute, Canada's top ranked think tank and among the top 15 globally, according to the University of Pennsylvania's *Global Go To Think Tanks Report*. Niels has written six books and more than 50 peer-reviewed studies on a wide range of economic topics. In 2011, he was awarded (along with his co-authors) the prestigious Sir Antony Fisher International Memorial Award for the best-selling book, *The Canadian Century*.

Niels is in high demand for his opinions and perspectives on major economic and social issues, appearing regularly on radio and television programs across Canada and in the United States. He has written more than 200 commentaries that have appeared in over 50 newspapers including the *Globe and Mail, Wall Street Journal, National Post*, and the Economist.

Niels is best known for his ability to explain matters of economics and government policy in a down-to-earth manner, making them easily understandable. He travels widely across North America, speaking to business groups, corporate gatherings, voluntary organizations, and students. In 2011, Niels led a discussion between former US Presidents Bill Clinton and George W. Bush at the Surrey Economic Forum.

In 2010, he was named one of Vancouver's Top 40 under 40 by Business in Vancouver. Niels is a member of the Young Presidents Organization.

WANG Huiyao Dr. Huiyao (Henry) WANG is the Founder and President of Center for China and Globalization (CCG), the leading Chinese nongovernment think tank. Chinese Premier Li Keqiang appointed Dr. Wang as a Counselor of China State Council, China's cabinet in 2015.

Dr. Wang is also Vice-Chairman of China Association for International Economic Cooperation Association of the Ministry of Commerce and Chairman of China global Talent Society under Ministry of Human Resources and Social Security. In addition, he is the Dean of Institute of Development Studies of China Southwestern University of Finance and Economics and a Vice-Chairman of China Western (Overseas) Returned Scholars Association.

Dr. Wang is a steering committee member of Paris Peace Forum initiated by French President Macron. He also sits on the Migration Advisory Board of International Organization of Migration (IOM) of the United Nation. He is also a member of Yale University Asia Development Advisory Council and a member of Duke Kunshan University Advisory Council.

Dr. Wang served as an official with Chinese Ministry of Foreign Economic Relations and Trade in charge of Chinese companies going global. He had also worked as Director for Asia at SNC-Lavalin in Montreal and served as Chief Trade Representative of Canada Quebec Government office in Hong Kong and greater China.

Dr. Wang pursued his Ph.D. studies in International business and global management at University of Western Ontario and University of Manchester. He was a Senior Fellow at Harvard Kennedy School and a Visiting Fellow at Brookings Institution as well as a Senior Fellow at Asia Pacific Foundation of Canada. He has taught at Peking University, Tsinghua University and University of Western Ontario as adjunct professor. He has also authored and edited over 70 books and more than 100 articles and papers in both Chinese and English on global trade, global governance, global migration, China outbound and inbound investment, Chinese Diasporas, and Chinese think tanks.

Dr. Wang is also frequently invited to speak at international conferences, such as Davos World Economic Forum, Munich Security Conference, Paris Peace Forum, China Development Forum, Munk Debates, Berlin Policy Forum, Milken Global Forum and so on.

WOLFF Guntram Guntram Wolff is Director of Bruegel. His research focuses on the European economy and governance, on fiscal and monetary policy and global finance. He regularly testifies to the European Finance Ministers' ECOFIN meeting, the European Parliament, the German Parliament (Bundestag), and the French Parliament (Assemblée

Nationale). From 2012 to 2016, he was a member of the French Prime Minister's Conseil d'Analyze Économique.

Guntram Wolff is also a member of the Solvay Brussels School's international advisory board of the Brussels Free University. He joined Bruegel from the European Commission, where he worked on the macroeconomics of the euro area and the reform of euro-area governance. Prior to joining the Commission, he was coordinating the research team on fiscal policy at Deutsche Bundesbank. He also worked as an adviser to the International Monetary Fund.

He holds a Ph.D. from the University of Bonn; he studied economics at the Universities of Bonn, Toulouse, Pittsburgh and Passau, and he taught economics at the University of Pittsburgh. He published a number of articles in various acclaimed economic journals.

Latest publications include: *From climate change to cyber-attacks: Incipient financial-stability risks for the euro area*, *Hybrid and cybersecurity threats and the European Union's financial system*, and *The threats to the European Union's economic sovereignty*.

YADLIN Amos Amos Yadlin was named Executive Director of Tel Aviv University's Institute for National Security Studies (INSS) in November 2011, after more than 40 years of service in the Israel Defense Forces, nine of which he was a member of the IDF General Staff.

From 2006 to 2010, Maj. Gen. (ret.) Yadlin served as the IDF's chief of Military Intelligence. Prior to that, he served as the IDF attaché to the United States. In February 2002, he earned the rank of major general and was named commander of the IDF Military Colleges and the National Defense College.

Maj. Gen. (ret.) Yadlin, a former deputy commander of the Israel Air Force, has commanded two fighter squadrons and two airbases. He has also served as Head of IAF Planning Department (1990–1993). He accumulated about 5000 flight hours and flew more than 250 combat missions behind enemy lines. He participated in the Yom Kippur War (1973), Operation Peace for Galilee (1982), and Operation Tamuz—the destruction of the Osirak nuclear reactor in Iraq (1981).

Maj. Gen. (ret.) Yadlin earned a B.A. with honors in economics and business administration from Ben-Gurion University of the Negev (1985). He also holds a Master's degree in Public Administration from the John F. Kennedy School of Government at Harvard University.

Maj. Gen. (ret.) Yadlin's primary areas of expertise and major topics on which he has written include strategy and national security; the changes in the Middle East; the Iranian nuclear challenge; United States–Israel relations; force buildup and the defense budget; intelligence; cyber-related challenges; civil–military relations, and the military ethics of fighting terror.

YERLAN Abil Rector of the Academy of Public Administration under the President of the Republic of Kazakhstan.

Born on September 18, 1973 in Zhezkazgan. In 1990 he graduated from Kazakh secondary school No. 8 in Zhezkazgan. In 1995 he graduated from Zhezkazgan Institute of Mining and Technology.

Some of his work experience include becoming head of Economy Management Department, Institute of Governance, Academy of Public Administration under the President of the Republic of Kazakhstan, Astana (July 2013–November 2016) and acting Director, Institute of Governance, Academy of Public Administration under the President of the Republic of Kazakhstan, Astana (November 2016–January 2017).

He is a Candidate of Economic Science and has Honorary Employee of Education award.

BIBLIOGRAPHY

INTRODUCTION

Abelson, Donald E. 2000. Do Think Tanks Matter? Opportunities, Constraints and Incentives for Think Tanks in Canada and the United States. *Global Society* 14 (2): 213–236.

Ahmad, Mahmood. 2008. US Think Tanks and the Politics of Expertise: Role, Value and Impact. *The Political Quarterly* 79 (4): 529–555.

Dabrowski, Marek. 2014. Center for Social and Economic Research (CASE): Think Tanks in the Era of Globalization. In *How Think Tanks Shape Social Development Policies*, ed. J.G. McGann, A. Viden, and J. Rafferty, 213–230. Philadelphia, PA: University of Pennsylvania Press.

Dickinson, Paul. 1972. *Think Tanks*. New York: Atheneum.

Dror, Yehezkel. 1980. Think Tanks: A New Invention in Government. In *Making Bureaucracies Work*, ed. Carol H. Weiss and Allen H. Barton, 139–152. Beverly Hills, London: Sage.

Hary, Nicoletta M. 1996. American Philanthropy in Europe: The Collaboration of the Carnegie Endowment for International Peace with the Vatican Library. *Libraries & Culture* 31 (2): 364–379.

Hernando, M.G., P. Hartwig, and D. Stone. 2018a. Think Tanks in 'Hard Times'—The Global Financial Crisis and Economic Advice. *Policy and Society* 37 (2): 125–139.

Levien, Roger E. 1969. Independent Public Policy Analysis Organization—A Major Social Invention. In *Rand Papers Series*, ed. Rand Corporation. Santa Monica: Rand Corporation.

McGann, James G. 2006. Think Tanks and Civil Societies 2006 Survey. University of Pennsylvania.

© The Editor(s) (if applicable) and The Author(s), under exclusive
license to Springer Nature Switzerland AG 2021
J. McGann, *The Future of Think Tanks and Policy Advice
Around the World*, https://doi.org/10.1007/978-3-030-60379-3

McGann, James G. 2008. *Think Tank Assessment Study; Initial Global Trend Report*. Philadelphia: Think Tanks and Civil Societies Program, Foreign Policy Research Institute.

McGann, James G. 2019. *2018 Global Go to Think Tank Index Report*. Philadelphia: Think Tanks and Civil Societies Program, University of Pennsylvania.

McGann, James G. 2020. *2019 Global Go to Think Tank Index Report*. Philadelphia: Think Tanks and Civil Societies Program, University of Pennsylvania.

McGann, James G., and R. Sabatini. 2010. *Global Think Tanks: Policy Networks and Governance*. New York: Routledge.

McGann, James G., and L.C. Whelan. 2020. *Global Think Tanks: Policy Networks and Governance*. New York: Taylor & Francis.

Montoya, S., and R. Swanger. 2007. Ideas for Policymakers: Enhancing the Impact of Think Tanks. *Pardee RAND Graduate School: Policy Insight* 1 (2): 1–2.

Orlans, Harold. 1972. *The Nonprofit Research Institute: Its Operation, Origins, Problems, and Prospects*. New York: McGraw-Hill.

Pacheco-Vega, Raul. (2015). Transnational Environmental Activism in North America: Wielding Soft Power through Knowledge Sharing? *Review of Policy Research, 32*(1): 146–162.

Schneider, Jiri. 2003. Globalizations and Think Tanks; Security Policy Networks. In *Proceedings from the SAREM International Seminar*, May 30, Istanbul, Turkey.

Stone, Diane. 2013. *Capturing the Political Imagination: Think Tanks and the Policy Process*. London: Routledge.

Struyk, R.J. 2002. Management of Transnational Think Tank Networks. *International Journal of Politics, Culture, and Society* 15 (4): 625–638.

Troy, T. 2012. Devaluing the Think Tank. *National Affairs*, Winter 2012. https://www.nationalaffairs.com. Accessed 23 March 2020.

Weaver, Kent R. 1989. The Changing World of Think Tanks. *Political Science and Politics* 22 (3): 563–578.

Wihardja, M.M. 2014. Center for Strategic and International Studies (CSIS): Shaping Development Policy in a Globalized World. In *How Think Tanks Shape Social Development Policies*, ed. J.G. McGann, A. Viden, and J. Rafferty, 185–199. Philadelphia, PA: University of Pennsylvania Press.

Winthrop, Rebecca. 2014. Brookings Institution: The Case for Global Education. In *How Think Tanks Shape Social Development Policies*, ed. J.G. McGann, A. Viden, and J. Rafferty, 65–75. Philadelphia, PA: University of Pennsylvania Press.

Submissions

Abelson, Donald E. From Generation to Generation, Reflections on the Evolution of Think Tanks.

African Capacity Building Foundation. 2017. The ACBF Strategy for 2017–2021: Skilled People and Strong Institutions Transforming Africa.

African Capacity Building Foundation. 2019. 6th Africa Think Tank Summit: Tackling Implementation Challenges for Africa's Sustainable Development. In *Proceedings of the Summit*, 24–26 April 2019, Nairobi, Kenya.

African Union. 2013. Agenda 2063. https://au.int/en/agenda2063/overview.

Asia Maritime Transparency Initiative. 9 May 2018. An Accounting of China's Deployments to the Spratly Islands. The Center for Strategic and International Studies. https://amti.csis.org/accounting-chinas-deployments-spratly-islands/.

Barnes-Huggins, Tiffany. 2019. New Knowledge Briefs on Lessons from the Think Tank Initiative. Think Tank Initiative. http://www.thinktankinitiative.org/blog/new-knowledge-briefs-lessons-think-tank-initiative.

Bennett, Amanda. 5 October 2015. Are Think Tanks Obsolete? *Washington Post: In Theory*. https://www.washingtonpost.com/news/in-theory/wp/2015/10/05/are-think-tanks-obsolete/. Accessed 7 February 2020.

Bergamini, Enrico. 19 December 2019. 2019 on #econtwitter, in a Million Tweets. Bruegel. https://bruegel.org/2019/12/2019-on-econtwitter-in-a-million-tweets/.

Cairney, Paul. 2016. *The Politics of Evidence-Based Policy Making*. London: Springer.

Carafano, James Jay. 21 October 2015. Think-Tanks Aren't Going Extinct. But They Have to Evolve. *The National Interest*. https://nationalinterest.org/feature/think-tanks-arent-going-extinct-they-have-evolve-14137. Accessed 8 February 2020.

Centers for Disease Control and Prevention. 31 January 2019. Lassa Fever. https://www.cdc.gov/vhf/lassa/index.html.

Centre for International Governance Innovation. 2019. CIGI-Ipsos Global Survey on Internet Security and Trust. https://www.cigionline.org/internet-survey-2019.

CNBC. Asia-Pacific News: Southeast Asia. https://www.cnbc.com/id/10000021.

Dalberg. 2013. *Evaluation of ACBF Supported Policy Centres and Think Tanks in Sub-Saharan Africa*. Harare: African Capacity Building Foundation.

Desch, Michael C. 27 February 2019. How Political Science Became Irrelevant. The Chronicle of Higher Education. https://www.chronicle.com/article/How-Political-Science-Became/245777.

European Union. June 2016. Shared Vision, Common Action: A Stronger Europe. http://eeas.europa.eu/archives/docs/top_stories/pdf/eugs_review_web.pdf.

Everyaction. Resource Library. https://www.everyaction.com/resource-library.

Fagan, Myron C. December 1966. CFR Completely Unmasked as "Illuminati" in U.S. No. 123. Cinema Educational Guild, Inc. https://www.amazon.com/CFR-Completely-Unmasked-Illuminati-US/dp/B005J1P0QE.

Financial Times. Britain Has Had Enough of Experts, Says Gove. https://www.ft.com/content/3be49734-29cb-11e6-83e4-abc22d5d108c.

Fransman, Jude, and Kate Newman. 2019. Rethinking Research Partnerships: Evidence and the Politics of Participation in Academic-INGO Research Partnerships for International Development. *Journal of International Development* (advance online publication).

Gatterer, Harry. The 5 Most Important Megatrends for Companies in the 2020s. zukunftsInstitut. https://www.zukunftsinstitut.de/artikel/die-5-wichtigsten-megatrends-fuer-unternehmern-in-den-2020ern/.

Geneva Environment Network. 2020. COVID-19 and the Environment. https://www.genevaenvironmentnetwork.org/covid19.html.

Georgalakis, James, and Pauline Rose. 2019. Introduction: Identifying the Qualities of Research-Policy Partnerships in International Development—A New Analytical Framework. *IDS Bulletin* 50: 1–20.

Google Trends. 2020. Interest over Time: Machine Learning. https://trends.google.com/trends/explore?date=all&q=machine%20learning. Accessed 1 February 2020.

Google Trends. 2020. Interest over Time: Web Scraping. https://trends.google.com/trends/explore?date=all&q=%2Fm%2F07ykbs. Accessed 1 February 2020.

Grose, Peter. 2006. *Continuing the Inquiry: The Council on Foreign Relations from 1921 to 1996*. New York, NY: Council on Foreign Relations Press.

Hernando, Marcos Gonzalez, Hartwig Pautz, and Diane Stone. 2018. Think Tanks in 'Hard Times'—The Global Financial Crisis and Economic Advice. *Policy and Society* 37 (2): 125–139.

Hildebrand, Philipp, and Tom Donilon. 2020. Davos Brief. Black-Rock Investment Institute. https://www.blackrock.com/ch/individual/en/insights/davos-brief-2020#sustainability.

Hills, Thomas T. Mass Proliferation of Information Evolving Beyond Our Control.

Hills, Thomas T. The Dark Side of Information Proliferation.

Hollis, Paul. 2011. *The Problem with the "Information Age" Is the Proliferation of Wrong Information*.

Hutter, Swen, & Edgar Grande. 2016. *Politicising Europe: Integration and Mass Politics*. Cambridge University Press, online publication March 2016. https://doi.org/10.1017/CBO9781316422991.002.

IPCC—Intergovernmental Panel on Climate Change. 2018. Global Warming of 1.5°C. An IPCC Special Report.

Jahn, Thomas, Matthias Bergmann, and Florian Keil. 2012. Transdisciplinarity: Between Mainstreaming and Marginalization. *Ecological Economics* 79: 1–10.

Jones, Basil. 2011. Linking Research to Policy: The African Development Bank as Knowledge Broker. African Development Bank. Working Paper No. 131.

Kelly, Eamonn. 2015. *Business Ecosystem Come of Age*. Westlake, TX: Deloitte University Press.

Kraemer, Andreas. 2014. The Ecologic Institute and Its Influence on Policies in Germany and the EU. In *How Think Tanks Shape Social Development Policies*, ed. James G. McGann, Anna Viden, and Jillian Rafferty, 129–147. Philadelphia, PA: University of Pennsylvania Press.

Kraemer, Andreas. 2017a. Digital Disruptions and the Emergence of Virtual Think Tanks. In *Phantom Ex Machina: Digital Disruption's Role in Business Model Transformation*, ed. A. Khare, R. Schatz, and B. Steward, 281–295. Cham, New York, Heidelberg, Berlin etc.: Springer.

Kraemer, Andreas. 2017b. The Co-Transformation of Energy & Transport: Outlook for the Wider Atlantic. In *Energy and Transportation in the Atlantic Basin: Implications for the European Union and Other Atlantic Actors*, ed. Paul Isbell and Eloy Alvarez Pelegry, 3–16. Washington, DC: Brookings Institution Press.

Lazarević, Milena, and Miloš Đinđić. 2018. Western Balkan PAR Monitor 2017/2018. Think for Europe Network. European Policy Center, 25–27. https://weber-cep.s3.amazonaws.com/data/attachment_978/western_balkan_par_monitor.pdf.

Le Miere, Jason. 27 November 2018. Donald Trump Says 'My Gut Tells Me More Sometimes Than Anybody Else's Brain Can Ever Tell Me.' Newsweek. https://www.newsweek.com/donald-trump-gut-brain-climate-change-fed-1234540.

Mandaville, A. 2004. *Legislatures and Civil Society: Potential Partners in Poverty Reduction*. Washington, DC: NDI.

McGann, James G. 2015. 2015 Global Think Tank Innovations Summit Report: The Think Tank of the Future Is Here Today. TTCSP Global and Regional Think Tanks Summit Reports. http://repository.upenn.edu/ttcsp_summitreports/15.

McGann, James G. 2016. *The Fifth Estate: Think Tanks, Public Policy, and Governance*. Washington, DC: Brookings Institution Press.

McGann, James G. 2017. 2017 Latin America Think Tank Summit Report: Global Challenges from a Regional Perspective: The Role of Think

Tanks in Latin America. TTCSP Global and Regional Think Tanks Summit Reports. https://repository.upenn.edu/cgi/viewcontent.cgi?article=1020&context=ttcsp_summitreports.

McGann, James G. 2018. 2018 Latin America Think Tank Summit Report: Think Tanks: A Bridge Over Troubled Waters and Turbulent Times. TTCSP Global and Regional Think Tanks Summit Reports. https://repository.upenn.edu/cgi/viewcontent.cgi?article=1022&context=ttcsp_summitreports.

McGann, James G. 2019. 2018 Global Go to Think Tank Index Report. TTCSP Global Go to Think Tank Index Reports. https://repository.upenn.edu/think_tanks/16.

McGann, James G. 2020. 2019 Global Go to Think Tank Index Report. TTCSP Global Go to Think Tank Index Reports.

McGann, James G., Landry Signé, and Monde Muyangwa. 2017. *The Crisis of African Think Tanks: Challenges and Solutions*. Brookings.

McGlade, Katriona, Lucy Olivia Smith, R. Andreas Kraemer, and Elizabeth Tedsen JD. 2016. Human Environmental Dynamics and Responses in the Atlantic Space. In *Atlantic Future. Shaping a New Hemisphere for the 21st century: Africa, Europe and the Americas*, ed. Jordi Bacaria and Laia Tarragona, 69–85. Barcelona: CIDOB.

Mendizabal, Enrique. 28 January 2013. Think tanks in Latin America: What Are They and What Drives Them? On Think Tanks. https://onthinktanks.org/articles/think-tanks-in-latin-america-what-are-they-and-what-drives-them/.

Mendizabal, Enrique. 2020. Reclaiming the Think Tank Space in the 2020s. On Think Tanks.

Mooney, Chris, and Brady Dennis. 29 January 2019. Trump Always Dismisses Climate Change When It's Cold: Not so Fast, Experts Say. *The Washington Post*. https://www.washingtonpost.com/climate-environment/2019/01/29/trump-always-dismisses-climate-change-when-its-cold-not-so-fast-experts-say/?noredirect=on&utm_term=.b8e827b30b86.

OECD. 2008. *Endowments for Think-Tanks in Developing Countries: What Role for Private Foundations and Official Donors?*. Paris: OECD.

Office of the Prime Minister. 13 December 2019. Minister of Foreign Affairs Mandate Letter. https://pm.gc.ca/en/mandate-letters/2019/12/13/minister-foreign-affairs-mandate-letter.

Ordoñez, Andrea. 29 August 2013. Five Challenges Think Tanks Face to Influence International Policy. *On Think Tanks*. https://onthinktanks.org/articles/five-challenges-think-tanks-face-to-influence-international-policy/.

Ordonez, Andrea. 2019. Development Effectiveness from Within: Emerging Issues from Recipient Countries. Southern Voice. http://southernvoice.org/development-effectiveness-from-within-emerging-issues-from-recipient-countries/.

Orion, Assaf, and Amos Yadlin. 14 May 2018. *Iran in the Nuclear Realm and Iran in Syria: A New State of Play*. The Institute for National Security Studies.   https://www.inss.org.il/publication/iran-nuclear-realm-iran-syria-new-state-play/?fbclid=IwAR0BQmTvWywAHNoSooPXW6IpsXgDWHq 1W3820V7o0O7NrTmwGrxZhhA8fL0.

Overl, IIndra, and Benjamin K. Sovacool. 2020. The Misallocation of Climate Research Funding. *Energy Research and Social Science*, 62: 101349.

PERFORM—Performing and Responsive Social Sciences. Serbia. http://www.perform.network/page/serbia/context.

Petropoulos, George. 24 December 2019. AI and the Productivity Paradox. Bruegel. https://bruegel.org/2019/12/ai-and-the-productivity-paradox/.

Petropoulos, George et al. 9 July 2019. Digitalisation and European welfare states. Bruegel. https://bruegel.org/2019/07/digitalisation-and-european-welfare-states/.

PWC. Megatrends. https://www.pwc.co.uk/issues/megatrends.html.

Renda, Guido, and Giacomo G.M. Cojazzi. 2018. Open Source Information Analysis in Support to Non-proliferation—A Systems Thinking Approach.

Revich, Boris A., and Marina A. Podolnaya. 21 November 2011. Thawing of Permafrost May Disturb Historic Cattle Burial Grounds in East Siberia. *Global Health Action*. https://doi.org/10.3402/gha.v4i0.8482.

Rich, Andrew. Think Tanks, Public Policy, and the Politics of Expertise.

Ritchie, Euan, and Charles Kenny. 2019. *The UK Needs a New Formula for ODA-Funded Research*. Center for Global Development. https://www.cgdev.org/blog/uk-needs-new-formula-oda-funded-research.

Rockström, Johan, et al. 2009. A Safe Operating Space for Humanity. *Nature*, 461, October: 472–475. Online publication 23 September 2009.

Roy, Katica. 26 November 2019. How Is the Fourth Industrial Revolution Changing our Economy? World Economic Forum. https://www.weforum.org/agenda/2019/11/the-fourth-industrial-revolution-is-redefining-the-economy-as-we-know-it/.

Schultz, Jeff. 6 August 2019. How Much Data Is Created on the Internet Each Day? Microfocus Blog. https://blog.microfocus.com/how-much-data-is-created-on-the-internet-each-day/.

Spinney, Laura. 28 March 2020. Is Factory Farming to Blame for Coronavirus? *The Guardian*. https://www.theguardian.com/world/2020/mar/28/is-factory-farming-to-blame-for-coronavirus.

Srinivasan, Madhav. The Inevitable Proliferation of Information Technology.

Sriram, Ramya. 12 April 2017. Nonprofit Organizations: Can They Benefit from Data Science? Kolabtree Blog. https://www.kolabtree.com/blog/nonprofit-data-science/.

Steffen, Will, et al. 2015. Planetary Boundaries: Guiding Human Development on a Changing Planet. *Sciences* 347 (6223): 1259855.

Stone, Diane. 2000. Think Tank Transnationalization and Non-Profit Analysis. *Advice and Advocacy. Global Society* 14 (2): 153–172.

Taleb, Nassim Nicholas. 16 September 2016. The Intellectual Yet Idiot. Medium. https://medium.com/incerto/the-intellectual-yet-idiot-13211e2d0577.

Tanji, Michael. 2010. The Think Tank Is Dead: Long Live the Think Tank. http://www.haftofthespear.com/wp-content/uploads/2010/08/The-Think-Tank-is-Dead-Final-Online.pdf. Accessed 8 February 2020.

Tocci, Nathalie. December 2018. Policy Relevant Scholarship? The Value of Creating, Framing and Storytelling. EU-LISTCO. https://www.eu-listco.net/publications/2018/12/13/policy-relevant-scholarship-the-value-of-creating-framing-and-storytelling.

Tsvetov, Anton. The Centers Cannot Hold: What's the Next Step for Think Tanks?

United Nations Environment Programme. 2019. *Emissions Gap Report 2019*. Nairobi: UNEP.

University of Vermont. 15 March 2012. With Climate Change, US Could Face Risk from Chagas Disease. *Science Daily*. https://www.sciencedaily.com/releases/2012/03/120315140225.htm.

Vidal, John. 2 April 2020. Don't Blame Bats or Pangolins. Human Actions Caused the Coronavirus. Yes! https://www.yesmagazine.org/environment/2020/04/02/coronavirus-destruction-environment-bats/.

Wackernagel, Mathis, and Bert Beyers. 2019. *Ecological Footprint: Managing Our Biocapacity Budget*. Gabriola Island, BC: New Society.

Walsh, Michael G., et al. 18 June 2018. Climatic Influence on Anthrax Suitability in Warming Northern Latitudes. *Scientific Reports* 8 (1): 1–9. https://doi.org/10.1038/s41598-018-27604-w.

Walter, Isabel, Sandra M. Nutley, and H.T.O. Davies. 2007. *Using Evidence: How Research Can Inform Public Services*, ed. H.T.O. Davies, I. Walter, and H.T.O. Davies. Bristol: Bristol, UK: Policy Press.

Wang, Huiyao, and Lv. Miao. 2014. Global Think Tanks. People's Publishing House: 10.

WBGU—German Advisory Council on Global Change. 2011. World in Transition—A Social Contract for Sustainability.

Wu, Xiao, and Rachel C. Nethery, et al. 2020. COVID-19 PM 2.5. Harvard University. https://projects.iq.harvard.edu/covid-pm.

World Health Organization. Global Environmental Change. https://www.who.int/globalchange/climate/summary/en/index5.html.

Zhang, Zuo-Feng, and Yan Cui, et al. 20 November 2003. Air Pollution and Case Fatality of SARS in the People's Republic of China: An Ecologic Study. *Environmental Health* 2(15). https://doi.org/10.1186/1476-069X-2-15.

Zick, Andreas, and Beate Küpper, and Wilhelm Berghan. 2018/2019: Verlorene Mitte - Feindselige Zustände. Rechtsextreme Einstellungen in Deutschland 2018/19. Hg. für die Friedrich-Ebert-Stiftung v. Franziska Schröter.

ZukunftsInstitut. Megatrends. https://www.zukunftsinstitut.de/dossier/megatrends/.

CONCLUSION

Avins, Jeremy. 25 November 2013. Strategy Is a Fundraising Necessity, Not a Luxury. *On Think Tanks.* https://onthinktanks.org/articles/strategy-is-afundraising-necessity-not-a-luxury/. Accessed 7 November 2018.

Bennett, Amanda. 5 October 2015. Are Think Tanks Obsolete? *The Washington Post.* https://www.washingtonpost.com/news/in-theory/wp/2015/10/05/are-think-tanksobsolete/?noredirect=on&utm_ter&utm_term=.20802394eb95. Accessed 7 November 2018.

Henke, Nicolaus, Jacques Bughin, Michael Chui, James Manyika, Tamim Saleh, Bill Wiseman, and Guru Sethupathy. December 2016. The Age of Analytics: Competing in a Data-driven World. McKinsey Global Institute. https://www.mckinsey.com/business-functions/mckinsey analytics/our insights/the age-of-analytics-competing-in-a-data-driven-world. Accessed 6 November 2018.

Kuntz, Fred. 11 July 2013. Communications and Impact Metrics for Think Tanks. Centre for International Governance Innovation. http://www.cigionline.org/articles/communications-and-impact-metrics-think-tanks. Accessed 7 November 2018.

Lipton, Eric, and Brooke Williams. 20 January 2018. How Think Tanks Amplify Corporate America's Influence. *The New York Times.* http://www.nytimes.com/2016/08/08/us/politics/think-tanks-research-andcorporate-lobby. Accessed 7 November 2018.

McGann, James G. 9 February 2016. 2015 Global Go to Think Tank Index Report. Scholarly Commons, University of Pennsylvania. https://repository.upenn.edu/think_tanks/10/. Accessed 7 November 2018.

Numanović, Amar. 11 July 2017. Data Science: The Next Frontier for Data-Driven Policy Making? Medium. https://medium.com/@numanovicamar/https-medium-com-numanovicamar-datascience-the-next-frontier-for-data-driven-policy-making-8abe98159748. Accessed 7 November 2018.

Ovans, Andrea. 6 December 2017. What Is a Business Model? *Harvard Business Review.* https://hbr.org/2015/01/what-is-a-business-model. Accessed 7 November 2018.

Ralphs, Gerard. 14 June 2016. Think Tank Business Models: The Business of Academia and Politics. *On Think Tanks.* https://onthinktanks.org/articles/

think-tank-business-models-the-business-ofacademia-and-politics/. Accessed 7 November 2018.

Zhu, Xufeng. 23 June 2017. A New Ranking: The 2016 Big Data Report on Chinese Think Tanks. *On Think Tanks*. https://onthinktanks.org/resources/a-new-ranking-the-2016-big-data-report-onchinese-think-tanks/. Accessed 7 November 2018.

The manufacturer's authorised representative in the EU is Springer
Nature Customer Service Centre GmbH, Europaplatz 3, 69115 Heidelberg,
Germany. If you have any concerns regarding our products, please
contact ProductSafety@springernature.com

Printed and bound by CPI Group (UK) Ltd, Croydon, CR0 4YY

29/04/2026

02099478-0012